The Poetry of Rilke

TRANSLATED AND EDITED BY *Edward Snow*

RAINER MARIA RILKE was born in Prague in 1875 and traveled throughout Europe for much of his adult life, returning frequently to Paris. His last years were spent in Switzerland, where he completed his two poetic masterworks, the *Duino Elegies* and the *Sonnets to Orpheus*. He died of leukemia in December 1926.

Edward Snow is a professor of English at Rice University. He is the recipient of an American Academy of Arts and Letters Award for his Rilke translations and has twice received the Academy of American Poets' Harold Morton Landon Translation Award.

The Poetry of Rilke

The Poetry of Rilke

BILINGUAL EDITION

TRANSLATED AND EDITED BY *Edward Snow*

INTRODUCTION BY *Adam Zagajewski*

NORTH POINT PRESS

A DIVISION OF FARRAR, STRAUS AND GIROUX

NEW YORK

North Point Press
A division of Farrar, Straus and Giroux
18 West 18th Street, New York 10011

Translation copyright © 2009 by Edward Snow
Introduction copyright © 2009 by Adam Zagajewski
Distributed in Canada by D&M Publishers, Inc.
Printed in the United States of America
Published in 2009 by North Point Press
First paperback edition, 2011

The Library of Congress has cataloged the hardcover edition as follows:
Rilke, Rainer Maria, 1875–1926.
 [Poems. English & German. Selections]
 The poetry of Rilke / translated and edited by Edward Snow ;
introduction by Adam Zagajewski. — 1st ed.
 p. cm.
 Includes bibliographical references and indexes.
 ISBN: 978-0-374-23531-4 (alk. paper)
 I. Snow, Edward A. II. Title.

 PT2635.I65A2 2009
 831'.912—dc22

 2009004721

Paperback ISBN: 978-0-374-53271-0

Designed by Jonathan D. Lippincott

www.fsgbooks.com

10 9 8 7 6 5 4 3 2

Contents

Introduction

REREADING RILKE by Adam Zagajewski

We read Rilke for his poetry, for his prose, for his novel *The Notebooks of Malte Laurids Brigge*, and for hundreds if not thousands of the letters he left, but there seems to be another important motive too: in our eyes his life presents itself as a flawless example of a modern artist's existence, an example purer perhaps than any other, perfect in its relentless pursuit of beauty.

In the German literary tradition it is Johann Wolfgang von Goethe who enjoyed for a very long time the status not only of an immense poet, playwright, and novelist but also of a sublime role model, an ideal human being, highly successful yet knowing the price of resignation, standing in the middle of a bourgeois society that had just rediscovered the value of intellectual accomplishment; Goethe, who happily accepted the position of someone who represented more than just his own singular destiny, graciously allowing others—through the numerous windows of his letters, diaries, and conversations—to have a look at him in his different hours and moods; Goethe, the scion of a patrician Frankfurt family, who as a young man became a minister at the Weimar court and a scientist entertaining each night in his lovely house on Frauenplan visitors from every imaginable country, explaining to them secrets of geology, biology, and literature—someone Napoleon would wish to meet and, as we know, did meet. Goethe, who renewed the German imagination even as he remained skeptical of the newborn nationalism of his compatriots during the Napoleonic Wars; Goethe, who was proud of his long life and didn't stop short of mocking others for dying too early; Goethe, a poet and thinker whose spiritual territory was so vast that it encompassed many elements of the Enlightenment but also involved vital ingredients of the Romantic era; and finally, Goethe, who knew well the silence of the writer's study but who also witnessed in 1792 the misery of premodern warfare in the mud, hunger, and hopelessness of an unsuccessful military campaign—not as a soldier but as an observer sharing the misery of others.

And then, next to this giant, Rainer Maria Rilke—a diffident, homeless poet born on the periphery of the Habsburg Empire, an artist who had to invent his own pedigree, who claimed an aristocratic lineage—the claim seems rather doubtful—an introvert, a lover of solitude, someone who, especially in his later years, didn't care much for publishing and remained until the end of his short life famous only among a rather small group of connoisseurs. Never

a minister like Goethe, never a senator like Yeats, never an ambassador like Saint-John Perse. Yes, he enjoyed the company of aristocrats, but not at any court; he'd only see them as private persons, gladly when they were set against the background of their natural environment, their castles and palaces: they were for him colorful relics of a more or less imaginary medieval Europe. The fact that Duino Castle—its name is forever linked to Rilke's poetry—which belonged to the Thurn und Taxis family, was destroyed in World War I (though later rebuilt) is symptomatic: the aristocrats Rilke knew were the shadows of once powerful magnates. None of the influential politicians of his time would have thought of meeting him. Clemenceau and Rilke? Lloyd George and Rilke? Lenin and Rilke? No, impossible, ridiculous: a joke. Paul Valéry? Yes, that makes sense; the two poets met and their meeting left a trace, a well-known photograph (but also and foremost Rilke's translations of Valéry's poetry).

What is so attractive for us in Rilke's symbolic status has almost nothing to do with the external circumstances of the period. Unlike Goethe, Rilke was not a robust representative of his epoch; he seemed to be, rather, an elegant question mark on the margin of history. Within the spectrum of literary modernism he stood among the antimoderns (in the sense of being hostile to many characteristics of the newly born industrial civilization), though he didn't care to develop his ideas in any coherent way. He was a poet, not a philosophical journalist, after all. He was like the Chopin of Gottfried Benn's marvelous poem: "when Delacroix propounded theories / he grew restless, for his part he could not / explain the Nocturnes."

It is his inner discipline, the discipline of his life, the sacrifices he made, that appeal to us. We cherish a certain intriguing narrowness of his external existence, which we can see and contemplate like an arrow ferociously speeding to its ultimate target: Rilke's poetic work. We believe we can see his rich inner life through the veil of his writings. If anything, Rilke was the epoch's secret voice, we think, the epoch's whisper, as opposed to its official expression. This, we think sometimes, is how his time should have been: not the absurd, terrifying killing fields of Verdun but the tranquillity of the poet's meditation in the midst of a great city or an Alpine meadow. His life spent in travels, his life as a search for the final illumination, fascinates us, but also his willingness to learn from Rodin and Cézanne and, later, to teach a young poet what poetry is about. We like to imagine lonely Rilke in Toledo or in Ronda in Spain, or think of him in Rome or in Cairo—and we always remember that from each of these travels he would bring with him a few pebbles we later find in the splendid mosaic of the *Duino Elegies*.

A lonely person he was, and yet not a stranger to social life. An incredibly prolific letter writer, he once told Merline—the nickname of Baladine Klossowska, the mother of Balthus—that he had to write 115 letters to make up for a backlog in his correspondence! These letters are extremely interesting, mostly written with the brio of the major artist he was, and should be seen as an important part of his oeuvre (as, for example, in the case of Elizabeth Bishop's letters).

The most mesmerizing part of this biography is Rilke's iron-willed waiting for the *Duino Elegies* to arrive, to visit his poetic mind. This is perhaps a unique case in the history of literature: a major poet who expected a certain poem for a long time—not any "great poem" but a particular one—apprehending its very nature, just not receiving it yet. We, the latecomers, know that the first four of the ten elegies were written between 1912 and 1914 and that he had to wait eight years for the rest of them. In this perspective, World War I can be regarded as just a very unpleasant nuisance that kept the poems from coming—which, by the way, is how Rilke himself often felt about the Great War. He didn't just wait—later, after the war was over and new possibilities opened up for him, he would, with some help from his friends, more or less actively look for a house, a tower, a quiet place on the planet in which to receive the Angel's message. For this he eventually chose Switzerland, one of the very few European countries not disfigured by the scars of trenches. The *Duino Elegies*, as we know, did eventually arrive and gave a glorious meaning to his entire pilgrimage, to his waiting, to his procrastinating, to his moving from one villa to another, to his patience. They gave Rilke's life the shape of a work of art, made him into a twentieth-century emblem of poetry.

Nobody will admire Rilke as a father or husband; his phobia of being loved doesn't necessarily convince us, but the form his life acquired through his poetic achievement is awe-inspiring. When Rilke dies in Val-Mont of leukemia (famously not willing to know the name of his illness), we weep, but perhaps a bit less than we would weep for other artists—didn't he announce that with the *Elegies* his work had come to a close? How could he live after them? As a retiree? Collecting stamps? Touring exotic countries with other retirees? Writing more mediocre French poems? Is it possible to be a poet in a more perfect way?

Yes, Rilke, the pure artist. At the same time, for some he will be more of a problematic figure, a freeloader, a half-ridiculous social climber, a snob who impressed a record number of princesses and countesses with his lofty comportment—but also with his writings. Few among the important modern poets have had so many admirers and so many detractors. Paul Claudel, for

instance, noted once in his diary: "This R. M. Rilke almost started a fight with me once he understood he meant nothing to me. He was bathed in sadness and mediocrity. Not really poor but a pauper. His poetry is unreadable." Auguste Rodin had at first almost no idea who his secretary was, what his value was. Much later W. H. Auden accepted Rilke's greatness only reluctantly. The list of those unseduced or seduced only against their will is much longer.

Rilke has often been presented as an example of an outstanding poet and writer whose beginnings were extremely unassuming, especially when compared to the early work of his peers, Hugo von Hofmannsthal or Thomas Mann, whose first publications conquered the reading public right away. Hofmannsthal was well known while still a high school student in Vienna; Mann published his *Buddenbrooks* at the age of twenty-six (Rilke, an unknown author then, wrote a brilliant review of the novel). Rilke also published as a very young man, but the acclaim he received then was scanty. An anecdote tells of the young Rilke running into the Poet Stefan George in the gardens of Florence (they had briefly met before in Berlin). George, who was seven years older and who then enjoyed a quiet reputation as someone who had breathed new life into German verse, supposedly told the future author of *Malte*: "You've started to publish too early." And we know this from Rilke, not from the other poet! This opinion is widespread even now. Rilke's first three poetry collections and his youthful naturalistic dramas are frequented by very few readers these days—probably only by the most conscientious scholars. Their author himself discarded them.

I've been struck by the fact that the reception of Rilke's work in the United States tends sometimes to obfuscate the context of his oeuvre. Rilke's poetry is often read without much attention to the historic moment in which it appeared—I mean both the history of literature and History as such. The second half of the nineteenth century is generally considered a low point in the ongoing saga of German poetry. After Goethe, Schiller, Hölderlin, and the outstanding Romantic poets (Platen, Eichendorff, Uhland, Mörike, Heine) came a time of severe drought. Paradoxically, it coincided with political success, with the unification of Germany executed under Bismarck's stern command; it seemed that the country of *"Dichter und Denker"* had to get rid of high culture (for which it was rightly famous) in order to establish an empire in this world, one not made out of dreams. And Bismarck most certainly was not a dreamer. There was almost nothing remarkable in German poetry at the time of Rilke's birth (1875), which of course helps to explain his own anemic beginnings. This was the time when the heart of European poetry

beat in Paris (who would believe it now!). And it was the same Stefan George who went to Paris and heard the word from the Master, from the very lips of Stéphane Mallarmé. The word was discipline, mystery, elegance, hatred of the bourgeois, rejection of mass production, art for art's sake. Baudelaire was influential too, and later Rimbaud. Without George's mediation, but also without the grace of Hofmannsthal's early poems, there would have been no Rilke masterpieces. They, George and Hofmannsthal, were the messengers of modernism in Germany; Rilke learned a lot from them—he stood on their shoulders.

Weak beginnings . . . Robert Musil, however, in his beautiful speech on Rilke pronounced after his death—a text that remains one of the best things ever written about the author of the *Duino Elegies*—saw a unity in the poet's work and wittily claimed that the younger Rilke simply imitated the older one. What a wonderful paradox! Yet it's quite clear that his early work simply reflected the ornamental taste of the time, the taste of art nouveau, which has dated quite badly, and which gradually evaporated from the pages of Rilke's books.

Compared to the other major poets, and not only in the German-speaking countries, Rilke embarked on the path that was supposed to lead him to the heights of poetry with a relatively poor knowledge of the German, or European, literary tradition. His formal education was rather thin. But he was lucky in other respects: he met in his youth several individuals who taught him a lot, who influenced him in the deepest possible way, though it's not easy to say what exactly he learned from them—maybe some kind of human format of greatness. His professors had little to do with any institution, even if he spent some time—though not much—listening to university lectures. His love affair with Lou Andreas-Salomé, which started when he was twenty-one and she thirty-six and which later was transformed into a lifelong friendship, was certainly highly educational, worth more than any Ivy League school. For a young poet from the provinces, meeting this strikingly original, courageous, and brilliant lady was immensely meaningful. That she was the only woman Friedrich Nietzsche ever fell in love with (though apparently she never reciprocated and, as we know from Malraux's memoirs, couldn't even remember if she'd exchanged a kiss with him), and that she then wrote one of the earliest well-informed books on the thinker of the eternal return, were of course of great significance. In the 1890s, when Lou Salomé and Rilke met, Nietzsche's fame was skyrocketing in Europe. He himself, as we know, never

recovered from the breakdown in Turin; he was still alive but practically unconscious, nursed by his obnoxious sister Elisabeth, later a Nazi, in Weimar. By then Nietzsche was a numb, humble shadow of the once blissful peripatetic philosopher who used to spend hours climbing the hills that dominated Rapallo and the shining Mediterranean in search of Zarathustra. It was a blessing for Rilke: to skip several rungs of the intellectual ladder thanks to a gracious and wise lady, a modern Diotima.

Lou Salomé was certainly one of the most dazzling women of her time; when the two of them walked in the meadows in the suburbs of Berlin, barefoot, as the fashion of the day required, they certainly spoke about the most important things, not just about the weather. She helped him as well with other things: meeting her contributed to tempering his *Exaltiertheit*—as she called his extravagant temperament. For Lou he changed his name—from René to Rainer—and the shape of his handwriting. That's easy to say, but what it amounts to is an identity transformation. Through her he also met many well-known Berlin intellectuals; thanks to her they noticed his literary existence.

Almost all the episodes in Rilke's youth seem to have been instilled with huge didactic value. There were the two trips to Russia (in both of them his companion was Lou Salomé, herself born in St. Petersburg, and speaking Russian perfectly): a short meeting with Tolstoy and a much longer one with the country of his dreams could not replace studying Slavic philology but nonetheless left an important trace on Rilke's entire life and on his poetic thinking. Then came Worpswede in northern Germany, a village that was just becoming famous for its artists' colony. Worpswede opened for him new vistas in the domain of the visual arts. He lived there for a short while with his wife, Clara, and their young daughter, Ruth. It was in Worpswede also that he would have long conversations with Paula Modersohn Becker, the most talented painter among the local artists. Next came his collaboration with Auguste Rodin, one of the most fascinating stories in the annals of modern art. We say today "collaboration," though for the famous elderly sculptor there was certainly very little symmetry in his dealings with *"un jeune Allemand"* who at the beginning of their acquaintance was merely a not very efficient secretary (a secretary who learned and improved his knowledge of French en route, probably sighing: Ah, all these accents!). Rodin not only could not read his "secretary's" poems but also, as Rilke described it in one of his letters, had no aptitude for foreignness, for the foreign sounds of strange languages; all non-French names were unpleasantly unpalatable for him.

The tentativeness of Rilke's beginnings also involved his standing outside any given set of traditions and myths. He was not German enough to wish to embrace—as a potential Wagner of poetry—German literary or mythical history (with the notable exception of his early prose work *The Lay of the Love and Death of Cornet Christopher Rilke*, the only book that brought him commercial success in his lifetime); neither was he Austrian enough to study—like Hofmannsthal—the glorious past of the Habsburgs who once reigned both in Vienna and in Madrid (and were portrayed by the best Spanish painters, including Velázquez). Prague, too provincial for him, was not significant enough in his eyes and remained forever blemished by the memory of his own difficult childhood, by the presence there of his imperfect parents, who obviously didn't fit into the legend of an old aristocratic family. Anyway, soon Paris—and not Berlin—would replace Prague in his heart and his poetic imagination. Early-twentieth-century Paris quickly became for Rilke the very embodiment of the glory and shame of modernity (he mostly saw the latter and didn't care much for the former). Russia came in handy too as a mysterious land, providing the poet with some hope for the future but also with glorious examples of a sacred territory that he had already discovered in human souls and old churches. (Rilke never took the Bolshevik revolution seriously, considering it just a tiny ripple on an ocean of eternal Russianness and refusing to discuss the meaning of the political upheaval.)

Other great modernist poets didn't need to borrow images from foreign sources: young W. B. Yeats could easily leaf through layers of Celtic memory and reverie and then dream of a revitalization of Irish culture; Lorca had rich mythical material around him right there in Andalusia; T. S. Eliot could rely on the suspension bridge that the migration of his ancestors had built between England and the United States; Mandelstam had at his disposal the domes of the Orthodox churches, Mozart's music, and Schubert's lieder. Rilke's detachment from any "organic" tradition resembled to some extent Pound's stance, but of course he would have never embarked on a hubristic perusal of a dozen different world cultures. Certainly pedantry (even a pedantry with the panache of Pound's fantasy) was not Rilke's forte. Russia was his China; the great modern city was his usury. The distance he kept from national traditions (didn't he publish a collection of poems in French, *Vergers?*) may have contributed to a certain "globalization" of his reputation in our day; today he is probably more read in the United States than in Germany.

Rilke's gift, one of many, was an uncanny capacity to approach the subject of his poems in the most direct way; his poem "The Panther" (*New Poems*) seems to pierce the animal, to X-ray it in one bold gesture:

His gaze has from the passing of the bars
become so tired that it holds nothing anymore.
It seems to him there are a thousand bars
and behind a thousand bars no world.

The supple pace of powerful soft strides,
turning in the very smallest circle,
is like a dance of strength around a center
in which a mighty will stands numbed.

Only at times the curtain of the pupils
soundlessly slides open——. Then an image enters,
glides through the limbs' taut stillness——
dives into the heart and dies.*

"Buddha in Glory" does something similar; in this poem there's again a fascination with the center of things and persons, an almost Aristotelian quest for the entelechy:

Center of all centers, core of cores,
almond, that closes tightly in and sweetens, —
all this world out to the farthest stars
is the flesh around your seed: we greet you.

The directness of the attack seems to announce to the reader: this poet needs no mythological system, he will tackle his subjects in a way that circumvents the mist of old myths. And certainly he will not remain with Buddha for long, he'll move on to other images and creeds. He will use the classical Greek myths at times, and how beautifully: in "Orpheus. Eurydice. Hermes," for instance. But in another of his great poems, "Corpse-Washing," the extreme situation doesn't require any preexisting system of myths of belief; this is a poem of radical bareness.

*I'm quoting this and all other poems of Rilke from Edward Snow's translations, whose power and brilliance I deeply admire.

Interestingly, this rootless poet, whenever he dwelled in manor houses or castles—in Denmark, in Sweden, in Switzerland, in Italy, in what is today the Czech Republic—he studied with great fervor biographical books and articles having to do with the local notables. Suddenly he would passionately try to reconstruct the roots of others, as if his free, homeless spirit liked the idea of playing with endless genealogies, as if, while moving from one place to another, he was always rehearsing the possibility of being a Swiss patrician, a Spanish hidalgo, a Danish aristocrat (like Malte, the hero of his eponymous novel), of becoming somebody *real*—as if he craved a final incarnation denied to him in his itinerant life. The topography of his last address, the now legendary Muzot tower, is very telling: it stands, as we know, in the canton of Valais in Switzerland, in the majestic valley carved by the young, serene Rhône. Rilke loved the place when he saw it for the first time. The valley, he said, combined the sweetness of Provence with the rougher character of the Spanish landscape, two of his favorite places. His last house was situated only a few kilometers from the linguistic frontier between French- and German-speaking towns. In Sierre, where the Muzot tower still rises in the same garden as it did seventy-five years ago—though dwarfed now by dozens of houses that didn't exist in the poet's time—you can hear light, clear French vowels fluttering like butterflies in the Alpine air, whereas in the medieval town of Leuk, just next to Sierre, your ear will receive the heavy blows of Germanic consonants. How perfect for our poet! To be nowhere would have been even better, but that is very difficult; to settle between languages and traditions, on a kind of San Andreas Fault of cultures, was just right for him. And then his grave, to which many poetry lovers make a pilgrimage, can be found outside the church in Raron, some twenty minutes by car from Sierre, in German-speaking territory. A few years in the French atmosphere, an eternity in German-soaked soil. On a modest tombstone we find these three lines every Rilke admirer knows by heart:

Rose, O pure contradiction, delight
in being no one's sleep under so many
eyelids.

Whoever visits the grave, contemplates it, and then turns away must be struck by the majesty of the deep and large Rhône Valley, which became the last landscape for the poet.

———

Rilke lived in imagination. When we look at his photographs, and there are many, we see a slender man with a narrow face that seems to expect something to happen more than to express any definable mood, a receiver more than a sender. We always see in them a very conventionally dressed gentleman; we guess that the quality of his suit is quite exceptional (never anything bohemian about his attire, never anything flashy). He is not handsome, but he always appears kind and quiet, peaceful and passive in these pictures, as only extremely polite people can be—but in fact we know that Rainer Maria Rilke could not be photographed at all. A good, accurate photograph of Rilke was impossible; it would have had to capture the invisible, to register the angel's wings, to represent shadows of medieval knights, to reflect long valleys where human souls were transformed, to include dawns in Italy and nights in Morocco. It's paradoxical that he was actually photographed, his face open like a full moon.

What's most interesting in the artistic biography of our hero is the fact that Rilke had been able, through all the years of his incessant traveling, through years of work and discipline, but also through months of silence, through the many spiritual deserts he patiently crossed, to transform the weakness of his beginnings into the most admirable strength: the universality of his middle and late poetry proves it triumphantly. His nonbelonging, nonclinging to what was given to him by his parents, his city, his biography, his Austrianness, his Germanness, crippled his writing early on to some extent, made him vulnerable to the fads of the day, yet later turned out to be one of his major assets, one of the sources of his enormous artistic force. If we attempt to elucidate the nature of this growing, the notion of an increasing degree of abstraction within the optics of his poetry may prove helpful, but an abstraction that never loses touch with the sensual, the concrete. When we think of Rilke and his connection to the world of visual arts, the name of Cézanne (next to Rodin) comes almost automatically to mind—and rightly so. We don't remember so well his significant interest in the work of Paul Klee; he talks about it, for instance, in his letter to Baladine Klossowska on February 23, 1921, late in his writing life, only one year before the explosion of his greatest poems. Klee's imagination was able to combine the abolition of a recognizable space governed by the laws of perspective with the preservation of the shapes and outlines of people, animals, and objects. Something parallel happens in Rilke's poems: in his early work we locate the poetic situations in different settings, be it Chartres, Bruges, or Paris. We also feel in them the age—the youngness—of the speaker's voice. It changes in the course of Rilke's maturing: objects never lose their vivid individuality, but

the air filling the poems becomes rarer, like the atmosphere in the high Alps. The geography of the Duino elegies (not to mention the even more elusive *Sonnets to Orpheus*) is different from that of earlier poems; it reminds us of the undefined landscapes old masters used to place as a background behind the subject they portrayed—as in Leonardo's *La Gioconda*. (By the way, the mysterious gorge in this picture could very well relate to the Rhône Valley, the same valley that the poet saw each day while he lived in the Muzot tower.) When I say "old masters," I mean also a quality that is easy to grasp and difficult to give a name to—a degree of authority, maybe also a degree of agelessness in the artist, a something in the voice that makes us obey, even if only for the time we spend with the book. Tolstoy's voice, for instance, is so authoritative that for half an hour we really believe "all happy families are alike," and only later revolt against this false axiom.

In the elegies we are not in Switzerland, nor in Austria, France, or Germany. *The Waste Land*, the Anglo-Saxon counterpart of Rilke's masterpiece, as we know, is set in London. The Duino elegies create a space that will never have its national flag or anthem; it's the human space par excellence, and in the post office mentioned in one of the elegies we could perhaps buy stamps (with what kind of money?), but they would be issued by the cosmos itself, not by any particular nation-state. Yet the human passions, longings, and situations depicted in the elegies we recognize right away as ours.

If we want to find a poem from before the last great period of his creation, a short poem that contains in a nutshell almost the entire appeal of Rilke's artistry, it would be, for the present writer, "Archaic Torso of Apollo."

We never knew his head and all the light
that ripened in his fabled eyes. But
his torso still burns like a streetlamp dimmed
in which his gaze, lit long ago,

holds fast and shines. Otherwise the surge
of the breast could not blind you, nor a smile
run through the slight twist of the loins
toward that center where procreation flared.

Otherwise this stone would stand cut off
and cold under the shoulders' transparent drop
and not glisten like a wild beast's fur

and not break forth from all its contours
like a star: for there is no place
that does not see you. You must change your life.

The poem was written in 1908 when the poet was thirty-three. It would be enough for a poet to have written only one poem like this to be remembered. This Apollo prepares us for the Angel that will turn up in the *Duino Elegies*—Apollo with his dormant cosmic force marks the appearance of a category of beings that are so much stronger than ourselves. We also have *"L'ange du méridien,"* the smiling angel that decorates the Chartres cathedral . . . and we have other figures.

"Archaic Torso" is one of his most remarkable poems. Here a sculpture, incomplete, maimed by time (and perhaps by early Christians as well—didn't they disfigure Greek statues to make them meek and sexless?), ceases to be an object; it's so full of meaning that it explodes and finally speaks to us, uttering the famous final injunction. The imperative comes as a surprise, but it had to come: if this torso of Apollo is more alive than we usually are, the electricity of its inner glory has to break open.

Let's look at yet another poem, also very well known—its title is "Autumn Day":

Lord: it is time. Your summer was superb.
Lay your shadows on the sundials,
and in the meadows let the winds go free.

Command the last fruits to be full;
give them only two more southern days,
urge them on to completion and chase
the last sweetness into the heavy wine.

Whoever has no house will never build one now.
Whoever is alone now will long remain so,
will stay awake, read books, write long letters
and wander restless back and forth
along the tree-lined streets, as the leaves drift down.

This poem from *The Book of Images* is situated at the intersection of the spiritual and the natural cruel determinism of nature. Among the many po-

ems on death in Rilke's collections this one is the most delicate; we don't hear the word "death" itself. Homelessness is one of Rilke's central themes—this poem (to which Paul Celan will reply with his "Corona") leads straight to the first of the Duino elegies with its complaint ("abiding is nowhere"), and yet its beauty is so different from the aesthetic of the *Elegies*, which relies on the quest for "general laws" ruling our human existence. Not so in this short poem: here we only have a snapshot of human life—but even here the later motif of building, of creating objects as a defense against the icy coldness of the universe, is already present; if somebody has already constructed a house, he will be safe.

Rilke's force increased steadily, each new book bringing new evidence of it. In the *New Poems* (1907), a collection that marked a turn in his poetry, he looks attentively at the world. This is the well-known phase of the *Dinggedicht*, the "thing poem," opposed to any impressionism, any subjectivism—should we say any confessionalism?—in writing. Rilke learned a lot from Rodin; in his studio Rodin certainly produced massive things, not moods. (He also had few moods in the sense of waiting for an inspiration—he just went to work every day, which deeply impressed the young poet.) In theory Rilke might also have overheard Stéphane Mallarmé talking to his friends. The same Paul Claudel who, we remember, didn't respect Rilke at all, raises an important point in his conversations with Jean Amrouche (*Mémoires improvisés*). Claudel, who for some time frequented the celebrated *mardis* (Tuesdays) in the rue de Rome apartment near the St. Lazare railway station, refers there to Mallarmé making a distinction between poets who describe people, objects, and situations, and poets who are rather interested in capturing not descriptions but *"qu'est-ce que ça veut dire,"* "what does it mean," or what do these people, objects, and situations "want to say," if we literally translate the beautiful French expression. This is what Rilke did in his poems: he didn't intend to describe objects—this would be a task for a lesser artist—he was entering them in order to find out what they were saying, what they wanted to say.

If some other poets from his generation and beyond tied both their spiritual disquietude and moments of inspiration to the cause of their nation, to the historic situation, or to their starkly accentuated biography, Rilke, we know, remained free in this respect; he kept his creative fire far from the furnaces of political or societal passions. There is one exception though: in August 1914 he briefly shared the enthusiasm of German crowds for the just-beginning Great War (he was strengthened in this by his recent discovery

of Friedrich Hölderlin's poetry, which could be read in a patriotic mode). This happened in his *Five Songs*, written in the first weeks of the war. These poems sang the praise of a god of war as a great renewer of humanity. Later on, Rilke never joined those poets who wept over the disaster of the same war, which failed to renew anything except the death industry.

The material absence of modern history in Rilke's work will intrigue or even dismay some of his readers. Let us quote one of them, Mieczyslaw Jastrun (1903–83), an eminent Polish poet and a seasoned translator of Rilke's (and Höderlin's) poetry.

I owe to Jastrun many rich hours and one particular luminous moment, many decades ago, when, still a high school student, I bought a slim, elegant book, *Duino Elegies*, in his translation. Standing in the street filled with the mediocre din of a lazy Communist afternoon, I read for the first time the magical sentences "Who, if I cried out, would hear me among the Angels' / Orders? And even if one of them pressed me / suddenly to his heart: I'd be consumed / in his more potent being. For beauty is nothing / but the beginning of terror, which we can still barely endure." The street suddenly disappeared, political systems evaporated, the day became timeless, I met eternity, poetry woke up.

This book was a jewel in my then still very modest library—as opposed to the library of my parents, which was quite well stocked, mostly with novels and short-story collections; don't we live in an age of prose? I loved the format of the Rilke volume—slightly bigger than the conventional size—and the sheer fact that this sequence of ten poems merited a separate edition. This was at a time when I was addicted to fat Russian novels I'd check out from the municipal library. The very slenderness of the *Elegies* made me wonder about the weight of words: if a thin volume can have so much significance, why carry the epic loads?

Here is what Mieczyslaw Jastrun said in the afterword to one of the many editions of his translations: "When, after World War II, during my stay in Switzerland, I visited the Muzot castle and Rilke's grave in Raron, I was no longer this young man who endlessly admired poems from *The Book of Hours* and *The Book of Images*. Rilke was never as remote for me as then, right after the war and the Nazi occupation had ended."

It's not difficult to guess why. Rilke's dialogue with gods and angels, his meditation on night and death (a quiet, aristocratic death, not the plebeian one having to do with machine guns or gas chambers), left out a whole territory of down-to-earth suffering, not sublime at all and yet craving recognition,

maybe needing its own poetry. Those of us who have witnessed (or even only read about) the several terrible sequels of World War I and understand that there are two contradictory betrayals lying in wait for every poet—one that consists in forgetting the pain of modern history for the sake of the spiritual life, untouched by the news, and another that has to do with paying close attention to the pain of modern history but forsaking the delicate, nameless substance of our interiority—will be probably more than willing to exonerate Rilke from this criticism. Mieczyslaw Jastrun, for whom every day and hour of the war and occupation could have been his last (he was Jewish and lived in hiding in Warsaw while at the same time actively participating in the underground literary life), himself returned later to Rilke's poetry; his rejection of the unpolitical sublime was only temporary. Once the evil shadow faded, he became again fascinated by the magnetism of this work.

While it is easy and even pleasant to exempt Rilke from the historicist's censure, the question remains and looms large on the horizon of Rilke studies. Yes, it's an unanswerable question. No Stalin ever flung him into a camp. Nobody, and fortunately so, ever sent the poet to the muddy trenches. The ridiculous episode of Rilke having been drafted in Vienna during the war (he held an Austrian passport at the time, after all), the comedy of the forty-year-old poet being for a short time subjected to the absurd ritual of a military drill he painfully remembered from the St. Polten school of his childhood, the stupidity of a larger-than-life sergeant humiliating the poet, mocking him for having a not very soldierly "Maria" as his middle name, and finally the successful rescue operation mounted by the influential and energetic Princess Maria von Thurn und Taxis, who delivered him from the barracks (once upon a time it was the knight who liberated the princess, but here the situation was reversed)—all remain parts of an isolated event in the otherwise well-protected if modest existence of our artist. The wise princess, who admired the poet but also knew well his weaknesses, liked to address Rilke in her letters and otherwise as Dottore Serafico—what a lovely, ironic sobriquet! How good for us, his readers, that he escaped the dungeons of the twentieth century. Nevertheless, some kind of modern evil that manifested itself in World War I and flourished in the following decades in many areas of our planet never made inroads into Rilke's poetic meditation. This is our loss. We've learned that to understand the nature of modern evil is an utterly difficult thing, perhaps impossible; having Rilke among the researchers working in this particular artistic laboratory would have been of inestimable value.

For me, the happy owner of the elegant slim book bought long ago, the

Elegies represented just the beginning of a long road leading to a better acquaintance with Rilke's entire oeuvre. The fiery invocation that starts "The First Elegy"—once again: "Who, if I cried out, would hear me among the Angels' / Orders? And even if one of them pressed me / suddenly to his heart: I'd be consumed / in his more potent being. For beauty is nothing / but the beginning of terror, which we can still barely endure"—had become for me a living proof that poetry hadn't lost its bewitching powers. At this early stage I didn't know Czeslaw Milosz's poetry; it was successfully banned by the Communist state from the schools, libraries, and bookstores—and from me. One of the first contemporary poets I read and tried to understand was Tadeusz Rozewicz, who then lived in the same city in which I grew up (Gliwice) and, at least hypothetically, might have witnessed the rapturous moment that followed my purchase of the *Duino Elegies* translated by Jastrun, might have seen a strangely immobile boy standing in the middle of a sidewalk, in the very center of the city, in its main street, at the hour of the local promenade when the sun was going down and the gray industrial city became crimson for fifteen minutes or so. Rozewicz's poems were born out of the ashes of the other war, World War II, and were themselves like a city of ashes. Rozewicz avoided metaphors in his poetry, considering any surplus of imagination an insult to the memory of the last war victims, a threat to the moral veracity of his poems; they were supposed to be quasi-reports from the great catastrophe. His early poems, written before Adorno uttered his famous dictum that after Auschwitz poetry's competence was limited—literally, he said, "It is barbaric to write poetry after Auschwitz"—were already imbued with the spirit of limitation and caution.

I admired the spartan sparseness of Rozewicz's language then, and for some time I did agree that poetry definitely must be tame, metaphorless, prosy, since history had delivered it such a deadly blow. Flights of imagination had to be strictly forbidden, I thought. Compared to the intentional flatness of Rozewicz's poetry, the wild opening of the first of the Duino elegies—but also everything that followed in this and the other elegies—was a welcome, almost unexpected confirmation that the poetic fire could still be alive, indeed was alive. Luckily, chronological (or, as the boring theorists of structuralism liked to say, diachronic) order doesn't apply to poetry at all, so that an earlier poem can contend with one written much later and thus can reassure the young reader: Don't listen to any contemporary commandments that seem to represent the verdict of the Zeitgeist itself. Listen to great poets only; sometimes a Catullus can save you from a literary dictatorship of some-

body who lives only five blocks away. And then perhaps you will see that under some circumstances the Zeitgeist may turn out to be no more convincing intellectually than a vulgar poltergeist.

These were the happy beginnings of my long acquaintance with Rilke's poetry. Later I also delighted in reading his prose: not so much the *Cornet Christopher Rilke* story, which somehow never appealed to me, but his only novel, the difficult *Malte*, which, with the density of an existentialist treatise, fascinated me. I also read with pleasure and profit Rilke's book on Rodin. Every young artist should read it: this beautiful praise of discipline exerts a stimulating effect on younger minds who may tend to overrate the irrational, purely inspirational ingredient of artistry. Even later I discovered the ocean of Rilke's letters. These letters contain everything from everyday gossip (but how elegant! how entertaining!) to the most sublime observations on life and art. In recent years I've read with the greatest interest his letters to Nanny Wunderly Volkart, a rich Swiss lady. There are two volumes of the correspondence, containing only the poet's letters; Wunderly Volkart decided to keep private her part of the exchange. These two volumes belong to the last chapter of Rilke's life, to the period when he left Munich, escaping political insecurity and the postwar misery of the Bavarian city, and went to Switzerland, at first with the idea of staying there for a short time only, but then, relishing the Swiss stability and lack of any revolutionary mood in the Alpine country, deciding to prolong his visit indefinitely.

The letters to Nanny Wunderly Volkart allow us a deep insight into Rilke's method of living and creating. The entire Dottore Serafico is in them: as the lady in question was quite powerful within the Swiss political and administrative network and the homeless poet's passport tended to lose its validity quite often, the letters are sometimes not free of supplicatory undertones. At the same time they never lose the air of a sovereign artistic dignity; Rilke rewarded his friend with the most generous pages, which reflected his spiritual quest in the new-for-him context of quotidian life in a Swiss villa or castle. For Rilke at this stage of his poetic pilgrimage, letters didn't represent just a way of communicating with friends and acquaintances; rather, they were the very content and substance of his life. In all these Swiss palaces he was only a guest, dependent on the whims of his hosts. He couldn't yet begin to write his great poems, his *Duino Elegies*, his *Sonnets to Orpheus*, and he knew it; he was still looking for a quiet place, for a poetic tower, which, as we know, he did find later in the canton of Valais. In the meantime, any villa he temporarily inhabited was only a waiting room. So—we know this from his letters—there

were days if not weeks entirely devoted to letter writing. Here the usual ratio between living a life and writing letters that would give an account of it was radically reversed. It was a life that consumed itself in endless missives whose addressees were mostly representatives of European nobility plus a few chosen anonymous people, mostly women, whom he considered his flock and looked after.

From the letters we learn about the rituals that accompanied Rilke's writing, what kind of paper was suitable, which inkpot and what kind of table were absolutely necessary. We also learn that many other letters had to be written; sometimes a letter to Nanny Wunderly Volkart has to be cut short because another must be urgently jotted down and soon after brought to a distant post office. Later, when the long-awaited avalanche of inspiration arrived, there were for quite a while no letters; their aim had been achieved, but at this preliminary juncture the correspondence filled his time and mind. At the same time it prevented him from writing poems he would consider minor.

Anyone who has spent several decades reading a major poet—of course always with some interruptions, we never dwell upon one poet for years continuously—will agree that this is a very complex story where fidelity and fickleness, even disloyalty, change places all the time, as in some elegant seventeenth-century dance—the minuet, let's say. Someone who loves C. P. Cavafy's work, for instance, will probably have to admit that, as much as he admires this poet, he has also known periods when passion for and interest in the modern Greek bard faded for a while—as if each act of reading poetry consisted in acquiring some kind of spiritual vitamins and in the process our inner voice would tell us from time to time: good, enough of this, give me a different nutrient now. So after the immense intelligence of Cavafy's historical poems the inner voice might be tempted to say: Please, give me a poet like Dylan Thomas now. Rilke is no exception to the rule; perhaps he's even one of those great poets whose grip on readers fluctuates the most. For one thing, there's almost no sense of humor in his poetry, as contrasted with his letters, which emanate a lovely understanding of the droll side of life—in the letters we hear the voice of Dottore Serafico, not a prophet. His poetry is almost always high-strung; in a way it represents the essence of poetry in the purity of its lyric song. Rilke's oeuvre, especially in his last years, is also characterized by a certain "passivity"; this is a poetry that receives, that listens to, that waits for a signal coming from the outside—as opposed, for instance, to many of W. H. Auden's later poems, where a muscular rhetoric is at work, a rhetoric

that gesticulates, posits, invents, denies, and moralizes all the time. Not so Rilke, who listens to the world, watches the world, who receives.

> And we, spectators, always, everywhere,
> looking at, never out of, everything!
> It fills us to overflowing. We arrange it. It falls apart.
> We rearrange it, and fall apart ourselves.
>
> ("The Eighth Elegy")

The poetic language has to follow the gaze, not the other way around. This is why he declares in "The Ninth Elegy":

> The traveler doesn't return to the valley from the mountainside
> with a handful of sod, around which all stand mute,
> but with a word he's won, a pure word, the yellow and blue
> gentian. What if we're only here to say: *house,*
> *bridge, fountain, gate, jug, fruit tree, window,* —
> at most: *column, tower* . . . but for *saying,* understand,
> oh for such saying as the things themselves
> never dreamt so intensely to be.

I have to confess my own fickleness in regard to Rilke's oeuvre. Even the *Duino Elegies*, the absolute summit of this poetic mountain range—the sequence of poems that was revealed to me in the shape of the slim book very early in the history of my reading, in the middle of an industrial city in Silesia—has in my life, known periods of oblivion, periods of gathering dust in a distant corner of my library. His wonderful requiems have known the same fate. Rilke's grip on an individual reader may indeed fluctuate strongly; nevertheless, his power of captivating new generations of readers is absolutely undiminished.

How to read the Duino elegies, those ten great poems that form the summit of Rilke's art? Should we try to understand them thoroughly or rush through them like children who run through the forest at night, half terrified, half elated? The question is almost pointless: whoever will risk an expedition to a good library will soon find an almost endless array of commentaries. Christian philosophers will inform us how Christian the Duino elegies are; existentialists will claim Rilke as one of their colleagues; Husserl's disciples will find here ten tons of phenomenology; other historians of ideas will in-

form us that this is simply Friedrich Nietzsche put into verse! Should we listen to them? Of course not. Or rather: we should know about these philosophical or ideological readings and then try to forget them. The elegies are like a forest; there's not a single line in them not written under the spell of inspiration, and truly poetic, not philosophical, inspiration. The elegies are an enchanted forest, and after a while an attentive reader will resemble not a child but a snowy owl flying silently between the dense spruce branches with the utmost facility—and with a kind of sad happiness that is, it seems, a proper response to great poetry. An attentive reader will understand that this is a poem that deals with ultimate questions, with unanswerable questions—who are we, what is death, are lovers the privileged ones, what can art give us . . .

Consider this strophe in "The Seventh Elegy":

> *Life* here is magic. Even *you* knew that, you girls
> who seemed so deprived of it, whose lives twisted down
> into the city's vilest streets, festering, or opened
> for the worst debris. There was an hour for each of you,
> perhaps not even an hour, but between two intervals
> a space scarcely measured by the rules of time—,
> when you *existed*. Completely. Veins filled with existence.
> But we so easily forget what our laughing neighbor
> neither covets nor confirms. We want to lift it up
> and show it, even though the most visible happiness
> only reveals itself when we've changed it, within.

Do we really need any commentary? We feel the poet has arrived here at the limit of the sayable and takes risks like a gambler who, shortly before the casino is going to close, puts on the table bills of the highest denomination: *life, existence, happiness.* The croupier looks at him with a condescending smile that says: Come on, I've seen it all hundreds of times. But the poet wins.

Maybe it's more interesting to see Rilke's work as not as virginal, not as ethereal, as it seems to many readers. After all, like the majority of literary modernists, he is an antimodern; one of the main impulses in his work consists in looking for antidotes to modernity. Heroes of his poems move in a spiritual space, not in the streets of New York or Paris, but they also, because of their intense existence, are meant to act against the supposed or real ugliness of the modern world. Even Rilke's snobbery, hypothetical or not, can be seen as corresponding more to his ideas than to the weaknesses of his charac-

ter: aristocrats represented for the poet the survivors of a better Europe, a chivalric continent, as opposed to the degradation caused by profit-oriented modernity, cherishing mass production and car races. He was not alone in representing this position—it will be enough to refer to the aesthetic movement and Walter Pater, who preceded him by one generation. Had Rilke met Marcel Proust, who was born only four years before our poet (they never met, but we know that Rilke admired the first volumes of *À la recherche du temps perdu*, published before his death), we can be sure there would have been between them no major disagreement concerning matters of philosophy, taste, and society. And certainly he would have readily agreed with his friend Paul Valéry when the French poet was sadly sighing at the sight of a new Europe of efficiency, labor, and military drill, and when, regretting the loss of the unhurried pace of intellectual work and musing in the past, he pronounced these beautiful words: *"Adieu, travaux infiniment lents . . ."*

Some of the more sharp-eyed scholars have even found one or two sentences in Rilke's letters in praise of Mussolini. This is not what I mean: I don't intend to accuse the superb poet of any political misdemeanor. What I want is simply also to see in his poetry a dimension that has a lot to do with the diversity of intellectual polemics, some of which are still ongoing. We're still pondering the value of modernity, as was Rilke, even if we do this using different notions and examples. We have a new sorrow today: after the terrible catastrophes of the twentieth century, after the disasters that entered both our memory and imagination, we tread gingerly at the point where poetry meets society; "Don't walk beyond this line," as the sign on every jetliner's wing warns us. And yet the central issue for us is probably the question of whether the mystery at the heart of poetry (and of art in general) can be kept safe against the assaults of an omnipresent talkative and soulless journalism and an equally omnipresent popular science—or pseudo-science. It also has a lot to do with the weighing of the advantages and vices of mass culture, with the influence of mass media, and with a difficult search for genuine expression inside the commercial framework that has replaced older, less vulgar traditions and institutions in our societies. In this respect, it's true, poets have less to fear than their friends the painters, especially the successful ones, who, because of the absurd prices their works can now command, will never see their canvases in the houses of their fellow artists, in the apartments of people like themselves, only in vaults belonging to oil or television moguls who don't even have time to look at them. Still, the stakes of the debate and its seriousness are not very different and not less important than a hundred years ago.

We know that the main domain of poetry is contemplation, through the riches of language, of human and nonhuman realities, in their separateness and in their numerous encounters, tragic or joyful. Rilke's powerful Angel standing at the gates of the *Elegies*, timeless as he is, is there to guard something that the modern era—which gave us so much in other fields—took away from us or only concealed: ecstatic moments, for instance, moments of wonder, hours of mystical ignorance, days of leisure, sweet slowness of reading and meditating. Ecstatic moments—aren't they one of the main reasons why poetry readers cannot live without Rilke's work? I mean here readers of contemporary poetry who otherwise are mostly kept on a rather meager diet of irony. The Angel is timeless, and yet his timelessness is directed against the deficiencies of a certain epoch. So is Rilke: timeless and deeply immersed in his own historic time. Not innocent, though; only silence is innocent, and he still speaks to us.

The translations from Rilke's *Book of Hours* included in this volume are presented here for the first time. All others are drawn from the volumes of Rilke's German poetry I have been translating since my version of the first part of Rilke's *New Poems* appeared in 1984. The present book is offered less as a selection than as a distillation of this work. I have felt free to revise and reinvent when new solutions emerged from this present vantage point. All the poems have been reconsidered, and many have changed dramatically. (The *Duino Elegies* offered here is virtually a new translation; the *Sonnets to Orpheus* has survived intact.) In this process of revision I am greatly indebted to Jonathan Galassi, whose generous response has kept encouraging me to urge the poems on to a new level of engagement with their great originals.

The Poetry of Rilke

From DAS STUNDEN-BUCH *(1905)*

From THE BOOK OF HOURS *(1905)*

Da neigt sich die Stunde und rührt mich an
mit klarem, metallenem Schlag:
mir zittern die Sinne. Ich fühle: ich kann—
und ich fasse den plastischen Tag.

Nichts war noch vollendet, eh ich es erschaut,
ein jedes Werden stand still.
Meine Blicke sind reif, und wie eine Braut
kommt jedem das Ding, das er will.

Nichts ist mir zu klein und ich lieb es trotzdem
und mal es auf Goldgrund und groß,
und halte es hoch, und ich weiß nicht wem
löst es die Seele los . . .

Now the hour bends down and touches me
with its clear, metallic ring:
my senses tremble. The feeling forms: *I can*—
and I grasp the malleable day.

Nothing was complete before I saw it,
all becoming stood still.
My eyes are ripe, and whatever they desire
approaches like a bride.

Nothing is too small: against a gold background
I paint it large and lovingly
and hold it high, and I will never know
whose soul it may release . . .

Ich lebe mein Leben in wachsenden Ringen,
die sich über die Dinge ziehn.
Ich werde den letzten vielleicht nicht vollbringen,
aber versuchen will ich ihn.

Ich kreise um Gott, um den uralten Turm,
und ich kreise jahrtausendelang;
und ich weiß noch nicht: bin ich ein Falke, ein Sturm
oder ein großer Gesang.

I live my life in widening circles
that drift out over the things.
I may not achieve the very last,
but it will be my aim.

I circle around God, around the age-old tower;
I've been circling for millennia
and still I don't know: am I a falcon, a storm,
or a sovereign song?

Ich habe viele Brüder in Sutanen
im Süden, wo in Klöstern Lorbeer steht.
Ich weiß, wie menschlich sie Madonnen planen,
und träume oft von jungen Tizianen,
durch die der Gott in Gluten geht.

Doch wie ich mich auch in mich selber neige:
Mein Gott ist dunkel und wie ein Gewebe
von hundert Wurzeln, welche schweigsam trinken.
Nur, daß ich mich aus *seiner* Wärme hebe,
mehr weiß ich nicht, weil alle meine Zweige
tief unten ruhn und nur im Winde winken.

I have many brothers who wear light cassocks
in the South, where in the cloisters there's laurel.
I know how humanly they make madonnas,
and I dream often of young Titians
through whom God moves in pure flame.

Yet here, where instincts turn inward:
My God is dark and like a web
of tangled roots all drinking soundlessly.
That out of this avid warmth I rise
is all I know: for my boughs keep perfect calm
and only rustle in the wind.

Du, Nachbar Gott, wenn ich dich manchesmal
in langer Nacht mit hartem Klopfen störe, —
so ists, weil ich dich selten atmen höre
und weiß: Du bist allein im Saal.
Und wenn du etwas brauchst, ist keiner da,
um deinem Tasten einen Trank zu reichen:
Ich horche immer. Gieb ein kleines Zeichen.
Ich bin ganz nah.

Nur eine schmale Wand ist zwischen uns,
durch Zufall; denn es könnte sein:
ein Rufen deines oder meines Munds—
und sie bricht ein
ganz ohne Lärm und Laut.

Aus deinen Bildern ist sie aufgebaut.

Und deine Bilder stehn vor dir wie Namen.
Und wenn einmal das Licht in mir entbrennt,
mit welchem meine Tiefe dich erkennt,
vergeudet sichs als Glanz auf ihren Rahmen.

Und meine Sinne, welche schnell erlahmen,
sind ohne Heimat und von dir getrennt.

～

You, neighbor God, if sometimes in the long night
I rouse you with my loud pounding, —
it's only that I so seldom hear you breathing
and know: you're in that huge room alone.
And should you need something, no one is there
to lift water to your lips.
I listen always. Give a small sign.
Feel me here.

Only a thin wall lies between us,
and that by purest chance: maybe just one call
from your mouth or mine—
and it would collapse
completely, without a sound.

It's a wall built from your images.

And your images stand before you like names.
And when the light within me kindles—
that light by which my inmost soul discerns you—
it glances off their frames like glare.

And my senses, which quickly fail,
are derelict, cut off from you.

Ich lebe grad, da das Jahrhundert geht.
Man fühlt den Wind von einem großen Blatt,
das Gott und du und ich beschrieben hat
und das sich hoch in fremden Händen dreht.

Man fühlt den Glanz von einer neuen Seite,
auf der noch Alles werden kann.

Die stillen Kräfte prüfen ihre Breite
und sehn einander dunkel an.

∾

I live at the very edge of the century.
One can feel the wind from a great page—
which God and you and I have filled with writing—
turning high above in foreign hands now.

One can feel the brightness of the new leaf,
on which anything can still be entered.

The silent forces test its breadth
and eye each other darkly.

Ich lese es heraus aus deinem Wort,
aus der Geschichte der Gebärden,
mit welchen deine Hände um das Werden
sich ründeten, begrenzend, warm und weise.
Du sagtest *leben* laut und *sterben* leise
und wiederholtest immer wieder: *Sein.*
Doch vor dem ersten Tode kam der Mord.
Da ging ein Riß durch deine reifen Kreise
und ging ein Schrein
und riß die Stimmen fort,
die eben erst sich sammelten
um dich zu sagen,
um dich zu tragen
alles Abgrunds Brücke—

Und was sie seither stammelten,
sind Stücke
deines alten Namens.

~

I read it in your word, learn it from the story
of those gestures with which your hands
cupped themselves around each fledgling thing—
warm, encompassing, wise.
You pronounced *live* strongly and *die* softly
and ceaselessly repeated: *Be.*
But before the first death murder came.
With that a rent tore through your perfect circles
and a scream broke in
and scattered all those voices
that had just then come together
to sing you,
to carry you about,
their bridge over all abysses—

And what they have been stammering since
are fragments
of your ancient name.

Ich bin, du Ängstlicher. Hörst du mich nicht
mit allen meinen Sinnen an dir branden?
Meine Gefühle, welche Flügel fanden,
umkreisen weiß dein Angesicht.
Siehst du nicht meine Seele, wie sie dicht
vor dir in einem Kleid aus Stille steht?
Reift nicht mein mailiches Gebet
an deinem Blicke wie an einem Baum?

Wenn du der Träumer bist, bin ich dein Traum.
Doch wenn du wachen willst, bin ich dein Wille
und werde mächtig aller Herrlichkeit
und ründe mich wie eine Sternenstille
über der wunderlichen Stadt der Zeit.

I am, you anxious one. Don't you hear me
surging against you with all my senses?
My feelings, which have found wings, circle
like white birds around your face.
And my soul—can't you see it there
standing before you in a robe of silence?
Doesn't my springtime prayer
ripen in your eyes as on a tree?

If you are the dreamer, I am your dream.
But if you choose to be awake, I am your will
and become the master of all majesty
and round to perfect stillness like a star
over the far-off city of time.

Mein Leben ist nicht diese steile Stunde,
darin du mich so eilen siehst.
Ich bin ein Baum vor meinem Hintergrunde,
ich bin nur einer meiner vielen Munde
und jener, welcher sich am frühsten schließt.

Ich bin die Ruhe zwischen zweien Tönen,
die sich nur schlecht aneinander gewöhnen:
denn der Ton Tod will sich erhöhn—

Aber im dunklen Intervall versöhnen
sich beide zitternd.
 Und das Lied bleibt schön.

My life is not this steep hour
through which you see me being swept.
I am a tree standing before my background,
of my many mouths I am but one—
the one, indeed, that's always first to close.

I am the space between two notes
which, if wed, ring crossly:
for the death note craves finality—

But in their dark interval the two meet,
embrace again, and tremble.
<div align="right">And the beautiful song goes on.</div>

Wenn ich gewachsen wäre irgendwo,
wo leichtere Tage sind und schlanke Stunden,
ich hätte dir ein großes Fest erfunden,
und meine Hände hielten dich nicht so,
wie sie dich manchmal halten, bang und hart.

Dort hätte ich gewagt, dich zu vergeuden,
du grenzenlose Gegenwart.
Wie einen Ball
hätt ich dich in alle wogenden Freuden
hineingeschleudert, daß einer dich finge
und deinem Fall
mit hohen Händen entgegenspringe,
du Ding der Dinge.

Ich hätte dich wie eine Klinge
blitzen lassen.
Vom goldensten Ringe
ließ ich dein Feuer umfassen,
und er müßte mirs halten
über die weißeste Hand.

Gemalt hätt ich dich: nicht an die Wand,
an den Himmel selber von Rand zu Rand,
und hätt dich gebildet, wie ein Gigant
dich bilden würde: als Berg, als Brand,
als Samum, wachsend aus Wüstensand—

oder
es kann auch sein: ich fand
dich einmal . . .
 Meine Freunde sind weit,
ich höre kaum noch ihr Lachen schallen;
und du: du bist aus dem Nest gefallen,

∾

If I'd grown up in a different land,
one with lighter days and slimmer hours,
I would have made for you a great fete,
and my hands would not have *held* you
the way they often do, clenched and afraid.

I would have been bold and squandered you,
you boundless Now.
I would have hurled you
like a ball
into every billowing delight, so that someone
could catch you and leap
with high hands to meet your fall,
you thing of things.

I would have had you flash and dash
like a cutlass.
I would have had your fire reset
on the most golden ring,
and I would have had it held out
above the whitest hand.

I would have painted you: not on the wall
but on the sky itself from edge to edge,
and would have sculpted you, the way a giant
would sculpt you: as mountain peak, as raging fire,
as simoom blasting out of desert sand—

or
in truth I may have found you
once . . .
 My boyhood friends are far away,
I can barely still hear their ringing laughter;
and you: you've fallen out of the nest,

bist ein junger Vogel mit gelben Krallen
und großen Augen und tust mir leid.
(Meine Hand ist dir viel zu breit.)
Und ich heb mit dem Finger vom Quell einen Tropfen
und lausche, ob du ihn lechzend langst,
und ich fühle dein Herz und meines klopfen
und beide aus Angst.

you're a young bird and have yellow claws
and big eyes and you pierce my heart.
(My hand must seem gigantic.)
And my fingertip lifts one drop from the well
and as I listen, listen, for some sound from your thirst
I feel your heart and mine beating
and both from fear.

Ich finde dich in allen diesen Dingen,
denen ich gut und wie ein Bruder bin;
als Samen sonnst du dich in den geringen
und in den großen giebst du groß dich hin.

Das ist das wundersame Spiel der Kräfte,
daß sie so dienend durch die Dinge gehn:
in Wurzeln wachsend, schwindend in die Schäfte
und in den Wipfeln wie ein Auferstehn.

∾

In all these *things* toward which I feel
this kinship and closeness, I always find you:
basking like seed in the very smallest
and giving yourself greatly to the great.

Such is the wondrous game the forces play
as they flow so selflessly through the things:
swelling in roots, narrowing in the long stems,
and in the blooming crowns: a resurrection.

Was wirst du tun, Gott, wenn ich sterbe?
Ich bin dein Krug (wenn ich zerscherbe?)
Ich bin dein Trank (wenn ich verderbe?)
Bin dein Gewand und dein Gewerbe,
mit mir verlierst du deinen Sinn.

Nach mir hast du kein Haus, darin
dich Worte, nah und warm, begrüßen.
Es fällt von deinen müden Füßen
die Samtsandale, die ich bin.

Dein großer Mantel läßt dich los.
Dein Blick, den ich mit meiner Wange
warm, wie mit einem Pfühl, empfange,
wird kommen, wird mich suchen, lange—
und legt beim Sonnenuntergange
sich fremden Steinen in den Schooß.

Was wirst du tun, Gott? Ich bin bange.

❧

What will you do, God, when I die?
I am your jug (and I will shatter)
I am your drink (and I'll go bad)
I am your clothing and your calling,
you'll lose all reason, losing me.

With me gone, you'll have no house
where warm words will welcome you.
Without me, you'll have no sandals:
your exhausted feet will wander bare.

Your mighty cloak will fall away.
Your gaze, which my cheek took in
soft and warm, like a pillow,
will arrive here, look, search long—
and finally at the end of sunset
lie down in the lap of alien stones.

What will you do, God? I'm afraid.

Dein allererstes Wort war: *Licht*:
da ward die Zeit. Dann schwiegst du lange.
Dein zweites Wort ward Mensch und bange
(wir dunkeln noch in seinem Klange)
und wieder sinnt dein Angesicht.

Ich aber will dein drittes nicht.

Ich bete nachts oft: Sei der Stumme,
der wachsend in Gebärden bleibt
und den der Geist im Traume treibt,
daß er des Schweigens schwere Summe
in Stirnen und Gebirge schreibt.

Sei du die Zuflucht vor dem Zorne,
der das Unsagbare verstieß.
Es wurde Nacht im Paradies:
sei du der Hüter mit dem Horne,
und man erzählt nur, daß er blies.

Your first word was: *Light*:
and time began. After long silence
your second word was Man and there was fear
(we still darken in its sound)
before your face resumed its brooding.

Yet I am loath to hear your third.

I often pray at night: be the mute one,
the one growing steadily in gestures
and driven by the spirit in dream
to inscribe the heavy sum of silence
on mountain peaks and human brows.

Be the refuge from that wrath
that cast out the ineffable.
Night fell in Paradise:
be the herdsman whose horn sounded once—
but only as our ancient stories tell.

Ihr vielen unbestürmten Städte,
habt ihr euch nie den Feind ersehnt?
O daß er euch belagert hätte
ein langes schwankendes Jahrzehnt.

Bis ihr ihn trostlos und in Trauern,
bis daß ihr hungernd ihn ertrugt;
er liegt wie Landschaft vor den Mauern,
denn also weiß er auszudauern
um jene, die er heimgesucht.

Schaut aus vom Rande eurer Dächer:
da lagert er und wird nicht matt
und wird nicht weniger und schwächer
und schickt nicht Droher und Versprecher
und Überreder in die Stadt.

Er ist der große Mauerbrecher,
der eine stumme Arbeit hat.

O you many unassaulted cities,
have you never longed for the enemy?
If only he'd lay siege to you
for ten long tremulous years.

Till you knew hunger and sorrow
and grieving and desperation utterly;
he spreads out before walls like countryside,
and in wars of endurance he knows
how to outlast whoever is inside.

Look out from your rooftop's edge:
there he camps and his will hasn't weakened
and his numbers haven't diminished
and he has dispatched no one into the city
to bargain or reason or warn.

He is the great demolisher of walls,
and his work goes on in silence.

Gott spricht zu jedem nur, eh er ihn macht,
dann geht er schweigend mit ihm aus der Nacht.
Aber die Worte, eh jeder beginnt,
diese wolkigen Worte, sind:

Von deinen Sinnen hinausgesandt,
geh bis an deiner Sehnsucht Rand;
gieb mir Gewand.

Hinter den Dingen wachse als Brand,
daß ihre Schatten, ausgespannt,
immer mich ganz bedecken.

Laß dir Alles geschehn: Schönheit und Schrecken.
Man muß nur gehn: Kein Gefühl ist das fernste.
Laß dich von mir nicht trennen.
Nah ist das Land,
das sie das Leben nennen.

Du wirst es erkennen
an seinem Ernste.

Gieb mir die Hand.

God talks to each of us as he creates us,
then walks with us silently out of night.
But the words, spoken to us before we start,
those cloudy words, are these:

Sent forth by your senses,
go to the very edge of your desire;
invest me.

Back behind the things grow as fire,
so that their shadows, lengthened,
will always and completely cover me.

Let everything happen to you: beauty and terror.
Only press on: no feeling is final.
Don't let yourself be cut off from me.
Nearby is that country
known as Life.

You will recognize it
by its seriousness.

Give me your hand.

Lösch mir die Augen aus: ich kann dich sehn,
wirf mir die Ohren zu: ich kann dich hören,
und ohne Füße kann ich zu dir gehn,
und ohne Mund noch kann ich dich beschwören.
Brich mir die Arme ab, ich fasse dich
mit meinem Herzen wie mit einer Hand,
halt mir das Herz zu, und mein Hirn wird schlagen,
und wirfst du in mein Hirn den Brand,
so werd ich dich auf meinem Blute tragen.

Put my eyes out: I can see you,
seal my ears shut: I can hear you,
and without feet I can walk toward you,
and without a mouth I can still beseech you.
Break my arms off, with my heart
I will grasp you as with a hand,
tear my heart out and my brain will beat,
and if you put a torch to my brain
I will bear you through all my blood.

Jetzt reifen schon die roten Berberitzen,
alternde Astern atmen schwach im Beet.
Wer jetzt nicht reich ist, da der Sommer geht,
wird immer warten und sich nie besitzen.

Wer jetzt nicht seine Augen schließen kann.
gewiß, daß eine Fülle von Gesichten
in ihm nur wartet bis die Nacht begann,
um sich in seinem Dunkel aufzurichten: —
der ist vergangen wie ein alter Mann.

Dem kommt nichts mehr, dem stößt kein Tag mehr zu,
und alles lügt ihn an, was ihm geschieht;
auch du, mein Gott. Und wie ein Stein bist du,
welcher ihn täglich in die Tiefe zieht.

Already the red barberries are ripening,
old asters are breathing weakly in their beds.
Whoever lacks riches now, with summer's passing,
will always wait and even lack himself.

Whoever cannot close his eyes now,
confident that inside him endless visions
are only waiting for the night to start
so that they can rise up in his darkness: —
his life is over, he's like an old man.

Nothing else will come, no more days will flare,
and what does happen will leave him feeling cheated;
even you, my God. And you're like a stone
that each day pulls him deeper down.

Du mußt nicht bangen, Gott. Sie sagen: *mein*
zu allen Dingen, die geduldig sind.
Sie sind wie Wind, der an die Zweige streift
und sagt: *mein* Baum.

Sie merken kaum,
wie alles glüht, was ihre Hand ergreift, —
so daß sie's auch an seinem letzten Saum
nicht halten könnten ohne zu verbrennen.

Sie sagen *mein*, wie manchmal einer gern
den Fürsten Freund nennt im Gespräch mit Bauern,
wenn dieser Fürst sehr groß ist und—sehr fern.
Sie sagen *mein* von ihren fremden Mauern
und kennen gar nicht ihres Hauses Herrn.
Sie sagen *mein* und nennen das Besitz,
wenn jedes Ding sich schließt, dem sie sich nahn,
so wie ein abgeschmackter Charlatan
vielleicht die Sonne sein nennt und den Blitz.
So sagen sie: mein Leben, meine Frau,
mein Hund, mein Kind, und wissen doch genau,
daß alles: Leben, Frau und Hund und Kind
fremde Gebilde sind, daran sie blind
mit ihren ausgestreckten Händen stoßen.
Gewißheit freilich ist das nur den Großen,
die sich nach Augen sehnen. Denn die Andern
wollens nicht hören, daß ihr armes Wandern
mit keinem Dinge rings zusammenhängt,
daß sie, von ihrer Habe fortgedrängt,
nicht anerkannt von ihrem Eigentume,
das Weib so wenig *haben* wie die Blume,
die eines fremden Lebens ist für alle.

℘

You mustn't worry, God. They say *mine*
to all patient, unprotesting things.
They're like the wind that gusts through branches
and says *my* tree.

They scarcely notice
how everything their hand reaches for
burns bright: they couldn't hold
even its outmost edge and not be singed.

They say *mine* as sometimes among villagers
one talking will call the prince his friend,
especially when this prince is very great—and far away.
They say *mine* of their foreign walls
and know nothing of their house's lord.
They say *mine* and claim possession
(though each thing shuts at their approach)
the way some arrant charlatan
might call the sun and lightning his.
So they say: my life, my spouse,
my dog, my child, and know quite well
that all of them—life, spouse, dog, and child
are foreign forms they sometimes blindly
stumble onto with their outstretched arms.
Alas, only those who long for eyes
confirm this truth. The others *will not hear*
that in their threadbare wandering
they connect with not one thing on their way;
that they, cast out by their possessing,
disavowed by their belongings,
can *have* wives as little as they can have flowers,
whose lives are foreign and apart for all.

Falle nicht, Gott, aus deinem Gleichgewicht.
Auch der dich liebt und der dein Angesicht
erkennt im Dunkel, wenn er wie ein Licht
in deinem Atem schwankt, —besitzt dich nicht.
Und wenn dich einer in der Nacht erfaßt,
so daß du kommen mußt in sein Gebet:
 Du bist der Gast,
 der wieder weiter geht.

Wer kann dich halten, Gott? Denn du bist dein,
von keines Eigentümers Hand gestört,
so wie der noch nicht ausgereifte Wein,
der immer süßer wird, sich selbst gehört.

God, don't lose your equanimity.
Even he who loves you and discerns your face
in darkness, when he trembles like a light
flickering beneath your breath—does not possess you.
And if at night someone takes hold of you
so fiercely that you must appear in his prayer:
>You are the guest
>who goes away again.

Who can hold you, God? For you are *yours*,
no possessor's hand disturbs you:
just as the not yet fully ripened wine
turns sweeter and sweeter and is all its own.

In tiefen Nächten grab ich dich, du Schatz.
Denn alle Überflüsse, die ich sah,
sind Armut und armsäliger Ersatz
für deine Schönheit, die noch nie geschah.

Aber der Weg zu dir ist furchtbar weit
und, weil ihn lange keiner ging, verweht.
O du bist einsam. Du bist Einsamkeit,
du Herz, das zu entfernten Talen geht.

Und meine Hände, welche blutig sind
vom Graben, heb ich offen in den Wind,
so daß sie sich verzweigen wie ein Baum.
Ich sauge dich mit ihnen aus dem Raum
als hättest du dich einmal dort zerschellt
in einer ungeduldigen Gebärde,
und fielest jetzt, eine zerstäubte Welt,
aus fernen Sternen wieder auf die Erde
sanft wie ein Frühlingsregen fällt.

∾

In the deep nights I dig for you, you treasure.
For all visible riches have been only
poverty and wretched simulacrum
of your beauty, which still waits undisclosed.

But the path to you is far and long unwalked
and covered over almost past discerning.
You are alone. You are solitude itself,
you heart, roaming valleys with far-off hills.

And my hands, which are bloody from digging:
I lift them, hold them open in the wind,
spread them so they can branch out like a tree.
And with them I suck you from the sky
as if you'd exploded there in a million pieces
from some rash gesture you had made
and fell now, a disintegrated world,
from distant stars once more upon the earth—
gently, the way a Spring rain falls.

Vielleicht, daß ich durch schwere Berge gehe
in harten Adern, wie ein Erz allein;
und bin so tief, daß ich kein Ende sehe
und keine Ferne: alles wurde Nähe
und alle Nähe wurde Stein.

Ich bin ja noch kein Wissender im Wehe, —
so macht mich dieses große Dunkel klein;
bist *Du* es aber: mach dich schwer, brich ein:
daß deine ganze Hand an mir geschehe
und ich an dir mit meinem ganzen Schrein.

It's as if I'm pushing through massive mountains
through hard veins, like solitary ore;
and I'm so deep that I can see no end
and no distance: everything became nearness
and all the nearness turned to stone.

I'm still a novice in the realm of pain, —
so this enormous darkness makes me small;
But if it's *You*—steel yourself, break in:
that your whole hand will grip me
and my whole scream will seize you.

∾

O Herr, gieb jedem seinem eignen Tod.
Das Sterben, das aus jenem Leben geht,
darin er Liebe hatte, Sinn und Not.

~

O Lord, give us each our own death. Grant us
the dying that comes forth from that life in which
we knew love, grappled with meaning, felt need.

From DAS BUCH DER BILDER

(1902, 1906)

From THE BOOK OF IMAGES

(1902, 1906)

Wer du auch seist: am Abend tritt hinaus
aus deiner Stube, drin du alles weißt;
als letztes vor der Ferne liegt dein Haus:
wer du auch seist.
Mit deinen Augen, welche müde kaum
von der verbrauchten Schwelle sich befrein,
hebst du ganz langsam einen schwarzen Baum
und stellst ihn vor den Himmel: schlank, allein.
Und hast die Welt gemacht. Und sie ist groß
und wie ein Wort, das noch im Schweigen reift.
Und wie dein Wille ihren Sinn begreift,
lassen sie deine Augen zärtlich los . . .

ENTRANCE

Whoever you are: in the evening step
out of your room, where you know everything;
yours is the last house before the distant:
whoever you are.
With your eyes, which wearily
just free themselves of the worn-out threshold,
very slowly you raise one black tree
and set it against the sky: slender, alone.
And you've made the world. And it's immense
and like a word ripening in silence.
And as your will reaches for its meaning,
tenderly your eyes let it go . . .

Wieder duftet der Wald.
Es heben die schwebenden Lerchen
mit sich den Himmel empor, der unseren Schultern schwer war;
zwar sah man noch durch die Äste den Tag, wie er leer war,—
aber nach langen, regnenden Nachmittagen
kommen die goldübersonnten
neueren Stunden,
vor denen flüchtend an fernen Häuserfronten
alle die wunden
Fenster furchtsam mit Flügeln schlagen.

Dann wird es still. Sogar der Regen geht leiser
über der Steine ruhig dunkelnden Glanz.
Alle Geräusche ducken sich ganz
in die glänzenden Knospen der Reiser.

Again the woods smell sweet.
The soaring larks lift up with them
the sky, which weighed so heavy on our shoulders;
through bare branches one still saw the day, standing empty—
but after long rain-filled afternoons
come the golden sun-drenched
newer hours,
before which, on distant housefronts,
all the wounded
windows flee fearful with beating wings.

Then it goes still. Even the rain runs softer
over the stones' quietly darkening glow.
All noises slip entirely away
into the brushwood's glimmering buds.

DIE ENGEL

Sie haben alle müde Münde
und helle Seelen ohne Saum.
Und eine Sehnsucht (wie nach Sünde)
geht ihnen manchmal durch den Traum.

Fast gleichen sie einander alle;
in Gottes Gärten schweigen sie,
wie viele, viele Intervalle
in seiner Macht und Melodie.

Nur wenn sie ihre Flügel breiten,
sind sie die Wecker eines Winds:
als ginge Gott mit seinen weiten
Bildhauerhänden durch die Seiten
im dunklen Buch des Anbeginns.

They all have tired mouths
and bright, seamless souls.
And a longing (as for sin)
sometimes haunts their dream.

They're all almost alike;
in God's gardens they keep still,
like many, many intervals
in his might and melody.

Only when they spread their wings
are they the wakers of a wind:
as if God with his broad sculptor's
hands were turning pages
in the dark book of the beginning.

Da rinnt der Schule lange Angst und Zeit
mit Warten hin, mit lauter dumpfen Dingen.
O Einsamkeit, o schweres Zeitverbringen . . .
Und dann hinaus: die Straßen sprühn und klingen
und auf den Plätzen die Fontänen springen
und in den Gärten wird die Welt so weit—.
Und durch das alles gehn im kleinen Kleid,
ganz anders als die andern gehn und gingen—:
O wunderliche Zeit, o Zeitverbringen,
o Einsamkeit.

Und in das alles fern hinauszuschauen:
Männer und Frauen; Männer, Männer, Frauen
und Kinder, welche anders sind und bunt;
und da ein Haus und dann und wann ein Hund
und Schrecken lautlos wechselnd mit Vertrauen—:
O Trauer ohne Sinn, o Traum, o Grauen,
o Tiefe ohne Grund.

Und so zu spielen: Ball und Ring und Reifen
in einem Garten, welcher sanft verblaßt,
und manchmal die Erwachsenen zu streifen,
blind und verwildert in des Haschens Hast,
aber am Abend still, mit kleinen steifen
Schritten nachhaus zu gehn, fest angefaßt—:
O immer mehr entweichendes Begreifen,
o Angst, o Last.

Und stundenlang am großen grauen Teiche
mit einem kleinen Segelschiff zu knien;
es zu vergessen, weil noch andre, gleiche
und schönere Segel durch die Ringe ziehn,
und denken müssen an das kleine bleiche
Gesicht, das sinkend aus dem Teiche schien—:

School's long anxiety and time slips by
in waiting, in endless dreary things.
O solitude, O heavy spending on and on of time . . .
And then outside: the streets flash and ring
and on the squares the fountains leap
and the world becomes boundless in the gardens.
And to walk through it all in one's small suit,
so unlike the way the others walked and sauntered—:
O wondrous time, O spending on and on of time,
O solitude.

And to look far off into it all:
men and women; men, more men, women
and then children, who are different and bright;
and here a house and now and then a dog
and fear changing places soundlessly with trust—:
O sadness without cause, O dream, O dread,
O endless depth.

And so to play: ball and hoop and handstands
in a garden that keeps softly fading,
and to collide sometimes with grownups
blindly and wildly in the rush of tag,
but at evening quietly, with small, stiff steps
to walk back home, your hand firmly held—:
O ever more escaping grasp of things,
O weight, O fear.

And for hours at the big gray pond
to kneel entranced with a small sailboat;
to neglect it, because other, identical yet
more beautiful sails glide through the rings,
and to have to think about the small pale face
that sinking gazed back out of the pond—:

O Kindheit, o entgleitende Vergleiche.
Wohin? Wohin?

O childhood, O likeness gliding off . . .
Where? Where?

Das Dunkeln war wie Reichtum in dem Raume,
darin der Knabe, sehr verheimlicht, saß.
Und als die Mutter eintrat wie im Traume,
erzitterte im stillen Schrank ein Glas.
Sie fühlte, wie das Zimmer sie verriet,
und küßte ihren Knaben: Bist du hier? . . .
Dann schauten beide bang nach dem Klavier,
denn manchen Abend hatte sie ein Lied,
darin das Kind sich seltsam tief verfing.

Es saß sehr still. Sein großes Schauen hing
an ihrer Hand, die ganz gebeugt vom Ringe,
als ob sie schwer in Schneewehn ginge,
über die weißen Tasten ging.

FROM A CHILDHOOD

The darkening was like treasures in the room
in which the boy, so deeply hidden, sat.
And when as in a dream his mother entered,
a glass shook on the silent shelf.
She felt how the room was giving her away,
and kissed her boy: So, you're here? . . .
Then both gazed fearfully toward the piano,
for many an evening she would play a song
in which the child got strangely, deeply caught.

He sat stock-still. His wide gaze hung
on her hand, which, weighed down by the ring,
as if it were walking in deep snow,
wandered across the white keys.

Ich möchte einer werden so wie die,
die durch die Nacht mit wilden Pferden fahren,
mit Fackeln, die gleich aufgegangnen Haaren
in ihres Jagens großem Winde wehn.
Vorn möcht ich stehen wie in einem Kahne,
groß und wie eine Fahne aufgerollt.
Dunkel, aber mit einem Helm von Gold,
der unruhig glänzt. Und hinter mir gereiht
zehn Männer aus derselben Dunkelheit
mit Helmen, die, wie meiner, unstät sind,
bald klar wie Glas, bald dunkel, alt und blind.
Und einer steht bei mir und bläst uns Raum
mit der Trompete, welche blitzt und schreit,
und bläst uns eine schwarze Einsamkeit,
durch die wir rasen wie ein rascher Traum:
Die Häuser fallen hinter uns ins Knie,
die Gassen biegen sich uns schief entgegen,
die Plätze weichen aus: wir fassen sie,
und unsre Rosse rauschen wie ein Regen.

I want to be like one of those
who ride through the night with wild horses,
with torches, which, like loosened hair,
stream back in the great wind of their pursuit.
I want to stand up front as in a boat,
huge and unfurled like a flag.
Dark, but with a golden helmet that
gleams restlessly. And lined up behind me
ten men of that same darkness
with helmets that flash the way mine does,
now clear as glass, now dark, and old, and blind.
And one at my side blasts us space
with his trumpet, which shines and screams out,
and blasts us a black solitude
we race through like an instant dream:
behind us the houses fall on their knees,
the streets slope back away from us,
the squares try to escape us: we take them,
and our horses sweep down like rain.

Ich möchte jemanden einsingen,
bei jemandem sitzen und sein.
Ich möchte dich wiegen und kleinsingen
und begleiten schlafaus und schlafein.
Ich möchte der Einzige sein im Haus,
der wüßte: die Nacht war kalt.
Und möchte horchen herein und hinaus
in dich, in die Welt, in den Wald.
Die Uhren rufen sich schlagend an,
und man sieht der Zeit auf den Grund.
Und unten geht noch ein fremder Mann
und stört einen fremden Hund.
Dahinter wird Stille. Ich habe groß
die Augen auf dich gelegt;
und sie halten dich sanft und lassen dich los,
wenn ein Ding sich im Dunkel bewegt.

I'd like to sing someone to sleep,
sit beside someone and be there.
I'd like to rock you and sing softly
and go with you to and from sleep.
I'd like to be the one in the house
who knew: the night was cold.
And I'd like to hear every little stirring
in you, in the world, in the woods.
The clocks call to one another striking,
and one sees to the bottom of time.
And down below a last strange man walks by
and rouses a strange dog.
And after that comes silence.
I have laid my eyes upon you wide;
and they hold you gently and they let you go
when a thing moves in the dark.

Die Nächte sind nicht für die Menge gemacht.
Von deinem Nachbar trennt dich die Nacht,
und du sollst ihn nicht suchen trotzdem.
Und machst du nachts deine Stube licht,
um Menschen zu schauen ins Angesicht,
so mußt du bedenken: wem.

Die Menschen sind furchtbar vom Licht entstellt,
das von ihren Gesichtern träuft,
und haben sie nachts sich zusammengesellt,
so schaust du eine wankende Welt
durcheinandergehäuft.
Auf ihren Stirnen hat gelber Schein
alle Gedanken verdrängt,
in ihren Blicken flackert der Wein,
an ihren Händen hängt
die schwere Gebärde, mit der sie sich
bei ihren Gesprächen verstehn;
und dabei sagen sie: *Ich* und *Ich*
und meinen: Irgendwen.

Nights are not made for the masses.
Night cuts you off from your neighbor,
and you'd do well not to seek him out.
And if you light your room at night
so you can look deep into someone's eyes,
you'll end by asking: whose face is this?

Human beings are horribly warped by the light
that drips from their faces,
and if at night they've gathered together
you'll see a makeshift world
with no hope of holding.
On their foreheads yellow glare
has driven out all thought,
in their eyes the wine flickers,
on their hands hangs
the heavy gesture with which
they understand one another in their talks;
and with which they say: *I* and *I*
and mean: Anyone.

DER NACHBAR

Fremde Geige, gehst du mir nach?
In wieviel fernen Städten schon sprach
deine einsame Nacht zu meiner?
Spielen dich hunderte? Spielt dich einer?

Giebt es in allen großen Städten
solche, die sich ohne dich
schon in den Flüssen verloren hätten?
Und warum trifft es immer mich?

Warum bin ich immer der Nachbar derer,
die dich bange zwingen zu singen
und zu sagen: Das Leben ist schwerer
als die Schwere von allen Dingen.

THE NEIGHBOR

Strange violin, do you follow me?
In how many distant cities before this
did your lonely night speak to mine?
Do hundreds play you? Or is it only one?

Are there people in all the big cities
who without you would have long since
thrown themselves in the rivers?
And why does it always find *me*?

Why am *I* always the neighbor of those
who force you to sing out of fear
and say out loud: Life is heavier
than the weight of all things.

Der blinde Mann, der auf der Brücke steht,
grau wie ein Markstein namenloser Reiche,
er ist vielleicht das Ding, das immer gleiche,
um das von fern die Sternenstunde geht,
und der Gestirne stiller Mittelpunkt.
Denn alles um ihn irrt und rinnt und prunkt.

Er ist der unbewegliche Gerechte,
in viele wirre Wege hingestellt;
der dunkle Eingang in die Unterwelt
bei einem oberflächlichen Geschlechte.

PONT DU CARROUSEL

The blind man standing on the bridge,
gray like a boundary stone of nameless kingdoms:
he is perhaps that one unchanging thing
around which the far-off stellar hours revolve,
the silent midpoint of the constellations.
For everything around him strays and struts and runs.

He is the immovable upright one
set down in many tangled paths;
the dark entrance to the underworld
among a surface-dwelling race.

Pont du Carrousel: A bridge over the Seine to the Place du Carrousel in Paris.

footer

DER EINSAME

Wie einer, der auf fremden Meeren fuhr,
so bin ich bei den ewig Einheimischen;
die vollen Tage stehn auf ihren Tischen,
mir aber ist die Ferne voll Figur.

In mein Gesicht reicht eine Welt herein,
die vielleicht unbewohnt ist wie ein Mond,
sie aber lassen kein Gefühl allein,
und alle ihre Worte sind bewohnt.

Die Dinge, die ich weither mit mir nahm,
sehn selten aus, gehalten an das Ihre—:
in ihrer großen Heimat sind sie Tiere,
hier halten sie den Atem an vor Scham.

THE SOLITARY

I'm like one who's traveled foreign oceans
among these so eternally at home;
the full days stand rote at their tables:
for me the distant roils with dream.

Deep inside my face a world reaches,
maybe uninhabited like a moon;
but they leave no feeling unexplored,
and all their words are taken.

The things I brought with me from far away
appear outlandish next to theirs——:
in their great homeland they were wild animals;
here they hold their breath for shame.

DIE ASCHANTI
(Jardin d'Acclimatation)

Keine Vision von fremden Ländern,
kein Gefühl von braunen Frauen, die
tanzen aus den fallenden Gewändern.

Keine wilde fremde Melodie.
Keine Lieder, die vom Blute stammten,
und kein Blut, das aus den Tiefen schrie.

Keine braunen Mädchen, die sich samten
breiteten in Tropenmüdigkeit;
keine Augen, die wie Waffen flammten,

und die Munde zum Gelächter breit.
Und ein wunderliches Sich-verstehen
mit der hellen Menschen Eitelkeit.

Und mir war so bange hinzusehen.

O wie sind die Tiere so viel treuer,
die in Gittern auf und niedergehn,
ohne Eintracht mit dem Treiben neuer
fremder Dinge, die sie nicht verstehn;
und sie brennen wie ein stilles Feuer
leise aus und sinken in sich ein,
teilnahmslos dem neuen Abenteuer
und mit ihrem großen Blut allein.

THE ASHANTI
(Jardin d'Acclimatation)

No vision of lush, far-off countries.
No feeling of brown, vivid women
dancing slowly out of falling garments.

No wild, unheard-of melodies.
No songs that issued from the blood,
no blood that screamed out of the depths.

No brown girls who stretched
velvetlike in tropical exhaustion;
no eyes that blazed like weapons

and the broad mouth shaped for laughter.
And a bizarre accommodation
with the light-skinned humans' vanity.

And it made me shudder seeing that.

O how much truer are the animals
pacing up and down in their steel cages,
unrelated to the antics of these new strange
beings, which they do not understand;
and they burn out softly like
a silent fire and subside into themselves,
indifferent to the new adventure
and alone with their untouchable blood.

Ashanti: A region in West Africa, now part of Ghana; here signifying the inhabitants of or
from that region.
Jardin d'Acclimatation: An amusement park with zoo in the Bois de Boulogne, Paris.

Im welken Walde ist ein Vogelruf,
der sinnlos scheint in diesem welken Walde.
Und dennoch ruht der runde Vogelruf
in dieser Weile, die ihn schuf,
breit wie ein Himmel auf dem welken Walde.
Gefügig räumt sich alles in den Schrei:
Das ganze Land scheint lautlos drin zu liegen,
der große Wind scheint sich hineinzuschmiegen,
und die Minute, welche weiter will,
ist bleich und still, als ob sie Dinge wüßte,
an denen jeder sterben müßte,
aus ihm herausgestiegen.

APPREHENSION

In the faded forest is a birdcall
that seems meaningless in this faded forest.
And yet the rounded birdcall rests
in this interim that shaped it,
wide as a sky upon the faded forest.
Everything pliantly makes room in the cry:
The whole landscape seems to lie there soundlessly,
the great wind seems to nestle inside,
and time, which wants to move on,
has, pale and silent, as if it knew things
for which one has to die,
risen out of it.

KLAGE

O wie ist alles fern
und lange vergangen.
Ich glaube, der Stern,
von welchem ich Glanz empfange,
ist seit Jahrtausenden tot.
Ich glaube, im Boot,
das vorüberfuhr,
hörte ich etwas Banges sagen.
Im Hause hat eine Uhr
geschlagen . . .
In welchem Haus? . . .
Ich möchte aus meinem Herzen hinaus
unter den großen Himmel treten.
Ich möchte beten.
Und einer von allen Sternen
müßte wirklich noch sein.
Ich glaube, ich wüßte,
welcher allein
gedauert hat, —
welcher wie eine weiße Stadt
am Ende des Strahls in den Himmeln steht . . .

LAMENT

O how far away and long gone
everything is.
I believe the star
whose brightness I take in
has been dead a thousand years.
I believe that in the boat
gliding by I heard
something fearful being said.
In the house a clock
just struck . . .
What house? . . .
I'd like to step out of my heart
and be under the great sky.
I'd like to pray.
And surely one of all those stars
must still exist.
I believe I'd know
which one alone
has lasted, —
which one like a white city
stands at its light's end in the sky . . .

EINSAMKEIT

Die Einsamkeit ist wie ein Regen.
Sie steigt vom Meer den Abenden entgegen;
von Ebenen, die fern sind und entlegen,
geht sie zum Himmel, der sie immer hat.
Und erst vom Himmel fällt sie auf die Stadt.

Regnet hernieder in den Zwitterstunden,
wenn sich nach Morgen wenden alle Gassen
und wenn die Leiber, welche nichts gefunden,
enttäuscht und traurig von einander lassen;
und wenn die Menschen, die einander hassen,
in *einem* Bett zusammen schlafen müssen:

dann geht die Einsamkeit mit den Flüssen . . .

SOLITUDE

Solitude is like a rain.
Toward evening it rises from the sea;
from plains that are distant and remote
it migrates to the sky, where it always is.
And only then it falls from the sky on the city.

It rains down in the in-between hours,
when toward dawn all the streets turn around again,
and when those bodies that found nothing
leave each other sad and disappointed;
and when those people who detest each other
have to sleep together in one bed:

then solitude runs with the rivers . . .

Herr: es ist Zeit. Der Sommer war sehr groß.
Leg deinen Schatten auf die Sonnenuhren,
und auf den Fluren laß die Winde los.

Befiehl den letzten Früchten voll zu sein;
gieb ihnen noch zwei südlichere Tage,
dränge sie zur Vollendung hin und jage
die letzte Süße in den schweren Wein.

Wer jetzt kein Haus hat, baut sich keines mehr.
Wer jetzt allein ist, wird es lange bleiben,
wird wachen, lesen, lange Briefe schreiben
und wird in den Alleen hin und her
unruhig wandern, wenn die Blätter treiben.

AUTUMN DAY

Lord: it is time. Your summer was superb.
Lay your shadows on the sundials,
and in the meadows let the winds go free.

Command the last fruits to be full;
give them only two more southern days,
urge them on to completion and chase
the last sweetness into the heavy wine.

Whoever has no house will never build one now.
Whoever is alone now will long remain so,
will stay awake, read books, write long letters
and wander restless back and forth
along the tree-lined streets, as the leaves drift down.

ERINNERUNG

Und du wartest, erwartest das Eine,
das dein Leben unendlich vermehrt;
das Mächtige, Ungemeine,
das Erwachen der Steine,
Tiefen, dir zugekehrt.

Es dämmern im Bücherständer
die Bände in Gold und Braun;
und du denkst an durchfahrene Länder,
an Bilder, an die Gewänder
wiederverlorener Fraun.

Und da weißt du auf einmal: das war es.
Du erhebst dich, und vor dir steht
eines vergangenen Jahres
Angst und Gestalt und Gebet.

MEMORY

And you wait, you wait for that one thing
that will infinitely enlarge your life;
the gigantic, the stupendous,
the awakening of stones,
depths turned round toward you.

The volumes bound in rust and gold
flicker dimly on the shelves;
and you think of lands traveled across,
of paintings, of the clothes of
women found and lost.

And then suddenly you know: it was *then*.
You rise, and before you
stands the fear and prayer and shape
of a vanished year.

Die Blätter fallen, fallen wie von weit,
als welkten in den Himmeln ferne Gärten;
sie fallen mit verneinender Gebärde.

Und in den Nächten fällt die schwere Erde
aus allen Sternen in die Einsamkeit.

Wir alle fallen. Diese Hand da fällt.
Und sieh dir andre an: es ist in allen.

Und doch ist Einer, welcher dieses Fallen
unendlich sanft in seinen Händen hält.

AUTUMN

The leaves are falling, falling as from far away,
as if distant gardens withered in the skies;
they fall with gestures saying "No."

And in the nights the heavy earth falls
from a multitude of stars into aloneness.

We are all falling. This hand is falling.
And look at the others: it's inside them all.

And yet there's one who with infinite
tenderness holds this falling in his hands.

Meine Stube und diese Weite,
wach über nachtendem Land, —
ist Eines. Ich bin eine Saite,
über rauschende breite
Resonanzen gespannt.

Die Dinge sind Geigenleiber,
von murrendem Dunkel voll;
drin träumt das Weinen der Weiber,
drin rührt sich im Schlafe der Groll
ganzer Geschlechter . . .
Ich soll
silbern erzittern: dann wird
Alles unter mir leben,
und was in den Dingen irrt,
wird nach dem Lichte streben,
das von meinem tanzenden Tone,
um welchen der Himmel wellt,
durch schmale, schmachtende Spalten
in die alten
Abgründe ohne
Ende fällt . . .

My room and this vastness,
awake above the darkening land, —
are one. I am a string,
stretched tightly over wide
raging resonances.

Things are bodies of violins
full of grumbling darkness:
in it dreams the grief of women,
in it the resentment of whole
generations stirs in its sleep . . .
I shall vibrate
like silver; then everything
beneath me will live,
and whatever wanders lost in things
will strive toward the light
that from my dancing note,
around which the heavens pulse,
through thin, pining rifts
into the old
abysses endlessly
falls . . .

Nacht, stille Nacht, in die verwoben sind
ganz weiße Dinge, rote, bunte Dinge,
verstreute Farben, die erhoben sind
zu Einem Dunkel Einer Stille, —bringe
doch mich auch in Beziehung zu dem Vielen,
das du erwirbst und überredest. Spielen
denn meine Sinne noch zu sehr mit Licht?
Würde sich denn mein Angesicht
noch immer störend von den Gegenständen
abheben? Urteile nach meinen Händen:
Liegen sie nicht wie Werkzeug da und Ding?
Ist nicht der Ring selbst schlicht
an meiner Hand, und liegt das Licht
nicht ganz so, voll Vertrauen, über ihnen, —
als ob sie Wege wären, die, beschienen,
nicht anders sich verzweigen, als im Dunkel? . . .

PRAYER

Night, silent night, into which are woven
pure white things, red, bright-patterned things,
scattered colors, which are gathered
into *one* darkness's *one* silence, —include me
also in the weft of that rich manifold
which you acquire and persuade. Do my senses
really still play too much with light?
Won't my face forever stand out
as an anomaly in the world of objects?
Judge by my hands instead:
Don't they lie there exactly
like tool and thing? Isn't the ring just *there*
on my finger, and doesn't the light
lie the same way, full of trust, across them, —
as if they were bright-lit paths
that diverge no differently in darkness? . . .

FORTSCHRITT

Und wieder rauscht mein tiefes Leben lauter,
als ob es jetzt in breitern Ufern ginge.
Immer verwandter werden mir die Dinge
und alle Bilder immer angeschauter.
Dem Namenlosen fühl ich mich vertrauter:
Mit meinen Sinnen, wie mit Vögeln, reiche
ich in die windigen Himmel aus der Eiche,
und in den abgebrochnen Tag der Teiche
sinkt, wie auf Fischen stehend, mein Gefühl.

And again my deep life rushes louder,
as if it moved now between steeper banks.
Objects grow ever more akin to me,
all images more intensely seen.
I've become more at home amid the nameless:
With my senses, as with birds, I reach up
into the windy heavens from the oak,
and in the small ponds' broken-off day
my feeling sinks, as if it stood on fishes.

VORGEFÜHL

Ich bin wie eine Fahne von Fernen umgeben.
Ich ahne die Winde, die kommen, und muß sie leben,
während die Dinge unten sich noch nicht rühren:
die Türen schließen noch sanft, und in den Kaminen ist Stille;
die Fenster zittern noch nicht, und der Staub ist noch schwer.

Da weiß ich die Stürme schon und bin erregt wie das Meer.
Und breite mich aus und falle in mich hinein
und werfe mich ab und bin ganz allein
in dem großen Sturm.

PRESENTIMENT

I'm like a flag surrounded by distances.
I can sense the coming winds, and have to live them,
while things down below don't stir yet:
the doors still close softly, and the chimneys hold silence;
the windows don't tremble yet, the dust lies calm.

Then all at once the squalls arrive and I'm embroiled like the sea.
And I spread myself out and plunge deep inside myself
and cast myself off and am entirely alone
in the great storm.

Der Park ist hoch. Und wie aus einem Haus
tret ich aus seiner Dämmerung heraus
in Ebene und Abend. In den Wind,
denselben Wind, den auch die Wolken fühlen,
die hellen Flüsse und die Flügelmühlen,
die langsam mahlend stehn am Himmelsrand.
Jetzt bin auch ich ein Ding in seiner Hand,
das kleinste unter diesen Himmeln. —Schau:

Ist das Ein Himmel?:
 Selig lichtes Blau,
in das sich immer reinere Wolken drängen,
und drunter alle Weiß in Übergängen,
und drüber jenes dünne, große Grau,
warmwallend wie auf roter Untermalung,
und über allem diese stille Strahlung
sinkender Sonne.

 Wunderlicher Bau,
in sich bewegt und von sich selbst gehalten,
Gestalten bildend, Riesenflügel, Falten
und Hochgebirge vor den ersten Sternen
und plötzlich, da: ein Tor in solche Fernen,
wie sie vielleicht nur Vögel kennen . . .

The park is high. And as out of a house
I step from its glimmering half-light
into openness and evening. Into the wind,
the same wind the clouds feel,
the bright rivers and the turning mills
that stand slowly grinding at the sky's edge.
Now I too am a thing held in its hand,
the smallest thing under this sky. —Look:

Is that *one* sky?:
 Blissful lucid blue,
in which throng ever purer clouds,
and under it all white in swift transitions,
and over it that huge thin swath of gray,
pulsing warm as on red underpaint,
and, over everything, this quiet radiance
of a setting sun.

 Wondrous structure,
quickened in itself and upheld by itself,
creating shapes, giant wings, chasms
and high mountain ridges before the first star
and suddenly, *there*: a gate into such
distances as perhaps only birds know . . .

ABEND

Der Abend wechselt langsam die Gewänder,
die ihm ein Rand von alten Bäumen hält;
du schaust: und von dir scheiden sich die Länder,
ein himmelfahrendes und eins, das fällt;

und lassen dich, zu keinem ganz gehörend,
nicht ganz so dunkel wie das Haus, das schweigt,
nicht ganz so sicher Ewiges beschwörend
wie das, was Stern wird jede Nacht und steigt—

und lassen dir (unsäglich zu entwirrn)
dein Leben bang und riesenhaft und reifend,
so daß es, bald begrenzt und bald begreifend,
abwechselnd Stein in dir wird und Gestirn.

EVENING

Slowly the evening puts on the clothes
held for it by a ridge of ancient trees;
you watch: and the lands divide from you,
one going heavenward, one sinking down;

and leave you, not quite belonging to either,
not quite so dark as the house cloaked in silence,
not quite so surely pledging the eternal
as that which becomes star each night and climbs—

and leave you (inexpressibly to untangle)
your life, immense and ripening and fearful,
so that now closed in, now reaching everywhere,
it grows alternately stone in you and star.

... Wie Vögel, welche sich gewöhnt ans Gehn
und immer schwerer werden, wie im Fallen:
die Erde saugt aus ihren langen Krallen
die mutige Erinnerung von allen
den großen Dingen, welche hoch geschehn,
und macht sie fast zu Blättern, die sich dicht
am Boden halten, —
wie Gewächse, die,
kaum aufwärts wachsend, in die Erde kriechen,
in schwarzen Schollen unlebendig licht
und weich und feucht versinken und versiechen, —
wie irre Kinder, —wie ein Angesicht
in einem Sarg, —wie frohe Hände, welche
unschlüssig werden, weil im vollen Kelche
sich Dinge spiegeln, die nicht nahe sind, —
wie Hülferufe, die im Abendwind
begegnen vielen dunklen großen Glocken, —
wie Zimmerblumen, die seit Tagen trocken,
wie Gassen, die verrufen sind, —wie Locken,
darinnen Edelsteine blind geworden sind, —
wie Morgen im April
vor allen vielen Fenstern des Spitales:
die Kranken drängen sich am Saum des Saales
und schaun: die Gnade eines frühen Strahles
macht alle Gassen frühlinglich und weit;
sie sehen nur die helle Herrlichkeit,
welche die Häuser jung und lachend macht,
und wissen nicht, daß schon die ganze Nacht
ein Sturm die Kleider von den Himmeln reißt,
ein Sturm von Wassern, wo die Welt noch eist,
ein Sturm, der jetzt noch durch die Gassen braust
und der den Dingen alle Bürde
von ihren Schultern nimmt, —
daß Etwas draußen groß ist und ergrimmt,

... Like birds that get used to walking
and become heavier and heavier, as if in free fall:
the earth sucks out of their long claws
the brave memory of all
the great things that happen up high,
and turns them almost into leaves that hold
close to the ground, —
like plants which,
loath to grow upward, pull back toward the soil,
sink weakly and softly and wetly
into black clods and sicken there lifelessly, —
like mad children, —like a face
in a coffin, —like happy hands
that grow hesitant, because in the full goblet
something is mirrored that isn't near, —
like shouts for help that in the evening wind
collide with many dark enormous bells, —
like houseplants that have dried for days,
like streets that are shunned, —like bright curls
within which jewels have grown blind, —
like early morning in April
before all the windows of the hospice:
the inmates crowd at the edge of the room
and gaze: the grace of a new light
makes all the streets spacious and springlike;
they see only the bright majesty
that makes the houses look young and gay,
and don't know that all night long
a storm ripped the clothes off the sky,
a storm of waters, where the world still freezes,
a storm which this very moment roars through the streets
and takes all burdens
off the shoulders of each thing, —
that Something outside is huge and incensed,

daß draußen die Gewalt geht, eine Faust,
die jeden von den Kranken würgen würde
inmitten dieses Glanzes, dem sie glauben. —

... Wie lange Nächte in verwelkten Lauben,
die schon zerrissen sind auf allen Seiten
und viel zu weit, um noch mit einem Zweiten,
den man sehr liebt, zusammen drin zu weinen, —
wie nackte Mädchen, kommend über Steine,
wie Trunkene in einem Birkenhaine, —
wie Worte, welche nichts Bestimmtes meinen
und dennoch gehn, ins Ohr hineingehn, weiter
ins Hirn und heimlich auf der Nervenleiter
durch alle Glieder Sprung um Sprung versuchen, —
wie Greise, welche ihr Geschlecht verfluchen
und dann versterben, so daß keiner je
abwenden könnte das verhängte Weh,
wie volle Rosen, künstlich aufgezogen
im blauen Treibhaus, wo die Lüfte logen,
und dann vom Übermut in großem Bogen
hinausgestreut in den verwehten Schnee, —
wie eine Erde, die nicht kreisen kann,
weil zuviel Tote ihr Gefühl beschweren,
wie ein erschlagener verscharrter Mann,
dem sich die Hände gegen Wurzeln wehren, —
wie eine von den hohen, schlanken, roten
Hochsommerblumen, welche unerlöst
ganz plötzlich stirbt im Lieblingswind der Wiesen,
weil ihre Wurzel unten an Türkisen
im Ohrgehänge einer Toten
stößt ...

Und mancher Tage Stunden waren *so*.
Als formte wer mein Abbild irgendwo,
um es mit Nadeln langsam zu mißhandeln.
Ich spürte jede Spitze seiner Spiele,
und war, als ob ein Regen auf mich fiele,
in welchem alle Dinge sich verwandeln.

that outside Power stalks, a fist
that would strangle each one of the sick
in the midst of this brilliance, which they believe in. —
. . . Like long nights in withered arbors
that are already torn on all sides
and much too open now to weep there together
with that one other whom one loves, —
like naked girls approaching over stones,
like drunkards in a birch grove, —
like words that mean nothing for sure
and yet go on, work their way into the ear,
enter the brain and secretly in every limb
at the nerve-branchings attempt leap after leap, —
like old men who curse their race
and then die, so no one ever can avert
the once-declared doom,
like full roses, raised speciously
in the blue hothouse where the air deceived,
and then after their exhilaration in great curves
cast out upon the scattered snow, —
like an earth that cannot orbit
because too many dead weigh on its feeling,
like a man killed and buried
whose hands are fighting roots, —
like one of the tall, slim, red
midsummer flowers that suddenly dies
unredeemed in its favorite meadow-wind,
because down below its roots strike turquoise
in the earring of a corpse
and halt . . .

And many a day's hours were like that.
As if someone stitched my likeness somewhere
so as to slowly torture it with needles.
I felt each sharp prick of his malice,
and it was: as if a rain fell on me
in which all things change.

Auf einmal weiß ich viel von den Fontänen,
den unbegreiflichen Bäumen aus Glas.
Ich könnte reden wie von eignen Tränen,
die ich, ergriffen von sehr großen Träumen,
einmal vergeudete und dann vergaß.

Vergaß ich denn, daß Himmel Hände reichen
zu vielen Dingen und in das Gedränge?
Sah ich nicht immer Großheit ohnegleichen
im Aufstieg alter Parke, vor den weichen
erwartungsvollen Abenden, —in bleichen
aus fremden Mädchen steigenden Gesängen,
die überfließen aus der Melodie
und wirklich werden und als müßten sie
sich spiegeln in den aufgetanen Teichen?

Ich muß mich nur erinnern an das Alles,
was an Fontänen und an mir geschah, —
dann fühl ich auch die Last des Niederfalles,
in welcher ich die Wasser wiedersah:
Und weiß von Zweigen, die sich abwärts wandten,
von Stimmen, die mit kleiner Flamme brannten,
von Teichen, welche nur die Uferkanten
schwachsinnig und verschoben wiederholten,
von Abendhimmeln, welche von verkohlten
westlichen Wäldern ganz entfremdet traten,
sich anders wölbten, dunkelten und taten
als wär das nicht die Welt, die sie gemeint . . .

Vergaß ich denn, daß Stern bei Stern versteint
und sich verschließt gegen die Nachbargloben?
Daß sich die Welten nur noch wie verweint
im Raum erkennen? —Vielleicht sind wir *oben*,
in Himmel andrer Wesen eingewoben,

Suddenly I know so much about fountains,
those incomprehensible trees of glass.
I could speak as though of my own tears,
which, in the grip of such fantastic dreaming,
I spilled lavishly and then forgot.

Did I forget that heaven extends hands
to many things and thrusts into our turmoil?
Did I not always see unrivaled greatness
in the rise of old parks before the prospect
of soft expectant evenings—in pale songs
that welled from unknown girls and ascended
through the melody until they overflowed
and became real, as if their shapes
must be reflected in the opened ponds?

I must only remember all those times
that fountains came alive in me, —
and I, too, feel the weight of the descent,
in which I saw the waters once again:
and can tell of branches that bent down,
of voices that burned with little flames,
of ponds, feebleminded and ineffectual,
that only repeated their sharp-edged banks;
of evening skies that from charred western forests
shrank back completely bewildered,
arched differently, darkened, and acted
as though this weren't the world they had expected . . .

Did I forget that star next to star grows hard
and shuts itself against its neighbor globe?
That worlds in space only recognize each other
as though through tears? —Perhaps we are *above*,
worked into the heaven of other beings

die zu uns aufschaun abends. Vielleicht loben
uns ihre Dichter. Vielleicht beten viele
zu uns empor. Vielleicht sind wir die Ziele
von fremden Flüchen, die uns nie erreichen,
Nachbaren eines Gottes, den sie meinen
in unsrer Höhe, wenn sie einsam weinen,
an den sie glauben und den sie verlieren,
und dessen Bildnis, wie ein Schein aus ihren
suchenden Lampen, flüchtig und verweht,
über unsere zerstreuten Gesichter geht . . .

who gaze toward us at evening. Maybe their
poets praise us. Maybe many of them
pray up toward us; maybe we are the goal
of strange curses that never reach us,
neighbors of a god whom they envision
far above, where we are, when they weep alone,
whom they believe in and yet lose,
and whose image, like a ray from their
searching lamps, fleeting and then gone,
passes across our scattered faces . . .

DIE STIMMEN
Neun Blätter mit einem Titelblatt

TITELBLATT

Die Reichen und Glücklichen haben gut schweigen,
niemand will wissen was sie sind.
Aber die Dürftigen müssen sich zeigen,
müssen sagen: ich bin blind
oder: ich bin im Begriff es zu werden
oder: es geht mir nicht gut auf Erden
oder: ich habe ein krankes Kind
oder: da bin ich zusammengefügt . . .

Und vielleicht, daß das gar nicht genügt.

Und weil alle sonst, wie an Dingen,
an ihnen vorbeigehn, müssen sie singen.

Und da hört man noch guten Gesang.

Freilich die Menschen sind seltsam; sie hören
lieber Kastraten in Knabenchören.

Aber Gott selber kommt und bleibt lang
wenn ihn *diese* Beschnittenen stören.

THE VOICES
Nine leaves with a title leaf

TITLE LEAF

The rich and the lucky can afford to be silent,
nobody wants to hear their stories anyway.
But the wretched have to advertise themselves,
have to say: I'm blind
or: I'm about to become so
or: Nothing on earth works out for me
or: I have a sick child
or: Here I am, all pieced together . . .

And probably even that won't be enough.

And, since otherwise people will pass them by
the way they pass things, they have to sing.

And then you hear *really* good singing.

People, though, are strange: they'd rather
hear castrati sing in boys' choirs.

But God himself comes and stays a long time
whenever *these* cut ones disturb him.

DAS LIED DES BETTLERS

Ich gehe immer von Tor zu Tor,
verregnet und verbrannt;
auf einmal leg ich mein rechtes Ohr
in meine rechte Hand.
Dann kommt mir meine Stimme vor
als hätt ich sie nie gekannt.

Dann weiß ich nicht sicher wer da schreit,
ich oder irgendwer.
Ich schreie um eine Kleinigkeit.
Die Dichter schrein um mehr.

Und endlich mach ich noch mein Gesicht
mit beiden Augen zu;
wie's dann in der Hand liegt mit seinem Gewicht
sieht es fast aus wie Ruh.
Damit sie nicht meinen ich hätte nicht,
wohin ich mein Haupt tu.

THE BEGGAR'S SONG

I go always from door to door,
rain-soaked and sun-scorched;
suddenly I'll lay my right ear
in my right hand.
Then my voice sounds to me
like something I've never heard before.

Then I can't say for sure who's screaming there,
I or someone else.
I scream out for some little trifle.
The poets scream for more.

And finally I'll close my face
using both eyes;
the way it lies then in my hand with its weight
looks almost like rest.
So they won't think I hadn't any place
to put my head.

DAS LIED DES BLINDEN

Ich bin blind, ihr draußen, das ist ein Fluch,
ein Widerwillen, ein Widerspruch,
etwas täglich Schweres.
Ich leg meine Hand auf den Arm der Frau,
meine graue Hand auf ihr graues Grau,
und sie führt mich durch lauter Leeres.

Ihr rührt euch und rückt und bildet euch ein
anders zu klingen als Stein auf Stein,
aber ihr irrt euch: ich allein
lebe und leide und lärme.
In mir ist ein endloses Schrein
und ich weiß nicht, schreit mir mein
Herz oder meine Gedärme.

Erkennt ihr die Lieder? Ihr sanget sie nicht,
nicht ganz in dieser Betonung.
Euch kommt jeden Morgen das neue Licht
warm in die offene Wohnung.
Und ihr habt ein Gefühl von Gesicht zu Gesicht
und das verleitet zur Schonung.

THE BLIND MAN'S SONG

I'm blind, you out there: that's a curse,
a countermanding, a contradiction,
something that weighs down daily.
I place my hand on the woman's arm,
gray of my hand on the gray of her grayness,
and she leads me through empty air.

You stir and shift and like to think
that you ring differently from stone on stone,
but you're wrong: I alone
live and feel pain and make noise.
Inside me there's an endless screaming,
and I don't know if it's my heart
that screams or my intestines.

Do you know the songs? You never sang them,
not with this accent anyway.
For you every morning the new light comes
warm into your open dwelling.
And you have a feeling of face to face
that lures you into caring.

DAS LIED DES TRINKERS

Es war nicht in mir. Es ging aus und ein.
Da wolt ich es halten. Da hielt es der Wein.
(Ich weiß nicht mehr was es war.)
Dann hielt er mir jenes und hielt mir dies
bis ich mich ganz auf ihn verließ.
Ich Narr.

Jetzt bin ich in seinem Spiel und er streut
mich verächtlich herum und verliert mich noch heut
an dieses Vieh, an den Tod.
Wenn der mich, schmutzige Karte, gewinnt,
so kratzt er mit mir seinen grauen Grind
und wirft mich fort in den Kot.

THE DRUNKARD'S SONG

It wasn't in me. It went out and in.
Then I tried to hold it. Then the wine held it.
(I don't remember what it was.)
Then the wine held me this and held me that
until I utterly relied on it.
Ass that I am.

Now I'm in its game and it deals me
scornfully and could lose me this very night
to that swine, Death.
If he does win me, filthy card,
he'll scratch his gray scabs with me
and toss me into the dung.

Also noch einen Augenblick.
Daß sie mir immer wieder den Strick
zerschneiden.
Neulich war ich so gut bereit
und es war schon ein wenig Ewigkeit
in meinen Eingeweiden.

Halten sie mir den Löffel her,
diesen Löffel Leben.
Nein ich will und ich will nicht mehr,
laßt mich mich übergeben.

Ich weiß das Leben ist gar und gut
und die Welt ist ein voller Topf,
aber mir geht es nicht ins Blut,
mir steigt es nur zu Kopf.

Andere nährt es, mich macht es krank;
begreift, daß man's verschmäht.
Mindestens ein Jahrtausend lang
brauch ich jetzt Diät.

THE SUICIDE'S SONG

All right: just one second more.
So once again they cut
my rope.
The other day I was so close:
I could even feel bits of eternity
in my intestines.

They hold the spoon out to me,
this spoon of life.
No, I *will* not and I *will* no longer,
let me vomit up myself.

I know that life is fine and good
and the world is a full pot,
but it doesn't get into my blood,
it only rushes to my head.

Others it nourishes, me it makes sick;
try to grasp: some people just can't stand it.
For at least a thousand years now
I'll have to diet.

DAS LIED DER WITWE

Am Anfang war mir das Leben gut.
Es hielt mich warm, es machte mir Mut.
Daß es das allen Jungen tut,
wie konnt ich das damals wissen.
Ich wußte nicht, was das Leben war—,
auf einmal war es nur Jahr und Jahr,
nicht mehr gut, nicht mehr neu, nicht mehr wunderbar,
wie mitten entzwei gerissen.

Das war nicht Seine, nicht meine Schuld;
wir hatten beide nichts als Geduld,
aber der Tod hat keine.
Ich sah ihn kommen (wie schlecht er kam),
und ich schaute ihm zu wie er nahm und nahm:
es war ja gar nicht das Meine.

Was war denn das Meine; Meines, Mein?
War mir nicht selbst mein Elendsein
nur vom Schicksal geliehn?
Das Schicksal will nicht nur das Glück,
es will die Pein und das Schrein zurück
und es kauft für alt den Ruin.

Das Schicksal war da und erwarb für ein Nichts
jeden Ausdruck meines Gesichts
bis auf die Art zu gehn.
Das war ein täglicher Ausverkauf
und als ich leer war, gab es mich auf
und ließ mich offen stehn.

THE WIDOW'S SONG

Life was good to me in the beginning.
It held me warmly, it gave me heart.
Of course it does the same with all the young,
but how could I have known that then?
I had no idea what life was like—,
then suddenly it was only year and year,
no longer sweet, no longer bright, no longer wondrous,
as if it had been torn in two.

It wasn't his fault, it wasn't mine;
we both had infinite patience,
but Death has none.
I saw him come (his walk was mean),
and I watched him as he took and took:
not one thing I could claim as mine.

What *was* mine, then: mine, my own?
Wasn't even my hoard of misery
only lent to me by Fate?
Fate wants not only the happiness,
he wants the pain and the screaming back,
and he buys the ruin secondhand.

Fate was there and for a pittance he acquired
all the expressions of my face
right down to the manner of my gait.
Every day was a closeout sale,
and when I was empty, he walked off
and left me standing open.

DAS LIED DES IDIOTEN

Sie hindern mich nicht. Sie lassen mich gehn.
Sie sagen es könne nichts geschehn.
Wie gut.
Es kann nichts geschehn. Alles kommt und kreist
immerfort um den heiligen Geist,
um den gewissen Geist (du weißt)—,
wie gut.

Nein man muß wirklich nicht meinen es sei
irgend eine Gefahr dabei.
Da ist freilich das Blut.
Das Blut ist das Schwerste. Das Blut ist schwer.
Manchmal glaub ich, ich kann nicht mehr—.
(Wie gut.)

Ah was ist das für ein schöner Ball;
rot und rund wie ein Überall.
Gut, daß ihr ihn erschuft.
Ob der wohl kommt wenn man ruft?

Wie sich das alles seltsam benimmt,
ineinandertreibt, auseinanderschwimmt:
freundlich, ein wenig unbestimmt.
Wie gut.

THE IDIOT'S SONG

They don't watch me. They let me go.
They say, "Nothing can happen."
That's good.
Nothing can happen. Everything comes and spins
round and round the Holy Ghost,
around that certain ghost (you know)——,
that's good.

No, no need to think there might be
any danger in it all.
Of course there is the blood.
Blood's the hardest. Blood's like stone.
Sometimes I think I can't go on——.
(That's good.)

Look what a lovely ball;
red and round like an Everywhere.
Good that you created it.
I wonder if it comes when called?

How strangely everything behaves,
drifting all together, swimming all apart;
friendly, a bit unclear.
That's good.

DAS LIED DER WAISE

Ich bin Niemand und werde auch Niemand sein.
Jetzt bin ich ja zum Sein noch zu klein;
aber auch später.

Mütter und Väter,
erbarmt euch mein.

Zwar es lohnt nicht des Pflegens Müh:
ich werde doch gemäht.
Mich kann keiner brauchen: jetzt ist es zu früh
und morgen ist es zu spät.

Ich habe nur dieses eine Kleid,
es wird dünn und es verbleicht,
aber es hält eine Ewigkeit
auch noch vor Gott vielleicht.

Ich habe nur dieses bißchen Haar
(immer dasselbe blieb),
das einmal Eines Liebstes war.

Nun hat er nichts mehr lieb.

THE ORPHAN GIRL'S SONG

I am nobody and I'll be nobody.
Now of course I'm still too small for being;
but later, too.

Mothers and fathers,
have pity on me.

Not that I'm worth the pain of raising:
I'll be reaped regardless.
No one can use me: today it's too early,
tomorrow too late.

I have only this one dress,
it fades and it wears thin,
but it will last an eternity
even in God's light perhaps.

I have only these locks of hair
(always they shine the same)
that once were someone's dearest love.

Now he loves nothing anymore.

DAS LIED DES ZWERGES

Meine Seele ist vielleicht grad und gut;
aber mein Herz, mein verbogenes Blut,
alles das, was mir wehe tut,
kann sie nicht aufrecht tragen.
Sie hat keinen Garten, sie hat kein Bett,
sie hängt an meinem scharfen Skelett
mit entsetztem Flügelschlagen.

Aus meinen Händen wird auch nichts mehr.
Wie verkümmert sie sind: sieh her:
zähe hüpfen sie, feucht und schwer,
wie kleine Kröten nach Regen.
Und das Andre an mir ist
abgetragen und alt und trist;
warum zögert Gott, auf den Mist
alles das hinzulegen.

Ob er mir zürnt für mein Gesicht
mit dem mürrischen Munde?
Es war ja so oft bereit, ganz licht
und klar zu werden im Grunde;
aber nichts kam ihm je so dicht
wie die großen Hunde.
Und die Hunde haben das nicht.

THE DWARF'S SONG

My soul may be straight and good,
but my heart, my hopelessly bent blood,
all that keeps hurting me inside,
it can't hold upright.
It has no garden, no bed,
it clings to my sharp skeleton
with a horrified beating of wings.

Nor will anything ever come of my hands.
Look at how stunted they are:
they hop sluggishly, damp and heavy,
like little toads after rain.
And all the rest of me is
worn out and old and dreary.
Why does God hesitate to toss it all
onto the junk heap?

Could it be he hates me for my face
with its grumpy jowls?
So often it was ready to be light
and clearness through and through.
But nothing ever came up to it
the way the big dogs do.
And the dogs couldn't care less.

DAS LIED DES AUSSÄTZIGEN

Sieh ich bin einer, den alles verlassen hat.
Keiner weiß in der Stadt von mir,
Aussatz hat mich befallen.
Und ich schlage mein Klapperwerk,
klopfe mein trauriges Augenmerk
in die Ohren allen
die nahe vorübergehn.
Und die es hölzern hören, sehn
erst gar nicht her, und was hier geschehn
wollen sie nicht erfahren.

Soweit der Klang meiner Klapper reicht
bin ich zuhause; aber vielleicht
machst Du meine Klapper so laut,
daß sich keiner in meine Ferne traut
der mir jetzt aus der Nähe weicht.
So daß ich sehr lange gehen kann
ohne Mädchen, Frau oder Mann
oder Kind zu entdecken.

Tiere will ich nicht schrecken.

Ende des Gedicht-Kreises »Die Stimmen«

THE LEPER'S SONG

Look, I'm one of those whom everything has abandoned.
No one in the city knows of me,
leprosy's my lot.
And I bang my clapper
and knock the sad sight of me
into the ears of all who
come close as they pass.
And they hear it woodenly, won't
look this way at all, and what happens here
they try not to know.

As far as the sound of my clapper reaches
I'm at home; but perhaps
You'll make its banging so loud
that they'll steer clear of my distance
the way they shun my nearness.
So I can go a very long way
without meeting girl, woman or man,
or child.

Animals I'll try not to frighten.

End of the poem cycle "The Voices"

From NEUE GEDICHTE *(1907)*

From NEW POEMS *(1907)*

FRÜHER APOLLO

Wie manches Mal durch das noch unbelaubte
Gezweig ein Morgen durchsieht, der schon ganz
im Frühling ist: so ist in seinem Haupte
nichts was verhindern könnte, daß der Glanz

aller Gedichte uns fast tödlich träfe;
denn noch kein Schatten ist in seinem Schaun,
zu kühl für Lorbeer sind noch seine Schläfe
und später erst wird aus den Augenbraun

hochstämmig sich der Rosengarten heben,
aus welchem Blätter, einzeln, ausgelöst
hintreiben werden auf des Mundes Beben,

der jetzt noch still ist, niegebraucht und blinkend
und nur mit seinem Lächeln etwas trinkend
als würde ihm sein Singen eingeflößt.

EARLY APOLLO

As sometimes between still leafless branches
a morning looks through that's already
consummate Spring; so nothing of his head
could prevent the splendor of all poems

from striking us with almost lethal force;
for there is yet no shadow in his gaze,
his temples are too cool still for the laurel,
and only later from his eyebrows' arches

will the rose garden rise up on long stems,
from which petals, released, one by one
will drift down on the trembling of his mouth,

which now is still quiet, never used, and gleaming
and only drinking something with its smile
as though the song were being infused in him.

Wie soll ich meine Seele halten, daß
sie nicht an deine rührt? Wie soll ich sie
hinheben über dich zu andern Dingen?
Ach gerne möcht ich sie bei irgendwas
Verlorenem im Dunkel unterbringen
an einer fremden stillen Stelle, die
nicht weiterschwingt, wenn deine Tiefen schwingen.
Doch alles, was uns anrührt, dich und mich,
nimmt uns zusammen wie ein Bogenstrich,
der aus zwei Saiten *eine* Stimme zieht.
Auf welches Instrument sind wir gespannt?
Und welcher Geiger hat uns in der Hand?
O süßes Lied.

How shall I keep my soul
from touching yours? How shall I
lift it up beyond you to other things?
Ah, I would gladly hide it
in darkness with something lost
in some silent foreign place
that doesn't tremble when your deeps stir.
Yet whatever touches *you* and *me*
blends us together the way a bow's stroke
draws *one* voice from two strings.
Across what instrument are we stretched taut?
And what player holds us in his hand?
O sweet song.

Wir gedenkens noch. Das ist, als müßte
alles dieses einmal wieder sein.
Wie ein Baum an der Limonenküste
trugst du deine kleinen leichten Brüste
in das Rauschen seines Bluts hinein:

—jenes Gottes.
 Und es war der schlanke
Flüchtling, der Verwöhnende der Fraun.
Süß und glühend, warm wie dein Gedanke,
überschattend deine frühe Flanke
und geneigt wie deine Augenbraun.

We keep remembering. It's as though
everything would have a second life.
Like a citrus tree along the Greek shore
you bore your small light breasts
into the surging of his blood:

—that god's.
 And he was the slender
fugitive, that admirer of women.
Tender, glowing, warm like your thought,
overshadowing your young thighs
and arched the way your eyebrows were.

Der König saß und sann den leeren Tag
getaner Taten, ungefühlter Lüste
und seiner Lieblingshündin, der er pflag—.
Aber am Abend wölbte Abisag
sich über ihm. Sein wirres Leben lag
verlassen wie verrufne Meeresküste
unter dem Sternbild ihrer stillen Brüste.

Und manchmal, als ein Kundiger der Frauen,
erkannte er durch seine Augenbrauen
den unbewegten, küsselosen Mund;
und sah: ihres Gefühles grüne Rute
neigte sich nicht herab zu seinem Grund.
Ihn fröstelte. Er horchte wie ein Hund
und suchte sich in seinem letzten Blute.

The king sat thinking through the empty day
of deeds done, pleasures never felt,
and his favorite dog, on whom he doted—.
But in the evening Abishag
arched over him. His tangled life
lay abandoned like an ill-famed coast
beneath the constellation of her silent breasts.

And now and then, as one adept with women,
he recognized through his eyebrows' thicket
the unmoved, unkissed mouth;
and saw: her feeling's green divining rod
did not point downward to his depths.
A chill went through him. He hearkened like a hound
and sought himself in his last blood.

1 Kings I:1–4: "And when the king [David] was old and burdened with years, he could not grow warm, even though they covered him with clothes. Then his servants said to him: 'Let there be sought for my lord the king a young girl, a virgin, who will stand before the king and care for him and sleep in his arms and warm my lord the king.' And they searched for a beautiful girl throughout all the lands of Israel, and found Abishag from Shunam, and brought her to the king. And she was indeed beautiful, and she cared for the king and served him. But the king knew her not."

Als ob er horchte. Stille: eine Ferne . . .
Wir halten ein und hören sie nicht mehr.
Und er ist Stern. Und andre große Sterne,
die wir nicht sehen, stehen um ihn her.

O er ist Alles. Wirklich, warten wir,
daß er uns sähe? Sollte er bedürfen?
Und wenn wir hier uns vor ihm niederwürfen,
er bliebe tief und träge wie ein Tier.

Denn das, was uns zu seinen Füßen reißt,
das kreist in ihm seit Millionen Jahren.
Er, der vergißt was wir erfahren
und der erfährt was uns verweist.

BUDDHA

As if he listened. Stillness: something distant . . .
We check ourselves—and cease to hear it.
And he is Star. And multitudes of giant stars
that we don't see stand all around him.

He is *everything*. Are we really waiting here
for him to see us? What would he require?
And if instead we threw ourselves before him,
he'd remain deep and idle as a cat.

For what drags us roughly to his feet
has circled in him for a million years.
He, who forgets what life instills in us,
and lives in the wisdom we're denied.

DIE FENSTERROSE

Da drin: das träge Treten ihrer Tatzen
macht eine Stille, die dich fast verwirrt;
und wie dann plötzlich eine von den Katzen
den Blick an ihr, der hin und wieder irrt,

gewaltsam in ihr großes Auge nimmt, —
den Blick, der, wie von eines Wirbels Kreis
ergriffen, eine kleine Weile schwimmt
und dann versinkt und nichts mehr von sich weiß,

wenn dieses Auge, welches scheinbar ruht,
sich auftut und zusammenschlägt mit Tosen
und ihn hineinreißt bis ins rote Blut—:

So griffen einstmals aus dem Dunkelsein
der Kathedralen große Fensterrosen
ein Herz und rissen es in Gott hinein.

THE ROSE WINDOW

In there: the lazy pacing of their paws
creates a stillness almost dizzying;
and as one of the cats then suddenly
takes the gaze carelessly watching

and pulls it into its own great eye, —
and that gaze, as if caught in a whirlpool's
spirals, for a time stays afloat
and then goes under, lost to oblivion,

when this eye, which apparently rests,
opens and crashes shut with a roar
and hauls it all the way into the blood—:

Thus in ancient times out of the darkness
the cathedrals' great rose windows
would seize hearts and drag them in to God.

DAS KAPITÄL

Wie sich aus eines Traumes Ausgeburten
aufsteigend aus verwirrendem Gequäl
der nächste Tag erhebt: so gehn die Gurten
der Wölbung aus dem wirren Kapitäl

und lassen drin, gedrängt und rätselhaft
verschlungen, flügelschlagende Geschöpfe:
ihr Zögern und das Plötzliche der Köpfe
und jene starken Blätter, deren Saft

wie Jähzorn steigt, sich schließlich überschlagend
in einer schnellen Geste, die sich ballt
und sich heraushält—: alles aufwärtsjagend,

was immer wieder mit dem Dunkel kalt
herunterfällt, wie Regen Sorge tragend
für dieses alten Wachstums Unterhalt.

As if escaping the creatures of a dream
engendered in the throes of anguish
the next day rises; so the vaulting's ribs
spring from the tangled capital

and leave that chaos of densely intertwined,
mysteriously winged creations:
their hesitance and the suddenness of the heads
and those strong leaves, whose sap

mounts like rising anger, finally spilling over
in a quick gesture that clenches
and thrusts out—: driving everything up

that always with darkness coldly
falls back again, like rain bearing worry
to keep this old growth alive.

Da liegen sie bereit, als ob es gälte,
nachträglich eine Handlung zu erfinden,
die mit einander und mit dieser Kälte
sie zu versöhnen weiß und zu verbinden;

denn das ist alles noch wie ohne Schluß.
Wasfür ein Name hätte in den Taschen
sich finden sollen? An dem Überdruß
um ihren Mund hat man herumgewaschen:

er ging nicht ab; er wurde nur ganz rein.
Die Bärte stehen, noch ein wenig härter,
doch ordentlicher im Geschmack der Wärter,

nur um die Gaffenden nicht anzuwidern.
Die Augen haben hinter ihren Lidern
sich umgewandt und schauen jetzt hinein.

MORGUE

They lie here ready, as if still waiting
for some rite to be invented
that would bind them to each other
and reconcile them to this cold;

for everything still lacks conclusion.
What sorts of names would they have carried
in their pockets? Around their mouths
the boredom has been sponged and scrubbed:

it didn't come off; it merely turned clean.
Their beards stand, perhaps a bit too stiff,
but more decent, their attendants feel,

to make sure no gawker is repulsed.
Behind their lids the eyes have pivoted
and are gazing now at what's within.

DER PANTHER
Im Jardin des Plantes, Paris

Sein Blick ist vom Vorübergehn der Stäbe
so müd geworden, daß er nichts mehr hält.
Ihm ist, als ob es tausend Stäbe gäbe
und hinter tausend Stäben keine Welt.

Der weiche Gang geschmeidig starker Schritte,
der sich im allerkleinsten Kreise dreht,
ist wie ein Tanz von Kraft um eine Mitte,
in der betäubt ein großer Wille steht.

Nur manchmal schiebt der Vorhang der Pupille
sich lautlos auf—. Dann geht ein Bild hinein,
geht durch der Glieder angespannte Stille—
und hört im Herzen auf zu sein.

THE PANTHER
In the Jardin des Plantes, Paris

His gaze has from the passing of the bars
become so tired that it holds nothing anymore.
It seems to him there are a thousand bars
and behind a thousand bars no world.

The supple pace of powerful soft strides,
turning in the very smallest circle,
is like a dance of strength around a center
in which a mighty will stands numbed.

Only at times the curtain of the pupils
soundlessly slides open——. Then an image enters,
glides through the limbs' taut stillness—
dives into the heart and dies.

DIE GAZELLE
Gazella dorcas

Verzauberte: wie kann der Einklang zweier
erwählter Worte je den Reim erreichen,
der in dir kommt und geht, wie auf ein Zeichen.
Aus deiner Stirne steigen Laub und Leier,

und alles Deine geht schon im Vergleich
durch Liebeslieder, deren Worte, weich
wie Rosenblätter, dem, der nicht mehr liest,
sich auf die Augen legen, die er schließt:

um dich zu sehen: hingetragen, als
wäre mit Sprüngen jeder Lauf geladen
und schösse nur nicht ab, solang der Hals

das Haupt ins Horchen hält: wie wenn beim Baden
im Wald die Badende sich unterbricht:
den Waldsee im gewendeten Gesicht.

THE GAZELLE
Gazella dorcas

Enchanted one: how shall the harmony
of two perfect words attain that rhyme
which ripples through you like a spell?
From your forehead rise leaf and lyre,

and all you are already moves in simile
through love songs whose words, softly
like rose petals, settle on the gaze of one
who, no longer reading, shuts his eyes:

and sees *you* there: transported, as if
each limb were loaded with leaps and only
deferred firing in that instant your neck

holds your head still, listening: as when a woman
bathing in a forest hears something stir:
the lake's reflection in her quick-turned face.

Wie ein Liegender so steht er; ganz
hingehalten von dem großen Willen.
Weitentrückt wie Mütter, wenn sie stillen,
und in sich gebunden wie ein Kranz.

Und die Pfeile kommen: jetzt und jetzt
und als sprängen sie aus seinen Lenden,
eisern bebend mit den freien Enden.
Doch er lächelt dunkel, unverletzt.

Einmal nur wird seine Trauer groß,
und die Augen liegen schmerzlich bloß,
bis sie etwas leugnen, wie Geringes,
und als ließen sie verächtlich los
die Vernichter eines schönen Dinges.

SAINT SEBASTIAN

Like someone lying down he stands erect;
entirely offered up by his mighty will.
Far removed, like mothers when they suckle,
and bound into himself like a wreath.

And the arrows come: *now* and *now*
and as if they sprang from his own loins,
iron-quivering with their free ends.
But he smiles darkly, unscathed.

Only once does his sorrow mount fearfully,
and his eyes sharpen their pain—
till they deny an impulse as unworthy,
and as if they were scornfully dismissing
the vandalizers of a hallowed thing.

Das war der Auftrag an die Malergilde.
Vielleicht daß ihm der Heiland nie erschien;
vielleicht trat auch kein heiliger Bischof milde
an seine Seite wie in diesem Bilde
und legte leise seine Hand auf ihn.

Vielleicht war dieses alles: *so* zu knien
(so wie es alles ist was wir erfuhren):
zu knien: daß man die eigenen Konturen,
die auswärtswollenden, ganz angespannt
im Herzen hält, wie Pferde in der Hand.

Daß wenn ein Ungeheueres geschähe,
das nicht versprochen ist und nieverbrieft,
wir hoffen könnten, daß es uns nicht sähe
und näher käme, ganz in unsre Nähe,
mit sich beschäftigt und in sich vertieft.

THE DONOR

That was the commission to the painter's guild.
Perhaps the Savior never appeared before him;
perhaps not even a holy bishop
stepped gently to his side as in this painting
and lightly laid his hand on him.

Perhaps this was all: to kneel *thus*
(just as it's all we witnessed):
to *kneel*: and thereby hold one's own
outward-willing contours tightly reined
in one's heart, like horses in hand.

So that if some enormity should appear,
something unpromised and never written,
we could hope that it wouldn't see us
and would come closer, all the way to us,
deep in itself and self-preoccupied.

Was aber hindert uns zu glauben, daß
(so wie wir hingestellt sind und verteilt)
nicht eine kleine Zeit nur Drang und Haß
und dies Verwirrende in uns verweilt,

wie einst in dem verzierten Sarkophag
bei Ringen, Götterbildern, Gläsern, Bändern,
in langsam sich verzehrenden Gewändern
ein langsam Aufgelöstes lag—

bis es die unbekannten Munde schluckten,
die niemals reden. (Wo besteht und denkt
ein Hirn, um ihrer einst sich zu bedienen?)

Da wurde von den alten Aquädukten
ewiges Wasser in sie eingelenkt—:
das spiegelt jetzt und geht und glänzt in ihnen.

But what prevents us from believing
(the way *we're* set down here and put in place)
that only for a short time rage and hate
and this confusion live in us,

just as once in this ornate sarcophagus
among ribbons, rings, images of gods,
in slowly disintegrating veils and garments
something lay slowly decomposing—

till it was swallowed by those unknown mouths
that never speak. (Where does a brain
wait and think that one day will employ them?)

Then from the ancient aqueducts
eternal water was channeled into them—:
where it shimmers now and laps and gleams.

DER SCHWAN .

Diese Mühsal, durch noch Ungetanes
schwer und wie gebunden hinzugehn,
gleicht dem ungeschaffnen Gang des Schwanes.

Und das Sterben, dieses Nichtmehrfassen
jenes Grunds, auf dem wir täglich stehn,
seinem ängstlichen Sich-Niederlassen—:

in die Wasser, die ihn sanft empfangen
und die sich, wie glücklich und vergangen,
unter ihm zurückziehn, Flut um Flut;
während er unendlich still und sicher
immer mündiger und königlicher
und gelassener zu ziehn geruht.

This heaviness, toiling on as if in bonds
through a landscape of things still undone,
is like the makeshift walking of the swan.

And dying—to feel slowly giving way
that ground on which we daily stand,
like his uneasy lowering of himself—:

into the water, which received him gently
and which, so serene in its passing,
withdraws beneath him, wave on wave;
while he, infinitely still and sure,
with ever greater confidence and kingship
and self-possession deigns to glide.

DER DICHTER

Du entfernst dich von mir, du Stunde.
Wunden schlägt mir dein Flügelschlag.
Allein: was soll ich mit meinem Munde?
mit meiner Nacht? mit meinem Tag?

Ich habe keine Geliebte, kein Haus,
keine Stelle auf der ich lebe.
Alle Dinge, an die ich mich gebe,
werden reich und geben mich aus.

THE POET

You're withdrawing from me, hour.
The beating of your wings leaves me bruised.
Alone: what shall I do with my mouth?
 my night? my day?

I have no loved one, no house,
no place to lead a life.
All the things to which I give myself
grow rich and spend me.

So wie der König auf der Jagd ein Glas
ergreift, daraus zu trinken, irgendeines, —
und wie hernach der welcher es besaß
es fortstellt und verwahrt als wär es keines:

so hob vielleicht das Schicksal, durstig auch,
bisweilen Eine an den Mund und trank,
die dann ein kleines Leben, viel zu bang
sie zu zerbrechen, abseits vom Gebrauch

hinstellte in die ängstliche Vitrine,
in welcher seine Kostbarkeiten sind
(oder die Dinge, die für kostbar gelten).

Da stand sie fremd wie eine Fortgeliehne
und wurde einfach alt und wurde blind
und war nicht kostbar und war niemals selten.

Just as the king out on a hunt picks up
a glass to drink from, any one at all, —
and afterward its owner puts it away
and guards it like some fabled chalice:

so perhaps Fate, who also thirsts, at times
raised a woman to its lips and drank,
whom then a small life, too much afraid
of breaking her, locked away from use

inside the tremulous glass cabinet
in which its most precious things are kept
(at least the things considered precious).

There she stood strange like something loaned
and became merely old and became blind
and was not precious and was never special.

Das alles stand auf ihr und war die Welt
und stand auf ihr mit allem, Angst und Gnade,
wie Bäume stehen, wachsend und gerade,
ganz Bild und bildlos wie die Bundeslade
und feierlich, wie auf ein Volk gestellt.

Und sie ertrug es; trug bis obenhin
das Fliegende, Entfliehende, Entfernte,
das Ungeheuere, noch Unerlernte
gelassen wie die Wasserträgerin
den vollen Krug. Bis mitten unterm Spiel,
verwandelnd und auf andres vorbereitend,
der erste weiße Schleier, leise gleitend,
über das aufgetane Antlitz fiel

fast undurchsichtig und sich nie mehr hebend
und irgendwie auf alle Fragen ihr
nur eine Antwort vage wiedergebend:
In dir, du Kindgewesene, in dir.

All of that stood on her and was the world
and stood on her with all its dread and grace
the way trees stand, rising and erect,
all image and imageless like the Ark of God
and solemnly, as if entrusted to a race.

And she bore it; bore high overhead
the flying, fleeting, far-receding,
the prodigious, the as-yet unlearned
as serenely as the water carrier
her brimful jug. Till in the midst of play,
changing and getting ready for other things,
the first white veil, descending lightly,
fell across her opened face

almost opaque and never again to lift
and somehow to all questions
vaguely returning to her one answer only:
In you, you onetime child, in you.

DIE ERBLINDENDE

Sie saß so wie die anderen beim Tee.
Mir war zuerst, als ob sie ihre Tasse
ein wenig anders als die andern fasse.
Sie lächelte einmal. Es tat fast weh.

Und als man schließlich sich erhob und sprach
und langsam und wie es der Zufall brachte
durch viele Zimmer ging (man sprach und lachte),
da sah ich sie. Sie ging den andern nach,

verhalten, so wie eine, welche gleich
wird singen müssen und vor vielen Leuten;
auf ihren hellen Augen die sich freuten
war Licht von außen wie auf einem Teich.

Sie folgte langsam und sie brauchte lang
als wäre etwas noch nicht überstiegen;
und doch: als ob, nach einem Übergang,
sie nicht mehr gehen würde, sondern fliegen.

She sat just like the others having tea.
First I noticed how she seemed to hold
her cup a bit differently from the others.
She smiled once. It almost hurt.

And when finally they rose and spoke
and slowly and as chance would have it
walked through many rooms (they talked and laughed),
I saw her. She walked behind the others,

restrained, like one who in a moment
will have to sing, and in front of many;
on her bright eyes that were rejoicing
light shone from outside, as on a pond.

She followed slowly and she needed time
as if something still were not surmounted;
and yet: as if, after a crossing over,
she would be done with walking, and would fly.

ABSCHIED

Wie hab ich das gefühlt was Abschied heißt.
Wie weiß ichs noch: ein dunkles unverwundnes
grausames Etwas, das ein Schönverbundnes
noch einmal zeigt und hinhält und zerreißt.

Wie war ich ohne Wehr, dem zuzuschauen,
das, da es mich, mich rufend, gehen ließ,
zurückblieb, so als wärens alle Frauen
und dennoch klein und weiß und nichts als dies:

Ein Winken, schon nicht mehr auf mich bezogen,
ein leise Weiterwinkendes—, schon kaum
erklärbar mehr: vielleicht ein Pflaumenbaum,
von dem ein Kuckuck hastig abgeflogen.

PARTING

How I have felt the shape that parting takes.
How I see it still: a dark invincible
cruel Something that holds out a fragile unity
and offers it and tears it straight in two.

How exposed I was, with my eyes fixed
on what, as it called to me, released its hold,
staying behind as though all womankind
yet small and white and nothing more than this:

A waving, already no longer linked with me,
a slight continuous waving—, already almost
inexplicable: maybe a plum-tree branch
from which a cuckoo has hastily taken flight.

TODES-ERFAHRUNG

Wir wissen nichts von diesem Hingehn, das
nicht mit uns teilt. Wir haben keinen Grund,
Bewunderung und Liebe oder Haß
dem Tod zu zeigen, den ein Maskenmund

tragischer Klage wunderlich entstellt.
Noch ist die Welt voll Rollen, die wir spielen.
Solang wir sorgen, ob wir auch gefielen,
spielt auch der Tod, obwohl er nicht gefällt.

Doch als du gingst, da brach in diese Bühne
ein Streifen Wirklichkeit durch jenen Spalt
durch den du hingingst: Grün wirklicher Grüne,
wirklicher Sonnenschein, wirklicher Wald.

Wir spielen weiter. Bang und schwer Erlerntes
hersagend und Gebärden dann und wann
aufhebend; aber dein von uns entferntes,
aus unserm Stück entrücktes Dasein kann

uns manchmal überkommen, wie ein Wissen
von jener Wirklichkeit sich niedersenkend,
so daß wir eine Weile hingerissen
das Leben spielen, nicht an Beifall denkend.

We know nothing of this going hence
that so excludes us. We have no grounds
for showing Death amazement and love
or hatred, since it wears the age-old mask

of tragedy that hopelessly contorts it.
The world is full of roles—which we still act.
As long as we keep striving for acclaim,
Death also plays its part—though always badly.

But when you went, a streak of reality
broke in upon the stage through that fissure
where you'd left: green of real green,
real sunshine, real forest.

We go on acting. Fearful and reciting
things difficult to learn and now and then
inventing gestures; but your existence,
withdrawn from us and taken from our play,

sometimes can come over us, like a knowledge
of that reality settling in,
so that for a time we act life
transported, not thinking of applause.

BLAUE HORTENSIE

So wie das letzte Grün in Farbentiegeln
sind diese Blätter, trocken, stumpf und rauh,
hinter den Blütendolden, die ein Blau
nicht auf sich tragen, nur von ferne spiegeln.

Sie spiegeln es verweint und ungenau,
als wollten sie es wiederum verlieren,
und wie in alten blauen Briefpapieren
ist Gelb in ihnen, Violett und Grau;

Verwaschnes wie an einer Kinderschürze,
Nichtmehrgetragnes, dem nichts mehr geschieht:
wie fühlt man eines kleinen Lebens Kürze.

Doch plötzlich scheint das Blau sich zu verneuen
in einer von den Dolden, und man sieht
ein rührend Blaues sich vor Grünem freuen.

BLUE HYDRANGEA

These leaves are like the last green
in the paint pots—dried up, dull, and rough,
behind the flowered umbels whose blue
is not their own, but mirrored from afar.

They reflect it tear-stained, vaguely,
as if deep down they hoped to lose it;
and as with old blue writing paper
there's yellow in them, violet and gray;

Washed out as on a child's pinafore,
things that are finished with, no longer worn:
the way one feels a small life's brevity.

But suddenly emotion seems to flare
in one of the umbels, and one sees
a moving blue as it takes joy in green.

VOR DEM SOMMERREGEN

Auf einmal ist aus allem Grün im Park
man weiß nicht was, ein Etwas, fortgenommen;
man fühlt ihn näher an die Fenster kommen
und schweigsam sein. Inständig nur und stark

ertönt aus dem Gehölz der Regenpfeifer,
man denkt an einen Hieronymus:
so sehr steigt irgend Einsamkeit und Eifer
aus dieser einen Stimme, die der Guß

erhören wird. Des Saales Wände sind
mit ihren Bildern von uns fortgetreten,
als dürften sie nicht hören was wir sagen.

Es spiegeln die verblichenen Tapeten
das ungewisse Licht von Nachmittagen,
in denen man sich fürchtete als Kind.

Suddenly from all the green in the park
something—you can't say what—has disappeared;
you feel the park come closer to the window
and silently gaze. From the copse

the calls of a plover, strong and urgent—
and you're reminded of a Saint Jerome:
so intensely do solitude and zeal arise
from that one voice, to which the downpour

will hearken. The walls of the great hall
have with their portraits moved away from us,
as if they shouldn't overhear us talking.

Reflected on the faded tapestries
is that uncertain light of afternoons,
in which as a child you felt afraid.

Wie sind sie alle um uns, diese Herrn
in Kammerherrentrachten und Jabots,
wie eine Nacht um ihren Ordensstern
sich immer mehr verdunkelnd, rücksichtslos,
und diese Damen, zart, fragile, doch groß
von ihren Kleidern, eine Hand im Schooß,
klein wie ein Halsband für den Bologneser:
wie sind sie da um jeden: um den Leser,
um den Betrachter dieser Bibelots,
darunter manches ihnen noch gehört.

Sie lassen, voller Takt, uns ungestört
das Leben leben wie wir es begreifen
und wie sie's nicht verstehn. Sie wollten blühn,
und blühn ist schön sein; doch wir wollen reifen,
und das heißt dunkel sein und sich bemühn.

How they're all around us, these gentlemen
in chamberlain's dress and jabots,
like a night growing ever darker
around its Order Star, implacably,
and these ladies, slight and fragile, yet
made large by their dresses, one hand in their laps,
small, like a tiny dog with its collar:
how they're around us all: around the reader,
around the peruser of these bibelots,
of which several remain their property.

Tactful, they let us live life undisturbed
as we conceive it and as they fail
to understand it. They wanted to blossom,
and blossoming is being beautiful. But we want to ripen,
and this means being dark and taking pains.

LETZTER ABEND
(Aus dem Besitze Frau Nonnas)

Und Nacht und fernes Fahren; denn der Train
des ganzen Heeres zog am Park vorüber.
Er aber hob den Blick vom Clavecin
und spielte noch und sah zu ihr hinüber

beinah wie man in einen Spiegel schaut:
so sehr erfüllt von seinen jungen Zügen
und wissend, wie sie seine Trauer trügen,
schön und verführender bei jedem Laut.

Doch plötzlich wars, als ob sich das verwische:
sie stand wie mühsam in der Fensternische
und hielt des Herzens drängendes Geklopf.

Sein Spiel gab nach. Von draußen wehte Frische.
Und seltsam fremd stand auf dem Spiegeltische
der schwarze Tschako mit dem Totenkopf.

LAST EVENING
(By permission of Frau Nonna)

And night and distant travel; for the train
of the full regiment passed by the park.
But he raised his eyes from the clavichord
and kept playing and gazed across at her

almost the way one looks into a mirror:
so intensely filled with his young features
and *knowing*, as they bore his sorrow,
beautiful and more seductive with each note.

But suddenly it was as if that blurred:
She stood as if with struggle in the window niche
and held in her heart's frantic pounding.

He broke off. A cold wind blew through.
And strangely alien on the mirrored table
stood the black shako with its silver skull.

Im Auge Traum. Die Stirn wie in Berührung
mit etwas Fernem. Um den Mund enorm
viel Jugend, ungelächelte Verführung,
und vor der vollen schmückenden Verschnürung
der schlanken adeligen Uniform
der Säbelkorb und beide Hände—, die
abwarten, ruhig, zu nichts hingedrängt.
Und nun fast nicht mehr sichtbar: als ob sie
zuerst, die Fernes greifenden, verschwänden.
Und alles andre mit sich selbst verhängt
und ausgelöscht als ob wirs nicht verständen
und tief aus seiner eignen Tiefe trüb—.

Du schnell vergehendes Daguerreotyp
in meinen langsamer vergehenden Händen.

Dream in the eyes. The brow as if in touch
with something far away. About the lips
immense youth, unsmiling seductiveness,
and across the full ornamental braids
of the slim aristocratic uniform
the saber's basket hilt and both the hands—
waiting, calmly, urged toward nothing.
And now scarcely visible: as if they would be
first, grasping the distant, to disappear.
And all the rest self-shrouded
and erased as if we didn't understand
and dimmed by something deep in its own depths—.

You swiftly fading daguerreotype
in my more slowly fading hands.

Des alten lange adligen Geschlechtes
Feststehendes im Augenbogenbau.
Im Blicke noch der Kindheit Angst und Blau
und Demut da und dort, nicht eines Knechtes
doch eines Dienenden und einer Frau.
Der Mund als Mund gemacht, groß und genau,
nicht überredend, aber ein Gerechtes
Aussagendes. Die Stirne ohne Schlechtes
und gern im Schatten stiller Niederschau.

Das, als Zusammenhang, erst nur geahnt;
noch nie im Leiden oder im Gelingen
zusammgefaßt zu dauerndem Durchdringen,
doch so, als wäre mit zerstreuten Dingen
von fern ein Ernstes, Wirkliches geplant.

The old long-noble family's
staying power in the eyebrows' build.
Still in the gaze the childhood fear and blue
and humility here and there, not slavish
but kin to a woman's and to those who serve.
The mouth made as mouths are, wide and straight,
not persuasive but good for impartial
speaking out. The forehead without guile
and happiest in the shade of quiet down-gazing.

This, as coherence, just barely glimpsed;
never as yet in grief or triumph
sealed into some final countenance,
—rather as though from far off, out of many scattered things,
a serious true work were being planned.

DIE KURTISANE

Venedigs Sonne wird in meinem Haar
ein Gold bereiten: aller Alchemie
erlauchten Ausgang. Meine Brauen, die
den Brücken gleichen, siehst du sie

hinführen ob der lautlosen Gefahr
der Augen, die ein heimlicher Verkehr
an die Kanäle schließt, so daß das Meer
in ihnen steigt und fällt und wechselt. Wer

mich einmal sah, beneidet meinen Hund,
weil sich auf ihm oft in zerstreuter Pause
die Hand, die nie an keiner Glut verkohlt,

die unverwundbare, geschmückt, erholt—.
Und Knaben, Hoffnungen aus altem Hause,
gehn wie an Gift an meinem Mund zugrund.

THE COURTESAN

In my hair the sun of Venice will
prepare a gold: all alchemy's
illustrious outcome. My eyebrows
are like her bridges. See

how they span the silent danger
of my eyes, which have a secret
commerce with her canals, so the sea
rises and falls and changes in them. Whoever

sees me once is envious of my dog,
since often on him in distracted pauses
my hand, never singed by any heat,

invulnerable and bejeweled, rests——.
And boys, the hopes of ancient houses,
perish at my mouth as if from poison.

BUDDHA

Schon von ferne fühlt der fremde scheue
Pilger, wie es golden von ihm träuft;
so als hätten Reiche voller Reue
ihre Heimlichkeiten aufgehäuft.

Aber näher kommend wird er irre
vor der Hoheit dieser Augenbraun:
denn das sind nicht ihre Trinkgeschirre
und die Ohrgehänge ihrer Fraun.

Wüßte einer denn zu sagen, welche
Dinge eingeschmolzen wurden, um
dieses Bild auf diesem Blumenkelche

aufzurichten: stummer, ruhiggelber
als ein goldenes und rundherum
auch den Raum berührend wie sich selber.

Even from afar the awestruck foreign
pilgrim feels how it drips from him like gold:
as if whole kingdoms full of penitence
had heaped up their secrecies.

But nearing, he becomes confused
before these eyebrows' loftiness:
for this is not their drinking cups
and the earrings of their women.

Is there anyone who *could* say
what things had been melted down
to erect this image on this calyx:

more hushed, more peacefully yellow
than golden things and all around
touching space the way it does itself.

RÖMISCHE FONTÄNE
Borghese

Zwei Becken, eins das andre übersteigend
aus einem alten runden Marmorrand,
und aus dem oberen Wasser leis sich neigend
zum Wasser, welches unten wartend stand,

dem leise redenden entgegenschweigend
und heimlich, gleichsam in der hohlen Hand,
ihm Himmel hinter Grün und Dunkel zeigend
wie einen unbekannten Gegenstand;

sich selber ruhig in der schönen Schale
verbreitend ohne Heimweh, Kreis aus Kreis,
nur manchmal träumerisch und tropfenweis

sich niederlassend an den Moosbehängen
zum letzten Spiegel, der sein Becken leis
von unten lächeln macht mit Übergängen.

ROMAN FOUNTAIN
Borghese

Two basins, one rising from the other
within a round, wide, ancient marble rim,
and from the high one, water overbrimming
softly down to water, which waits below,

receiving its gentle talk in silence
and secretly, as in the hollow of a hand,
showing it sky behind darkness and green
like some unfamiliar object; while it

drifts peacefully away in its own lovely bowl
in circle after circle, without nostalgia,
only sometimes dreamily and drop by drop

threading its way down on the mossy carvings
to the last mirror, which, from there below
gazing up, smiles, seeing all is transition.

DAS KARUSSELL
Jardin du Luxembourg

Mit einem Dach und seinem Schatten dreht
sich eine kleine Weile der Bestand
von bunten Pferden, alle aus dem Land,
das lange zögert, eh es untergeht.
Zwar manche sind an Wagen angespannt,
doch alle haben Mut in ihren Mienen;
ein böser roter Löwe geht mit ihnen
und dann und wann ein weißer Elefant.

Sogar ein Hirsch ist da, ganz wie im Wald,
nur daß er einen Sattel trägt und drüber
ein kleines blaues Mädchen aufgeschnallt.

Und auf dem Löwen reitet weiß ein Junge
und hält sich mit der kleinen heißen Hand,
dieweil der Löwe Zähne zeigt und Zunge.

Und dann und wann ein weißer Elefant.

Und auf den Pferden kommen sie vorüber,
auch Mädchen, helle, diesem Pferdesprunge
fast schon entwachsen; mitten in dem Schwunge
schauen sie auf, irgendwohin, herüber—

Und dann und wann ein weißer Elefant.

Und das geht hin und eilt sich, daß es endet,
und kreist und dreht sich nur und hat kein Ziel.
Ein Rot, ein Grün, ein Grau vorbeigesendet,
ein kleines kaum begonnenes Profil—.
Und manchesmal ein Lächeln, hergewendet,
ein seliges, das blendet und verschwendet
an dieses atemlose blinde Spiel . . .

THE CAROUSEL
Jardin du Luxembourg

With a canopy and its shade it turns
for a short while, this little herd
of many-colored horses, all from the land
that lingers long, then disappears.
Some, it's true, are hitched to carriages,
yet all have courage in their faces;
an angry red lion goes with them
and now and then a white elephant.

Even a stag is there, as in the woods,
except he wears a saddle and on top of it
a little blue girl sits all buckled in.

And on the lion rides a boy in white
who holds on tightly with his small, hot hand,
while the lion bares teeth and tongue.

And now and then a white elephant.

And on the horses they come skimming past—
girls in bright dresses also, almost too old
already for this leaping of horses; in the midst
of the lunge they look up, off, over here—

And now and then a white elephant.

And it goes on and hurries to be over
and only circles and turns and has no goal.
A red, a green, a gray coming past,
a little, scarcely formed profile—.
And from time to time a smile, turned this way,
elated and starry-eyed as it expends itself
on this blind, breathless play . . .

Wie in der Hand ein Schwefelzündholz, weiß,
eh es zur Flamme kommt, nach allen Seiten
zuckende Zungen streckt—: beginnt im Kreis
naher Beschauer hastig, hell und heiß
ihr runder Tanz sich zuckend auszubreiten.

Und plötzlich ist er Flamme, ganz und gar.

Mit einem Blick entzündet sie ihr Haar
und dreht auf einmal mit gewagter Kunst
ihr ganzes Kleid in diese Feuersbrunst,
aus welcher sich, wie Schlangen die erschrecken,
die nackten Arme wach und klappernd strecken.

Und dann: als würde ihr das Feuer knapp,
nimmt sie es ganz zusamm und wirft es ab
sehr herrisch, mit hochmütiger Gebärde
und schaut: da liegt es rasend auf der Erde
und flammt noch immer und ergiebt sich nicht—.
Doch sieghaft, sicher und mit einem süßen
grüßenden Lächeln hebt sie ihr Gesicht
und stampft es aus mit kleinen festen Füßen.

As in the hand a sulfur match flares white
and sends out flicking tongues on every side
before it bursts into flame——: in that ring
of crowding onlookers, hot, eager, and precise
her round dance begins to dart and spread.

And all at once it is entirely flame.

With a glance she sets her hair ablaze
and whirls suddenly with daring art
her slender dress into this fiery rapture,
from which, like snakes awakened,
two naked arms uncoil, aroused and rattling.

And then: as if she felt the fire grow tight,
she gathers it all up and casts it off
disdainfully, and watches with imperious
command: it lies there raging on the ground
and still flares up and won't surrender——.
But unwavering, assured, and with a sweet
welcoming smile she lifts her face
and stamps it out with rock-hard little feet.

QUAI DU ROSAIRE
Brügge

Die Gassen haben einen sachten Gang
(wie manchmal Menschen gehen im Genesen
nachdenkend: was ist früher hier gewesen?)
und die an Plätze kommen, warten lang

auf eine andre, die mit einem Schritt
über das abendklare Wasser tritt,
darin, je mehr sich rings die Dinge mildern,
die eingehängte Welt von Spiegelbildern
so wirklich wird wie diese Dinge nie.

Verging nicht diese Stadt? Nun siehst du, wie
(nach einem unbegreiflichen Gesetz)
sie wach und deutlich wird im Umgestellten,
als wäre dort das Leben nicht so selten;
dort hängen jetzt die Gärten groß und gelten,
dort dreht sich plötzlich hinter schnell erhellten
Fenstern der Tanz in den Estaminets.

Und oben blieb?––Die Stille nur, ich glaube,
und kostet langsam und von nichts gedrängt
Beere um Beere aus der süßen Traube
des Glockenspiels, das in den Himmeln hängt.

QUAI DU ROSAIRE
Bruges

The streets move forward with a gentle gait
(as convalescents will sometimes walk
thinking to themselves: what used to be here?)
and those that come to squares stand

waiting for another, which with one stride
leaps across the evening-clear water,
in which, as things adjacent lose their edge,
the in-hung world of mirrored images
takes on the reality those things never know.

Didn't this city fade? Now you see how
(obeying some unfathomable law)
it wakes and grows clear in the world transposed,
as if life there were not so scarce;
the gardens there hang large and liquid,
there suddenly behind swiftly brightened windows
the dance in the estaminets revolves.

And above?— —Only the silence, I believe,
slowly tasting and lazily savoring
berry after berry from the sweet
cluster of the carillon hanging from the sky.

Bruges: The poem plays throughout on the identity of Bruges as "Bruges-la-Morte," a famous and thriving medieval city that in its wane—owing in part to the loss of its natural harbor—became a symbol of mutability and transience.

In ihren langen Haaren liegen sie
mit braunen, tief in sich gegangenen Gesichtern.
Die Augen zu wie vor zu vieler Ferne.
Skelette, Munde, Blumen. In den Munden
die glatten Zähne wie ein Reise-Schachspiel
aus Elfenbein in Reihen aufgestellt.
Und Blumen, gelbe Perlen, schlanke Knochen,
Hände und Hemden, welkende Gewebe
über dem eingestürzten Herzen. Aber
dort unter jenen Ringen, Talismanen
und augenblauen Steinen (Lieblings-Angedenken)
steht noch die stille Krypta des Geschlechtes,
bis an die Wölbung voll mit Blumenblättern.
Und wieder gelbe Perlen, weitverrollte, —
Schalen gebrannten Tones, deren Bug
ihr eignes Bild geziert hat, grüne Scherben
von Salben-Vasen, die wie Blumen duften,
und Formen kleiner Götter: Hausaltäre,
Hetärenhimmel mit entzückten Göttern.
Gesprengte Gürtel, flache Skarabäen,
kleine Figuren riesigen Geschlechtes,
ein Mund der lacht und Tanzende und Läufer,
goldene Fibeln, kleinen Bogen ähnlich
zur Jagd auf Tier- und Vogelamulette,
und lange Nadeln, zieres Hausgeräte
und eine runde Scherbe roten Grundes,
darauf, wie eines Eingangs schwarze Aufschrift,
die straffen Beine eines Viergespannes.
Und wieder Blumen, Perlen, die verrollt sind,
die hellen Lenden einer kleinen Leier,
und zwischen Schleiern, die gleich Nebeln fallen,
wie ausgekrochen aus des Schuhes Puppe:
des Fußgelenkes leichter Schmetterling.

They lie in their long hair, with brown faces
that have gone deep into themselves.
The eyes closed, as if confronting endless distances.
Skeletons, mouths, flowers. In the mouths
the smooth teeth like a pocket chess set
arrayed in ivory rows.
And flowers, yellow pearls, slender bones,
hands and tunics, faded weavings
above the caved-in heart. But
there beneath those rings, talismans,
and blue-eyed stones (precious love charms)
the silent crypt of the sex still stands,
filled to its vaulted roof with flower petals.
And again yellow pearls, scattered everywhere —
Shallow fired-clay plates, whose curve
their own image once adorned, green shards
of ointment jars with scents like flowers,
and statues of small deities: household altars,
hetaerae heavens with enamored gods.
Unclasped waistbands, flat scarab stones,
small figures' giant phalluses,
a laughing mouth and dancing girls and runners,
golden brooches that look like tiny bows
for hunting beast- and bird-shaped amulets,
and long needles, ornamented household things,
and a roundish potsherd's reddish ground,
on which, like the dark writing over an entrance:
the stiff legs of a team-of-four.
And more flowers, scattered pearls,
the bright loins of a little lyre,
and between veils that fall like mist,
as if crept forth from the shoe's chrysalis,
the pale butterfly of an ankle.

Hetaerae: Courtesans or concubines in ancient Greece.

So liegen sie mit Dingen angefüllt,
kostbaren Dingen, Steinen, Spielzeug, Hausrat,
zerschlagnem Tand (was alles in sie abfiel),
und dunkeln wie der Grund von einem Fluß.

Flußbetten waren sie,
darüber hin in kurzen schnellen Wellen
(die weiter wollten zu dem nächsten Leben)
die Leiber vieler Jünglinge sich stürzten
und in denen der Männer Ströme rauschten.
Und manchmal brachen Knaben aus den Bergen
der Kindheit, kamen zagen Falles nieder
und spielten mit den Dingen auf dem Grunde,
bis das Gefälle ihr Gefühl ergriff:

Dann füllten sie mit flachem klaren Wasser
die ganze Breite dieses breiten Weges
und trieben Wirbel an den tiefen Stellen;
und spiegelten zum ersten Mal die Ufer
und ferne Vogelrufe—, während hoch
die Sternennächte eines süßen Landes
in Himmel wuchsen, die sich nirgends schlossen.

Thus they lie filled up with things—
jewels, precious objects, toys, household stuff,
broken trinkets (whatever fell into them)—
and darken like the bottom of a river.

And they *were* riverbeds,
across whom in short, swift waves
(each wanting to go on into the next life)
the bodies of many young men hurled themselves,
and in whom grown men's torrents rushed.
And sometimes boys broke out of the mountains
of childhood, came down in timid falls
and played with the things on the bottom
until the slope gripped their feeling:

Then they filled with smooth clear water
across the whole expanse of their wide course
and began eddying in their deep places;
and for the first time mirrored the shore
and distant birdcalls—, while on high
the starry nights of a sweet country
blossomed into heavens that closed nowhere.

Das war der Seelen wunderliches Bergwerk.
Wie stille Silbererze gingen sie
als Adern durch sein Dunkel. Zwischen Wurzeln
entsprang das Blut, das fortgeht zu den Menschen,
und schwer wie Porphyr sah es aus im Dunkel.
Sonst war nichts Rotes.

Felsen waren da
und wesenlose Wälder. Brücken über Leeres
und jener große graue blinde Teich,
der über seinem fernen Grunde hing
wie Regenhimmel über einer Landschaft.
Und zwischen Wiesen, sanft und voller Langmut,
erschien des einen Weges blasser Streifen,
wie eine lange Bleiche hingelegt.

Und dieses einen Weges kamen sie.

Voran der schlanke Mann im blauen Mantel,
der stumm und ungeduldig vor sich aussah.
Ohne zu kauen fraß sein Schritt den Weg
in großen Bissen; seine Hände hingen
schwer und verschlossen aus dem Fall der Falten
und wußten nicht mehr von der leichten Leier,
die in die Linke eingewachsen war
wie Rosenranken in den Ast des Ölbaums.
Und seine Sinne waren wie entzweit:
indes der Blick ihm wie ein Hund vorauslief,
umkehrte, kam und immer wieder weit
und wartend an der nächsten Wendung stand,—
blieb sein Gehör wie ein Geruch zurück.
Manchmal erschien es ihm als reichte es
bis an das Gehen jener beiden andern,
die folgen sollten diesen ganzen Aufstieg.

This was the souls' strange mine.
Like silent silver ore they wandered
through its dark like veins. Between roots
the blood welled up that makes its way to men,
and it looked hard as porphyry in the dark.
Nothing else was red.

Rocks were there
and unreal forests. Bridges spanning voids
and that huge gray blind unmoving lake
that hung above its distant bed
like rainy sky above a landscape.
And between meadows, soft and full of patience,
the pale stripe of the single path,
laid down like a long pallor being bleached.

And up this single path they came.

In front the slender man in the blue mantle,
who mute and impatient stared ahead.
His stride devoured the path in huge mouthfuls
without slowing to chew; his hands hung heavy
and clenched out of the falling folds
and were no longer conscious of the light lyre
that had twined itself into his left
like tendrils of roses in an olive bough.
And his senses were as if divided:
for while his sight raced ahead like a dog,
turned around, came back, and then stood
far away and waiting at the path's next turn,—
his hearing, like an odor, lagged behind.
Sometimes it seemed to him it reached
back to the steps of those two others
who were to follow for the whole ascent.

Dann wieder wars nur seines Steigens Nachklang
und seines Mantels Wind was hinter ihm war.
Er aber sagte sich, sie kämen doch;
sagte es laut und hörte sich verhallen.
Sie kämen doch, nur wärens zwei
die furchtbar leise gingen. Dürfte er
sich einmal wenden (wäre das Zurückschaun
nicht die Zersetzung dieses ganzen Werkes,
das erst vollbracht wird), müßte er sie sehen,
die beiden Leisen, die ihm schweigend nachgehn:

Den Gott des Ganges und der weiten Botschaft,
die Reisehaube über hellen Augen,
den schlanken Stab hertragend vor dem Leibe
und flügelschlagend an den Fußgelenken;
und seiner linken Hand gegeben: *sie.*

Die So-geliebte, daß aus einer Leier
mehr Klage kam als je aus Klagefrauen;
daß eine Welt aus Klage ward, in der
alles noch einmal da war: Wald und Tal
und Weg und Ortschaft, Feld und Fluß und Tier;
und daß um diese Klage-Welt, ganz so
wie um die andre Erde, eine Sonne
und ein gestirnter stiller Himmel ging,
ein Klage-Himmel mit entstellten Sternen—:
Diese So-geliebte.

Sie aber ging an jenes Gottes Hand,
den Schritt beschränkt von langen Leichenbändern,
unsicher, sanft und ohne Ungeduld.
Sie war in sich, wie Eine hoher Hoffnung,
und dachte nicht des Mannes, der voranging,
und nicht des Weges, der ins Leben aufstieg.
Sie war in sich. Und ihr Gestorbensein
erfüllte sie wie Fülle.
Wie eine Frucht von Süßigkeit und Dunkel,
so war sie voll von ihrem großen Tode,
der also neu war, daß sie nichts begriff.

Then again it was just his own climbing's echo
and his mantle's wind he heard behind him.
But he told himself they *were* coming,
said it aloud and heard the words die out.
They *were* coming, it was only that they walked
with frightening lightness. If he could only
turn around once (though any backward glance
would be death to the entire undertaking,
so near completion now), he would *have* to see them,
those two light-footed ones, who followed silently:

The god of faring and of distant messages,
eyes shining under the traveler's hood,
the slender staff held out before his body,
and at his ankles a fluttering of wings;
and entrusted to his left hand: *she.*

The one so loved that from a single lyre
came more lament than ever from lamenting women;
that from lament a world arose, in which
everything had second life: forest and valley
and road and village, field and flock and stream;
and that around this lament world, just as
around the other earth, a sun turned
and a star-filled silent heaven,
a lament heaven with devastated stars—:
This one so loved.

But now she walked at that god's hand,
her steps, constrained by long winding-sheets,
soft, uncertain, and without impatience.
She was in herself, like a woman near birth,
and thought not of the man, who walked ahead,
and not of the path, which ascended into life.
She was in herself. And her having died
filled her like abundance.
Like a fruit ripe with sweetness and night
she was filled with her great death,
which was so new that she understood nothing.

Sie war in einem neuen Mädchentum
und unberührbar; ihr Geschlecht war zu
wie eine junge Blume gegen Abend,
und ihre Hände waren der Vermählung
so sehr entwöhnt, daß selbst des leichten Gottes
unendlich leise, leitende Berührung
sie kränkte wie zu sehr Vertraulichkeit.

Sie war schon nicht mehr diese blonde Frau,
die in des Dichters Liedern manchmal anklang,
nicht mehr des breiten Bettes Duft und Eiland
und jenes Mannes Eigentum nicht mehr.

Sie war schon aufgelöst wie langes Haar
und hingegeben wie gefallner Regen
und ausgeteilt wie hundertfacher Vorrat.

Sie war schon Wurzel.

Und als plötzlich jäh
der Gott sie anhielt und mit Schmerz im Ausruf
die Worte sprach: Er hat sich umgewendet—,
begriff sie nichts und sagte leise: *Wer?*

Fern aber, dunkel vor dem klaren Ausgang,
stand irgend jemand, dessen Angesicht
nicht zu erkennen war. Er stand und sah,
wie auf dem Streifen eines Wiesenpfades
mit trauervollem Blick der Gott der Botschaft
sich schweigend wandte, der Gestalt zu folgen,
die schon zurückging dieses selben Weges,
den Schritt beschränkt von langen Leichenbändern,
unsicher, sanft und ohne Ungeduld.

She was in a new virginity
and untouchable; her sex had closed
like a young flower at approach of evening,
and her hands had been so weaned
from marriage, that even the light god's
infinitely soft, guiding touch
hurt her like too great a liberty.

She was no longer the blond wife
who echoed often in the poet's songs,
no longer the vast bed's scent and island,
and that one man's property no longer.

She was already loosened like long hair
and given over like fallen rain
and handed out like a limitless supply.

She was already root.

And when without warning
the god stopped her and with pain in his voice
uttered the words: *He has turned around—*,
she didn't understand, and answered softly: *Who?*

But there in the distance, dark against
the bright exit, stood someone whose features
could not be read. He stood and saw
how on that stripe of meadow path
with mournful look the god of messages
turned silently around, to follow the shape
already returning on that same path,
her steps, constrained by the long winding-sheets,
soft, uncertain, and without impatience.

Da plötzlich war der Bote unter ihnen,
hineingeworfen in das Überkochen
des Hochzeitsmahles wie ein neuer Zusatz.
Sie fühlten nicht, die Trinkenden, des Gottes
heimlichen Eintritt, welcher seine Gottheit
so an sich hielt wie einen nassen Mantel
und ihrer einer schien, der oder jener,
wie er so durchging. Aber plötzlich sah
mitten im Sprechen einer von den Gästen
den jungen Hausherrn oben an dem Tische
wie in die Höh gerissen, nicht mehr liegend,
und überall und mit dem ganzen Wesen
ein Fremdes spiegelnd, das ihn furchtbar ansprach.
Und gleich darauf, als klärte sich die Mischung,
war Stille; nur mit einem Satz am Boden
von trübem Lärm und einem Niederschlag
fallenden Lallens, schon verdorben riechend
nach dumpfem umgestandenen Gelächter.
Und da erkannten sie den schlanken Gott,
und wie er dastand, innerlich voll Sendung
und unerbittlich, —wußten sie es beinah.
Und doch, als es gesagt war, war es mehr
als alles Wissen, gar nicht zu begreifen.
Admet muß sterben. Wann? In dieser Stunde.

Der aber brach die Schale seines Schreckens
in Stücken ab und streckte seine Hände
heraus aus ihr, um mit dem Gott zu handeln.
Um Jahre, um ein einzig Jahr noch Jugend,
um Monate, um Wochen, um paar Tage,
ach, Tage nicht, um Nächte, nur um Eine,
um Eine Nacht, um diese nur: um die.
Der Gott verneinte, und da schrie er auf
und schrie's hinaus und hielt es nicht und schrie
wie seine Mutter aufschrie beim Gebären.

Then suddenly the messenger was with them,
tossed into the simmering wedding feast
like a fresh ingredient. But they all
went on drinking, and didn't feel
the god's secret entrance, as he held
his godhead tight against him like a wet
mantle and seemed just another guest
making his way. Until one of them,
engrossed in conversation, glanced up
and saw at the table's head their young host
no longer reclining but as if snatched to his feet,
and mirroring everywhere, with all his being,
a foreignness that fearfully addressed him.
And with that, as if the mixture cleared,
there was silence; just some dregs
of muddy noise on the floor and a sediment
of falling murmur, already rancid
with the smell of muffled ruined laughter.
Now they recognized the slender god,
and as he stood there, inwardly full of mission
and unentreatable, —they almost knew.
And yet, when it was uttered, it was beyond
comprehension, impossible to absorb.
Admetus must die. When? This very hour.

But then the shell of his terror cracked
and he shattered it and stretched his hands
out beyond, to bargain with the god:
for years, for a single year more of youth,
for months, for weeks, for a few days,
ah, not days then, nights, just one,
for just *one* night, just *this* one night: for *it*.
The god refused, and then Admetus screamed
and screamed it out, held nothing in and screamed
the way his mother had screamed in childbirth.

Und die trat zu ihm, eine alte Frau,
und auch der Vater kam, der alte Vater,
und beide standen, alt, veraltet, ratlos,
beim Schreienden, der plötzlich, wie noch nie
so nah, sie ansah, abbrach, schluckte, sagte:
Vater,
liegt dir denn viel daran an diesem Rest,
an diesem Satz, der dich beim Schlingen hindert?
Geh, gieß ihn weg. Und du, du alte Frau,
Matrone,
was tust du denn noch hier: du hast geboren.
Und beide hielt er sie wie Opfertiere
in Einem Griff. Auf einmal ließ er los
und stieß die Alten fort, voll Einfall, strahlend
und atemholend, rufend: Kreon, Kreon!
Und nichts als das; und nichts als diesen Namen.
Aber in seinem Antlitz stand das Andere,
das er nicht sagte, namenlos erwartend,
wie ers dem jungen Freunde, dem Geliebten
erglühend hinhielt übern wirren Tisch.
Die Alten (stand da), siehst du, sind kein Loskauf,
sie sind verbraucht und schlecht und beinah wertlos,
du aber, du, in deiner ganzen Schönheit—

Da aber sah er seinen Freund nicht mehr.
Er blieb zurück, und das, was kam, war *sie*,
ein wenig kleiner fast als er sie kannte
und leicht und traurig in dem bleichen Brautkleid.
Die andern alle sind nur ihre Gasse,
durch die sie kommt und kommt—: (gleich wird sie da sein
in seinen Armen, die sich schmerzhaft auftun).

Doch wie er wartet, spricht sie; nicht zu ihm.
Sie spricht zum Gotte, und der Gott vernimmt sie,
und alle hörens gleichsam erst im Gotte:

And she stepped toward him, an old woman,
and his father came with her, his ancient father,
and both stood, old, decrepit, perplexed,
beside their screaming son, who looked at them
(as if never before so close) and suddenly
broke off, swallowed, spoke: Father,
do you really covet these remains,
these dregs you choke on as you drink?
Go, empty them. And you, old woman,
my honored Mother,
what's left for you here: you have given birth.
And he held both like sacrificial beasts
tightly gripped. Suddenly he let go and pushed
the old couple aside, inspired, beaming
and breathing, calling: Creon! Creon!
And nothing else; nothing but the name.
But in his face was all he didn't say
as he extended it, glowing with hope,
to the young friend, the loved one,
across the tumult of the wedding table.
The old (it said), look, cannot serve as ransom,
they're used up and ruined and almost worthless,
but you, Creon, you, in all your beauty—

But with that he no longer saw his friend.
He shrank back, and *she* stepped forth instead,
looking even smaller than he knew her
and frail and sad in her pale wedding dress.
All the others serve as her avenue,
down which she comes—: (soon she'll be there
in his arms, which open painfully).

But as he waits, she speaks; though not to him.
She speaks to the god, and the god listens,
and all hear, as it were, only in the god.

Ersatz kann keiner für ihn sein. Ich *bins*.
Ich bin Ersatz. Denn keiner ist zu Ende
wie ich es bin. Was bleibt mir denn von dem
was ich hier war? Das *ists* ja, daß ich sterbe.
Hat sie dirs nicht gesagt, da sie dirs auftrug,
daß jenes Lager, das da drinnen wartet,
zur Unterwelt gehört? Ich nahm ja Abschied.
Abschied über Abschied.
Kein Sterbender nimmt mehr davon. Ich ging ja,
damit das Alles, unter Dem begraben
der jetzt mein Gatte ist, zergeht, sich auflöst—.
So führ mich hin: ich sterbe ja für ihn.

Und wie der Wind auf hoher See, der umspringt,
so trat der Gott fast wie zu einer Toten
und war auf einmal weit von ihrem Gatten,
dem er, versteckt in einem kleinen Zeichen,
die hundert Leben dieser Erde zuwarf.
Der stürzte taumelnd zu den beiden hin
und griff nach ihnen wie im Traum. Sie gingen
schon auf den Eingang zu, in dem die Frauen
verweint sich drängten. Aber einmal sah
er noch des Mädchens Antlitz, das sich wandte
mit einem Lächeln, hell wie eine Hoffnung,
die beinah ein Versprechen war: erwachsen
zurückzukommen aus dem tiefen Tode
zu ihm, dem Lebenden—

Da schlug er jäh
die Hände vors Gesicht, wie er so kniete,
um nichts zu sehen mehr nach diesem Lächeln.

No one can stand in for him. Take me.
I *am* a stand-in. No one's life is over
the way mine is. What remains to me
of all I was here? I'm *already* dying.
Didn't she tell you, when she charged you,
that the bed that waits inside there
belongs to the underworld? I've *said* farewell.
Farewell after farewell. No one dying
ever said more of them. I *have* departed,
so that all this, buried under the man
who is now my husband, dissolves, disappears—.
So lead me away: I *am* dying for him.

And as the wind veers around on high seas,
the god stepped almost as toward someone dead
and was suddenly distant from her husband,
to whom, in a quick unglimpsed gesture,
he tossed the hundred lifetimes of this earth.
The young man stumbled drunkenly toward the pair
and reached for them as in a dream. Already
they had neared the entrance, in which the women
crowded weeping. Then one last time
he saw the girl's face, as it turned around
with a smile, which shone like a hope
that was almost a promise: to come back
full-grown from the deeps of death
to him, the living one—

At that, kneeling there,
he threw his hands up to his face,
to see her smile—and nothing after.

An diesem Morgen nach der Nacht, die bang
vergangen war mit Rufen, Unruh, Aufruhr, —
brach alles Meer noch einmal auf und schrie.
Und als der Schrei sich langsam wieder schloß
und von der Himmel blassem Tag und Anfang
herabfiel in der stummen Fische Abgrund—:
gebar das Meer.

Von erster Sonne schimmerte der Haarschaum
der weiten Wogenscham, an deren Rand
das Mädchen aufstand, weiß, verwirrt und feucht.
So wie ein junges grünes Blatt sich rührt,
sich reckt und Eingerolltes langsam aufschlägt,
entfaltete ihr Leib sich in die Kühle
hinein und in den unberührten Frühwind.

Wie Monde stiegen klar die Kniee auf
und tauchten in der Schenkel Wolkenränder;
der Waden schmaler Schatten wich zurück,
die Füße spannten sich und wurden licht,
und die Gelenke lebten wie die Kehlen
von Trinkenden.

Und in dem Kelch des Beckens lag der Leib
wie eine junge Frucht in eines Kindes Hand.
In seines Nabels engem Becher war
das ganze Dunkel dieses hellen Lebens.
Darunter hob sich licht die kleine Welle
und floß beständig über nach den Lenden,
wo dann und wann ein stilles Rieseln war.
Durchschienen aber und noch ohne Schatten,
wie ein Bestand von Birken im April,
warm, leer und unverborgen, lag die Scham.

In the morning after that night which fearfully
had passed in outcry, tumult, uproar, —
the sea split open once again and screamed.
And as the scream slowly closed up
and from the sky's pale light and brightness
fell back into the silent fishes' chasm—:
the sea gave birth.

From first sun the hair-froth shimmered
in the wide cleft of wave, on whose rim
the girl stood—white, dripping, and confused.
As a blade of new green leaf stirs,
stretches, and, uncoiling, slowly opens,
her body unfolded into cool sea-air
and into untouched early morning breeze.

Like moons her knees rose brightly
and ducked into the cloud rims of her thighs;
her calves' slender shadows withdrew,
her feet flexed and turned luminous,
and her joints came alive
like the throats of drinkers.

And in the hips' chalice lay the belly,
like a young fruit nestled in a child's hand.
Within its navel's narrow goblet was
all the darkness this bright life contained.
Beneath it the small wave rose lightly
and lapped continuously toward the loins,
where now and then there was a silent ripple.
But translucent and still without shadow,
like a stand of birch trees in early April,
warm, empty, and unhidden, lay the sex.

Jetzt stand der Schultern rege Waage schon
im Gleichgewichte auf dem graden Körper,
der aus dem Becken wie ein Springbrunn aufstieg
und zögernd in den langen Armen abfiel
und rascher in dem vollen Fall des Haars.

Dann ging sehr langsam das Gesicht vorbei:
aus dem verkürzten Dunkel seiner Neigung
in klares, waagrechtes Erhobensein.
Und hinter ihm verschloß sich steil das Kinn.

Jetzt, da der Hals gestreckt war wie ein Strahl
und wie ein Blumenstiel, darin der Saft steigt,
streckten sich auch die Arme aus wie Hälse
von Schwänen, wenn sie nach dem Ufer suchen.

Dann kam in dieses Leibes dunkle Frühe
wie Morgenwind der erste Atemzug.
Im zartesten Geäst der Aderbäume
entstand ein Flüstern, und das Blut begann
zu rauschen über seinen tiefen Stellen.
Und dieser Wind wuchs an: nun warf er sich
mit allem Atem in die neuen Brüste
und fülte sie und drückte sich in sie, —
daß sie wie Segel, von der Ferne voll,
das leichte Mädchen nach dem Strande drängten.

So landete die Göttin.

Hinter ihr,
die rasch dahinschritt durch die jungen Ufer,
erhoben sich den ganzen Vormittag
die Blumen und die Halme, warm, verwirrt,
wie aus Umarmung. Und sie ging und lief.

Am Mittag aber, in der schwersten Stunde,
hob sich das Meer noch einmal auf und warf
einen Delphin an jene selbe Stelle.
Tot, rot und offen.

Now the shoulders' quick scales already stood
in perfect balance on the upright body,
which rose from the pelvis like a fountain
and fell hesitantly in the long arms
and more swiftly in the hair's cascade.

Then very slowly the face went past:
out of downtilted darkness
into clear, horizontal upliftedness.
And in its wake, the sharp closing of the chin.

Now, with the neck extending like a ray of light,
and like flower stalks in which the sap mounts,
the arms too stretched, like necks of swans
when they're searching for the shore.

Then into this body's dark dawning
came the first breath like morning wind.
In the vein-trees' tenderest branches
a whispering arose, and the blood began
rushing louder over its deep places.
And this wind increased: now it plunged
with all its might into the newborn breasts
and filled them and crowded into them, —
so that like sails full of distance
they drove the light girl toward the shore.

And so the goddess landed.

Behind her,
as she strode swiftly on across the young sands,
all morning long the flowers and grasses
sprang up, warm, confused,
as from embracing. And she walked and ran.

But at noon, in the heaviest hour,
the sea rose up once more and threw
a dolphin on that selfsame spot.
Dead, red, and open.

Zornige sahst du flackern, sahst zwei Knaben
zu einem Etwas sich zusammenballen,
das Haß war und sich auf der Erde wälzte
wie ein von Bienen überfallnes Tier;
Schauspieler, aufgetürmte Übertreiber,
rasende Pferde, die zusammenbrachen,
den Blick wegwerfend, bläkend das Gebiß
als schälte sich der Schädel aus dem Maule.

Nun aber weißt du, wie sich das vergißt:
denn vor dir steht die volle Rosenschale,
die unvergeßlich ist und angefüllt
mit jenem Äußersten von Sein und Neigen,
Hinhalten, Niemals-Gebenkönnen, Dastehn,
das unser sein mag: Äußerstes auch uns.

Lautloses Leben, Aufgehn ohne Ende,
Raum-brauchen ohne Raum von jenem Raum
zu nehmen, den die Dinge rings verringern,
fast nicht Umrissen-sein wie Ausgespartes
und lauter Inneres, viel seltsam Zartes
und Sich-bescheinendes—bis an den Rand:
ist irgend etwas uns bekannt wie dies?

Und dann wie dies: daß ein Gefühl entsteht,
weil Blütenblätter Blütenblätter rühren?
Und dies: daß eins sich aufschlägt wie ein Lid,
und drunter liegen lauter Augenlider,
geschlossene, als ob sie, zehnfach schlafend,
zu dämpfen hätten eines Innern Sehkraft.
Und dies vor allem: daß durch diese Blätter
das Licht hindurch muß. Aus den tausend Himmeln
filtern sie langsam jenen Tropfen Dunkel,
in dessen Feuerschein das wirre Bündel
der Staubgefäße sich erregt und aufbäumt.

THE BOWL OF ROSES

You've seen caged anger flare, seen two boys
knot themselves into a ball
of pure hatred, writhing on the ground
like an animal attacked by bees;
you've seen play-actors, sky-high exaggerators,
careening horses crashing down,
flinging their eyes around, baring their teeth
as if their muzzles were peeling away from their skulls.

But now you see how such things are forgotten:
for before you stands the full bowl of roses,
which is unforgettable and wholly filled
with that utmost of presence and promise,
of offering up, beyond any power to give, of being here,
that might be ours—*our* utmost as well.

Living in silence, endlessly opening,
making use of space without taking space
from the space adjacent things diminish,
barest hint of outline, like untouched ground
and pure withinness, all strangely soft
and self-illuminating—to the very edge:
is there anything we know like this?

And like this: that a feeling arises
because flower petals touch petals?
And this: that one opens like an eye,
and under it lie eyelid after eyelid,
all tightly closed, as if through tenfold sleep
they might curb an inner power of sight.
And this above all: that through these petals
light must pass. From a thousand skies
slowly they filter out the drop of darkness
within whose fiery glow the tangled pack
of stamens bestirs itself and springs erect.

Und die Bewegung in den Rosen, sieh:
Gebärden von so kleinem Ausschlagswinkel,
daß sie unsichtbar blieben, liefen ihre
Strahlen nicht auseinander in das Weltall.

Sieh jene weiße, die sich selig aufschlug
und dasteht in den großen offnen Blättern
wie eine Venus aufrecht in der Muschel;
und die errötende, die wie verwirrt
nach einer kühlen sich hinüberwendet,
und wie die kühle fühllos sich zurückzieht,
und wie die kalte steht, in sich gehüllt,
unter den offenen, die alles abtun.
Und *was* sie abtun, wie das leicht und schwer,
wie es ein Mantel, eine Last, ein Flügel
und eine Maske sein kann, je nach dem,
und *wie* sie's abtun: wie vor dem Geliebten.

Was können sie nicht sein: war jene gelbe,
die hohl und offen daliegt, nicht die Schale
von einer Frucht, darin dasselbe Gelb,
gesammelter, orangeröter, Saft war?
Und wars für diese schon zu viel, das Aufgehn,
weil an der Luft ihr namenloses Rosa
den bittern Nachgeschmack des Lila annahm?
Und die batistene, ist sie kein Kleid,
in dem noch zart und atemwarm das Hemd streckt,
mit dem zugleich es abgeworfen wurde
im Morgenschatten an dem alten Waldbad?
Und diese hier, opalnes Porzellan,
zerbrechlich, eine flache Chinatasse
und angefüllt mit kleinen hellen Faltern, —
und jene da, die nichts enthält als sich.

Und sind nicht alle so, nur sich enthaltend,
wenn Sich-enthalten heißt: die Welt da draußen
und Wind und Regen und Geduld des Frühlings
und Schuld und Unruh und vermummtes Schicksal

And the movement in the roses, look:
gestures from vibrations so minute
that they'd remain invisible, if their rays
did not fan out into the universe.

Look at that white one, blissfully opened
and standing there amid its spread of petals
like a Venus balanced on her shell;
and the blushing one, which as if flustered
turns across to one that is cool,
and how the cool one withdraws aloof,
and how that cold one stands, wrapped in itself,
among the open ones, that shed everything.
And *what* they shed: how it can be
at once light and heavy, a cloak, a burden,
a wing and a mask—it all depends—
and *how* they shed it: as before the loved one.

What can't they be: was that yellow one,
which lies there hollow and open, not the rind
of a fruit in which that very yellow,
more intense, more orange-red, was juice?
And was mere opening too much for this one,
since touched by air its inexpressible pink
has taken on the bitter aftertaste of lilac?
And that cambric one, is it not a dress
in which the shift still clings, soft and breath-warm,
both of them cast off together
in the morning shadows by the old woodland pond?
And this one, opalescent porcelain,
fragile, a shallow china cup
and full of tiny brilliant butterflies, —
and that one, containing nothing but itself.

And aren't they all that way, simply self-containing,
if self-containing means: to transform the world outside
and the wind and rain and patience of Spring
and guilt and restlessness and muffled fate

und Dunkelheit der abendlichen Erde
bis auf der Wolken Wandel, Flucht und Anflug,
bis auf den vagen Einfluß ferner Sterne
in eine Hand voll Innres zu verwandeln.

Nun liegt es sorglos in den offnen Rosen.

and the darkness of the evening earth
out to the roaming and flying and fleeing of the clouds
and the vague influence of distant stars
into a handful of inwardness.

Now it lies carefree in these opened roses.

From DER NEUEN GEDICHTE
ANDERER TEIL *(1908)*

Wir kannten nicht sein unerhörtes Haupt,
darin die Augenäpfel reiften. Aber
sein Torso glüht noch wie ein Kandelaber,
in dem sein Schauen, nur zurückgeschraubt,

sich hält und glänzt. Sonst könnte nicht der Bug
der Brust dich blenden, und im leisen Drehen
der Lenden könnte nicht ein Lächeln gehen
zu jener Mitte, die die Zeugung trug.

Sonst stünde dieser Stein entstellt und kurz
unter der Schultern durchsichtigem Sturz
und flimmerte nicht so wie Raubtierfelle;

und bräche nicht aus allen seinen Rändern
aus wie ein Stern: denn da is keine Stelle,
die dich nicht sieht. Du mußt dein Leben ändern.

We never knew his head and all the light
that ripened in his fabled eyes. But
his torso still burns like a streetlamp dimmed
in which his gaze, lit long ago,

holds fast and shines. Otherwise the surge
of the breast could not blind you, nor a smile
run through the slight twist of the loins
toward that center where procreation flared.

Otherwise this stone would stand cut off
and cold under the shoulders' transparent drop
and not glisten like a wild beast's fur;

and not break forth from all its contours
like a star: for there is no place
that does not see you. You must change your life.

Als ihn der Gott in seiner Not betrat,
erschrak er fast, den Schwan so schön zu finden;
er ließ sich ganz verwirrt in ihm verschwinden.
Schon aber trug ihn sein Betrug zur Tat,

bevor er noch des unerprobten Seins
Gefühle prüfte. Und die Aufgetane
erkannte schon den Kommenden im Schwane
und wußte schon: er bat um Eins,

das sie, verwirrt in ihrem Widerstand,
nicht mehr verbergen konnte. Er kam nieder
und halsend durch die immer schwächre Hand

ließ sich der Gott in die Geliebte los.
Dann erst empfand er glücklich sein Gefieder
und wurde wirklich Schwan in ihrem Schooß.

LEDA

When the god in his great need entered it,
he was shocked almost to find the swan so beautiful;
he disappeared inside it still surprised.
But his deceit propelled him toward the deed

before the senses of that untried life
could be explored. And the unguarded woman
saw at once who was coming in the swan
and knew too well: he begged that thing of her

which she, confused in her resistance,
no longer could conceal. The god came down,
and, necking through her ever softer hand,

released himself into the one he loved.
Then only—with what joy!—he felt his feathers,
and became truly swan within her womb.

FREMDE FAMILIE

So wie der Staub, der irgendwie beginnt
und nirgends ist, zu unerklärtem Zwecke
an einem leeren Morgen in der Ecke
in die man sieht, ganz rasch zu Grau gerinnt,

so bildeten sie sich, wer weiß aus was,
im letzten Augenblick vor deinen Schritten
und waren etwas Ungewisses mitten
im nassen Niederschlag der Gasse, das

nach dir verlangte. Oder nicht nach dir.
Denn eine Stimme, wie vom vorigen Jahr,
sang dich zwar an und blieb doch ein Geweine;
und eine Hand, die wie geliehen war,
kam zwar hervor und nahm doch nicht die deine.
Wer kommt denn noch? Wen meinen diese vier?

The way the dust, which begins somehow
and isn't anywhere, for an unknown reason
on an empty morning in that very corner
where one glances, jells as if on cue to gray,

so they took shape—who knows from what—
in the last instant before your footsteps,
and were an uncertain something
in the damp detritus of the side street,

that longed for you. Or not for you.
For a voice, as from the year just past,
did sing to you, and yet remained a weeping;
and a hand, which was as if extended,
did reach out, and yet didn't take your own.
Who else is coming? Who *are* these four?

Sie hatten sich an ihn gewöhnt. Doch als
die Küchenlampe kam und unruhig brannte
im dunkeln Luftzug, war der Unbekannte
ganz unbekannt. Sie wuschen seinen Hals,

und da sie nichts von seinem Schicksal wußten,
so logen sie ein anderes zusamm,
fortwährend waschend. Eine mußte husten
und ließ solang den schweren Essigschwamm

auf dem Gesicht. Da gab es eine Pause
auch für die zweite. Aus der harten Bürste
klopften die Tropfen; während seine grause
gekrampfte Hand dem ganzen Hause
beweisen wollte, daß ihn nicht mehr dürste.

Und er bewies. Sie nahmen wie betreten
eiliger jetzt mit einem kurzen Huster
die Arbeit auf, so daß an den Tapeten
ihr krummer Schatten in dem stummen Muster

sich wand und wälzte wie in einem Netze,
bis daß die Waschenden zu Ende kamen.
Die Nacht im vorhanglosen Fensterrahmen
war rücksichtslos. Und einer ohne Namen
lag bar und reinlich da und gab Gesetze.

CORPSE-WASHING

They had gotten used to him. But when
the kitchen lamp came and burned restlessly
in the dark draft, the one no one knew
turned utterly unknown. They washed his neck,

and since they knew nothing of his fate,
they made up another one with lies,
washing all the while. The first had to cough,
and set the heavy vinegar-soaked sponge

down on his face. Then there was a pause
while the other rested. The drops kept falling
from her hard brush; while his terrible
cramped hand tried to make the whole house
see that he no longer thirsted.

He got through to them. With a short cough,
as if embarrassed, they resumed the task
more urgently, so that on the wallpaper
their hunched shadows writhed and twisted

in the mute patterns as though in a net,
until the washings came to an end.
The night in the uncurtained window frame
was pitiless. And one without names
lay there bare and clean and gave commands.

EINE VON DEN ALTEN
Paris

Abends manchmal (weißt du, wie das tut?)
wenn sie plötzlich stehn und rückwärts nicken
und ein Lächeln, wie aus lauter Flicken,
zeigen unter ihrem halben Hut.

Neben ihnen ist dann ein Gebäude,
endlos, und sie locken dich entlang
mit dem Rätsel ihrer Räude,
mit dem Hut, dem Umhang und dem Gang.

Mit der Hand, die hinten unterm Kragen
heimlich wartet und verlangt nach dir:
wie um deine Hände einzuschlagen
in ein aufgehobenes Papier.

ONE OF THE OLD ONES
Paris

Sometimes at evening (do you know how it feels?)
when they suddenly stop and nod backward
and show you under their half-hats
a smile that seems all patches . . .

Next to them there's always a building,
endless, and they lure you along
with the riddle of their scabs—
with the hat, the shawl, and the gait.

With the hand, which curled under the collar
waits in secret and longs for you:
as if it wished to wrap your hands
in a scrap of picked-up paper.

EINE WELKE

Leicht, wie nach ihrem Tode
trägt sie die Handschuh, das Tuch.
Ein Duft aus ihrer Kommode
verdrängte den lieben Geruch,

an dem sie sich früher erkannte.
Jetzt fragte sie lange nicht, wer
sie sei (: eine ferne Verwandte),
und geht in Gedanken umher

und sorgt für ein ängstliches Zimmer,
das sie ordnet und schont,
weil es vielleicht noch immer
dasselbe Mädchen bewohnt.

FADED

Lightly, as after her death,
she wears her gloves, her shawl.
A fragrance from her bureau
has displaced the cherished scent

by which she used to know herself.
Now she's long stopped asking
who she is (: some distant relative),
and wanders lost in thought

and looks after a querulous room,
which she cares for and keeps arranged
because that same young girl
may live there yet.

Gemieden von dem Frühherbstmorgen, der
mißtrauisch war, lag hinter den versengten
Hauslinden, die das Heidehaus beengten,
ein Neues, Leeres. Eine Stelle mehr,

auf welcher Kinder, von Gott weiß woher,
einander zuschrien und nach Fetzen haschten.
Doch alle wurden stille, sooft er,
der Sohn von hier, aus heißen, halbveraschten

Gebälken Kessel und verbogne Tröge
an einem langen Gabelaste zog,—
um dann mit einem Blick als ob er löge
die andern anzusehn, die er bewog

zu glauben, was an dieser Stelle stand.
Denn seit es nicht mehr war, schien es ihm so
seltsam: phantastischer als Pharao.
Und er war anders. Wie aus fernem Land.

THE SITE OF THE FIRE

Avoided by the early autumn morning,
which was mistrustful, behind the scorched
lindens that crowded in around the heath house,
lay a newness, a blankness. One place more

in which children, god knows from where,
screamed back and forth and grabbed for scraps.
Yet they all fell silent whenever he,
the son who lived here, with a long, forked branch

fished a kettle or a twisted washtub
from under hot, half-incinerated beams,—
and then, with the look of someone lying,
gazed at the others, whom he strove

to convince of what stood on that spot.
For now that it was gone, it seemed to him
so strange: more fantastic than Pharaoh.
And *he* was foreign. As from a far-off land.

DIE GRUPPE
Paris

Als pflückte einer rasch zu einem Strauß:
ordnet der Zufall hastig die Gesichter,
lockert sie auf und drückt sie wieder dichter,
ergreift zwei ferne, läßt ein nahes aus,

tauscht das mit dem, bläst irgendeines frisch,
wirft einen Hund, wie Kraut, aus dem Gemisch
und zieht, was niedrig schaut, wie durch verworrne
Stiele und Blätter, an dem Kopf nach vorne

und bindet es ganz klein am Rande ein;
und streckt sich wieder, ändert und verstellt
und hat nur eben Zeit, zum Augenschein

zurückzuspringen mitten auf die Matte,
auf der im nächsten Augenblick der glatte
Gewichteschwinger seine Schwere schwellt.

THE GROUP
Paris

Like someone swiftly making a bouquet:
Chance hastily arranges all the faces,
loosens them, then squeezes tight again,
grabs two distant ones, omits one close,

transposes them, blows life into those drooping,
tosses a dog out of the mix like a weed,
pulls what looks lost or too small by the head
as if through tangled leaves and stems

and makes room for it up front, at the edge;
and reaches out again, alters and adjusts
and for inspection has just time enough

to spring back to the middle of the mat,
on which in the next instant the glistening
strongman begins to wield his weight.

SCHLANGEN-BESCHWÖRUNG

Wenn auf dem Markt, sich wiegend, der Beschwörer
die Kürbisflöte pfeift, die reizt und lullt,
so kann es sein, daß er sich einen Hörer
herüberlockt, der ganz aus dem Tumult

der Buden eintritt in den Kreis der Pfeife,
die will und will und will und die erreicht,
daß das Reptil in seinem Korb sich steife
und die das steife schmeichlerisch erweicht,

abwechselnd immer schwindelnder und blinder
mit dem, was schreckt und streckt, und dem, was löst——;
und dann genügt ein Blick: so hat der Inder
dir eine Fremde eingeflößt,

in der du stirbst. Es ist als überstürze
glühender Himmel dich. Es geht ein Sprung
durch dein Gesicht. Es legen sich Gewürze
auf deine nordische Erinnerung,

die dir nichts hilft. Dich feien keine Kräfte,
die Sonne gärt, das Fieber fällt und trifft;
von böser Freude steilen sich die Schäfte,
und in den Schlangen glänzt das Gift.

When the charmer, swaying in the market,
pipes on that flute of gourd, which lulls and rouses,
it can sometimes happen that he lures
a listener across, who steps from the tumult

of the stalls into the circle of the pipe,
which wills and wills and wills until at last
it makes the reptile stiffen in its basket
and fawns upon the stiffness till it softens,

alternating ever more blindly and dizzily
what startles and stretches with what unloosens—;
and then just a glance: and the Indian
has infused a foreignness in you,

in which you die. It's as though a blazing
sky crashed in on you. A crack
runs down your face. Spices pile themselves
upon your Nordic memory,

which is no help. No power is a charm,
the sun ferments, the fever falls and strikes;
the shafts rise up with a malicious joy,
and poison glistens in the snakes.

SCHWARZE KATZE

Ein Gespenst ist noch wie eine Stelle,
dran dein Blick mit einem Klange stößt;
aber da, an diesem schwarzen Felle
wird dein stärkstes Schauen aufgelöst:

wie ein Tobender, wenn er in vollster
Raserei ins Schwarze stampft,
jählings am benehmenden Gepolster
einer Zelle aufhört und verdampft.

Alle Blicke, die sie jemals trafen,
scheint sie also an sich zu verhehlen,
um darüber drohend und verdrossen
zuzuschauern und damit zu schlafen.
Doch auf einmal kehrt sie, wie geweckt,
ihr Gesicht und mitten in das deine:
und da triffst du deinen Blick im geelen
Amber ihrer runden Augensteine
unerwartet wieder: eingeschlossen
wie ein ausgestorbenes Insekt.

Even a ghost is like a place
your glance bumps into with a sound;
but here, in the thickness of this black fur,
your strongest gaze will be dissolved:

the way a madman, when in wild-eyed rage
he strides off into pure blackness,
stops short and feels his force evaporate
at the insensate padding of a cell.

All the glances that have ever met her
she seems to conceal about herself
so she can look them over,
morose and menacing, and sleep with them.
But all at once, as if awakened,
she turns her face straight into your own:
and unexpectedly you meet your gaze
in the yellow amber of her round eye-stones:
trapped there like some prehistoric fly.

Wie zuletzt, in einem Augenblick
aufgehäuft aus Hängen, Häusern, Stücken
alter Himmel und zerbrochnen Brücken,
und von drüben her, wie vom Geschick,
von dem Sonnenuntergang getroffen,
angeschuldigt, aufgerissen, offen—
ginge dort die Ortschaft tragisch aus:

fiele nicht auf einmal in das Wunde,
drin zerfließend, aus der nächsten Stunde
jener Tropfen kühlen Blaus,
der die Nacht schon in den Abend mischt,
so daß das von ferne Angefachte
sachte, wie erlöst, erlischt.

Ruhig sind die Tore und die Bogen,
durchsichtige Wolken wogen
über blassen Häuserreihn
die schon Dunkel in sich eingesogen;
aber plötzlich ist vom Mond ein Schein
durchgeglitten, licht, als hätte ein
Erzengel irgendwo sein Schwert gezogen.

How at the very last, in an instant
heaped up out of houses, hillsides, pieces
of old sky and broken bridges,
and from far away, as if by destiny,
struck by the setting sun,
accused, torn open, left exposed—
this little town would end in tragedy:

if suddenly from the next hour
there didn't fall into the wound, dissolving
coolly, that drop of tranquil blue,
which begins at once to blend night into the lateness,
so that things inflamed by distant fire
die out softly, as if redeemed.

The gates and arches are at rest,
transparent clouds
float over the pale house rows
that have already soaked up darkness;
but suddenly a shaft of moonlight
glides through, bright, as if somewhere
an archangel had unsheathed his sword.

Aus der vollgestellten Stadt, die lieber
schliefe, träumend von den hohen Thermen,
geht der grade Gräberweg ins Fieber;
und die Fenster in den letzten Fermen

sehn ihm nach mit einem bösen Blick.
Und er hat sie immer im Genick,
wenn er hingeht, rechts und links zerstörend,
bis er draußen atemlos beschwörend

seine Leere zu den Himmeln hebt,
hastig um sich schauend, ob ihn keine
Fenster treffen. Während er den weiten

Aquädukten zuwinkt herzuschreiten,
geben ihm die Himmel für die seine
ihre Leere, die ihn überlebt.

Exiting the cluttered city, which would rather
sleep, dreaming of the lofty Thermae,
the tomb road makes straight for the fever,
and the windows in the last farms

follow with an evil eye.
And it always has them at its back
as it continues on, wreaking havoc left and right,
until outside, breathlessly beseeching,

it lifts its emptiness up to the skies,
quickly looking all around to see
if any window watches. While it signals

the distant aqueducts to start marching,
the heavens take its emptiness
and give it their own, which will outlive it.

The tomb road: The Appian Way, ancient high road that runs through the Roman countryside to lower Italy and eventually enters the Pontine Marshes (hence, perhaps, the obscure *ins Fieber* of line 3). The ruins of the magnificent Thermae, or baths, of Caracalla are the last important building it passes before it leaves the city, and tombs line its passage through the countryside.

NÄCHTLICHE FAHRT
Sankt Petersburg

Damals als wir mit den glatten Trabern
(schwarzen, aus dem Orloff'schen Gestüt)—,
während hinter hohen Kandelabern
Stadtnachtfronten lagen, angefrüht,
stumm und keiner Stunde mehr gemäß—,
fuhren, nein: vergingen oder flogen
und um lastende Paläste bogen
in das Wehn der Newa-Quais,

hingerissen durch das wache Nachten,
das nicht Himmel und nicht Erde hat, —
als das Drängende von unbewachten
Gärten gärend aus dem Ljetnij-Ssad
aufstieg, während seine Steinfiguren
schwindend mit ohnmächtigen Konturen
hinter uns vergingen, wie wir fuhren—:

damals hörte diese Stadt
auf zu sein. Auf einmal gab sie zu,
daß sie niemals war, um nichts als Ruh
flehend; wie ein Irrer, dem das Wirrn
plötzlich sich entwirrt, das ihn verriet,
und der einen jahrelangen kranken
gar nicht zu verwandelnden Gedanken,
den er nie mehr denken muß: Granit—
aus dem leeren schwankenden Gehirn
fallen fühlt, bis man ihn nicht mehr sieht.

NIGHT DRIVE
Saint Petersburg

That time, when drawn by the sleek trotters
(black ones, bred on the Orloff stud)—,
while behind streetlamp sentinels
stood city-night facades, all tinged with dawn,
mute, no longer linked to any hour—,
we were driving, no: flying, disappearing,
careening around heavy palaces
out into the wind of the Neva's quays,

transported through the wakeful night
that hasn't earth and hasn't sky, —
as the urgings of unattended gardens
fermented up from the Letny Sad,
while the stone statues, dwindling there
haplessly with passive contours,
disappeared behind us as we drove—:

That time this city ceased
to be. All at once it admitted
that it never was, begging only peace;
like a lunatic, when the confusion
that betrayed him suddenly unravels,
and he feels a sickly years-long
utterly unalterable thought
that he never has to think again—granite—
fall from his empty reeling brain
until it vanishes from sight.

Letny Sad: A large park (literally, "Summer Garden") that belonged to the czars.

PAPAGEIEN-PARK
Jardin des Plantes, Paris

Unter türkischen Linden, die blühen, an Rasenrändern,
in leise von ihrem Heimweh geschaukelten Ständern
atmen die Ara und wissen von ihren Ländern,
die sich, auch wenn sie nicht hinsehn, nicht verändern.

Fremd im beschäftigten Grünen wie eine Parade,
zieren sie sich und fühlen sich selber zu schade,
und mit den kostbaren Schnäbeln aus Jaspis und Jade
kauen sie Graues, verschleudern es, finden es fade.

Unten klauben die duffen Tauben, was sie nicht mögen,
während sich oben die höhnischen Vögel verbeugen
zwischen den beiden fast leeren vergeudeten Trögen.

Aber dann wiegen sie wieder und schläfern und äugen,
spielen mit dunkelen Zungen, die gerne lögen,
zerstreut an den Fußfesselringen. Warten auf Zeugen.

PARROT PARK
Jardin des Plantes, Paris

Under blossoming Turkish lindens, at the grass's edge,
on stands rocked lightly by their languishings for home,
the Aras breathe and contemplate their countries,
which, even though their eyes aren't on them, never vary.

As out of place as a parade in all this busy green,
they put on airs and preen and feel above it all,
and with those precious beaks made out of jade and jasper
chew a gray something, find it dull, toss it away.

Below, the dreary doves pick up what they've disdained,
while from above the scornful birds make a mock-obedient bow
between the two squandered, nearly empty feeding trays.

But then they start rocking again and sleeping and watching,
and with dark tongues, which would gladly tell lies,
play distractedly with their foot chains. Waiting for witnesses.

VENEZIANISCHER MORGEN
Richard Beer-Hofmann zugeeignet

Fürstlich verwöhnte Fenster sehen immer,
was manchesmal uns zu bemühn geruht:
die Stadt, die immer wieder, wo ein Schimmer
von Himmel trifft auf ein Gefühl von Flut,

sich bildet ohne irgendwann zu sein.
Ein jeder Morgen muß ihr die Opale
erst zeigen, die sie gestern trug, und Reihn
von Spiegelbildern ziehn aus dem Kanale
und sie erinnern an die andern Male:
dann giebt sie sich erst zu und fällt sich ein

wie eine Nymphe, die den Zeus empfing.
Das Ohrgehäng erklingt an ihrem Ohre;
sie aber hebt San Giorgio Maggiore
und lächelt lässig in das schöne Ding.

VENETIAN MORNING
Dedicated to Richard Beer-Hofmann

Windows pampered like princes behold always
what on occasion deigns to draw our gaze:
the city that over and over, where a shimmer
of sky strikes a feeling of flood tide,

takes shape without yet agreeing to be.
Each new morning first must show her
the opals she wore yesterday, and lift
strings of reflections out of the canal
and remind her of all her former times:
only then does she consent and grow compliant

like a nymph acquiescing to great Zeus.
The dangling earrings chime at her ears:
but she lifts San Giorgio Maggiore
and smiles idly into that wondrous thing.

Nun treibt die Stadt schon nicht mehr wie ein Köder,
der alle aufgetauchten Tage fängt.
Die gläsernen Paläste klingen spröder
an deinen Blick. Und aus den Gärten hängt

der Sommer wie ein Haufen Marionetten
kopfüber, müde, umgebracht.
Aber vom Grund aus alten Waldskeletten
steigt Willen auf: also sollte über Nacht

der General des Meeres die Galeeren
verdoppeln in dem wachen Arsenal,
um schon die nächste Morgenluft zu teeren

mit einer Flotte, welche ruderschlagend
sich drängt und jäh, mit allen Flaggen tagend,
den großen Wind hat, strahlend und fatal.

Already the city no longer drifts
like a lure, catching the days as they surface.
The glassy palaces ring more brittle
against your gaze. And from the gardens

summer hangs like a heap of marionettes,
headlong, exhausted, done in.
But up from the ground, out of old forest skeletons,
volition rises: as if overnight

the General of the Sea were to double
the galleys in the sleepless Arsenal,
in order to tar the next morning breeze

with a fleet, which starts out rowing
and then suddenly, all its flags dawning,
seizes the great wind, radiant and dire.

SAN MARCO
Venedig

In diesem Innern, das wie ausgehöhlt
sich wölbt und wendet in den goldnen Smalten,
rundkantig, glatt, mit Köstlichkeit geölt,
ward dieses Staates Dunkelheit gehalten

und heimlich aufgehäuft, als Gleichgewicht
des Lichtes, das in allen seinen Dingen
sich so vermehrte, daß sie fast vergingen—.
Und plötzlich zweifelst du: vergehn sie nicht?

und drängst zurück die harte Galerie,
die, wie ein Gang im Bergwerk, nah am Glanz
der Wölbung hängt; und du erkennst die heile

Helle des Ausblicks: aber irgendwie
wehmütig messend ihre müde Weile
am nahen Überstehn des Viergespanns.

SAN MARCO
Venice

In this Interior, which curves and arches
inside its gold mosaic like a cave,
round-cornered, smoothed, oiled with exquisiteness,
this State's darkness was preserved

and secretly amassed, as counterbalance
to the light that multiplied so blindingly
in all its things, they almost disappeared——.
And suddenly you think: perhaps they *did*.

And you shove back the narrow gallery
that hangs like a catwalk in a mine
along the dome's brilliance: and see before you

the bright prospect, still intact: yet somehow
sadly measuring its rote endurance
against the bronze survival of the team-of-four.

Viergespann: Literally, a four-in-hand, or quadriga. The reference is almost certainly to the four
bronze horses of San Marco, treasures of antiquity that stand over the central porch of the west
front of St. Mark's. They were brought to Venice from Constantinople in 1204, as part of the
plunder when that city was taken in the Fourth Crusade.

Ich bin die Laute. Willst du meinen Leib
beschreiben, seine schön gewölbten Streifen:
sprich so, als sprächest du von einer reifen
gewölbten Feige. Übertreib

das Dunkel, das du in mir siehst. Es war
Tullias Dunkelheit. In ihrer Scham
war nicht so viel, und ihr erhelltes Haar
war wie ein heller Saal. Zuweilen nahm

sie etwas Klang von meiner Oberfläche
in ihr Gesicht und sang zu mir.
Dann spannte ich mich gegen ihre Schwäche,
und endlich war mein Inneres in ihr.

I am the lute. Should you wish to describe
my body, with its lovely arching stripes:
speak of me as you would of a ripe
full-bodied fig. Underscore

the darkness you see in me. This was
Tullia's darkness. There was so little
in her secret places, and her lustrous hair
was like a light-filled hall. Sometimes

she'd absorb some sound from my surfaces
into her features and sing while I played.
Then I'd tense myself against her easefulness,
and finally my soul found itself in her.

Tullia: Most commentators suggest Tullia d'Aragona, a famous courtesan (as well as poet and musician) of sixteenth-century Italy. But a still more famous Tullia is Cicero's daughter, whose body, according to legend, was found after fifteen hundred years in a monument along the Appian Way, with a lamp still burning there, before contact with the air turned both to dust. (Donne alludes to the legend, and to Tullia by name, in one of his epithalamiums.) The name should probably be allowed its mystery. It assumes an intimacy and a lived dimension that exclude us; as such it underscores the lute's inaccessibility, both as historical artifact and as Rilkean "thing."

Plötzlich tritt sie, in den Wind gehüllt,
licht in Lichtes, wie herausgegriffen,
während jetzt die Stube wie geschliffen
hinter ihr die Türe füllt

dunkel wie der Grund einer Kamee,
die ein Schimmern durchläßt durch die Ränder;
und du meinst der Abend war nicht, ehe
sie heraustrat, um auf das Geländer

noch ein wenig von sich fortzulegen,
noch die Hände, —um ganz leicht zu sein:
wie dem Himmel von den Häuserreihn
hingereicht, von allem zu bewegen.

Suddenly she steps, sheathed in the wind,
brightly into brilliance, as if singled out,
while the room behind her now slips in
to fit the door's outline,

darkly like the background of a cameo
that lets the merest glint in at the edges;
and you think the evening wasn't there
before she stepped out, and on the railing

set forth just a little of herself,
just her hands, —to be completely light:
so the house rows might pass her on
to the heavens, to be moved by everything.

ÜBUNG AM KLAVIER

Der Sommer summt. Der Nachmittag macht müde;
sie atmete verwirrt ihr frisches Kleid
und legte in die triftige Etüde
die Ungeduld nach einer Wirklichkeit,

die kommen konnte: morgen, heute abend—,
die vielleicht da war, die man nur verbarg;
und vor den Fenstern, hoch und alles habend,
empfand sie plötzlich den verwöhnten Park.

Da brach sie ab; schaute hinaus, verschränkte
die Hände; wünschte sich ein langes Buch—
und schob auf einmal den Jasmingeruch
erzürnt zurück. Sie fand, daß er sie kränkte.

PIANO PRACTICE

The summer drones. The afternoon drags on.
She flounced her crisp white dress distractedly
and put into that sharply etched étude
her impatience for a reality

that could come: tomorrow, this evening—,
that perhaps was there, but only hidden;
and at the windows, tall, in full possession,
she suddenly could feel the pampered park.

With that she broke off; gazed outside,
locked her hands; wished for a long book—
and in a burst of anger fought off
the jasmine scent. She found it sickened her.

Wo ist zu diesem Innen
ein Außen? Auf welches Weh
legt man solches Linnen?
Welche Himmel spiegeln sich drinnen
in dem Binnensee
dieser offenen Rosen,
dieser sorglosen, sieh:
wie sie lose im Losen
liegen, als könnte nie
eine zitternde Hand sie verschütten.
Sie können sich selber kaum
halten; viele ließen
sich überfüllen und fließen
über von Innenraum
in die Tage, die immer
voller und voller sich schließen,
bis der ganze Sommer ein Zimmer
wird, ein Zimmer in einem Traum.

Where is there an outside
for this inside? On what pain
is linen like this placed?
What skies find themselves reflected
in the inland lake
of these open roses,
these blissfully unworried ones:
see how neglectfully in all this looseness
they relax, as if no trembling hand
could ever spill them.
They scarcely can contain
themselves; many let themselves
fill up with inner space
until they overflow and stream
into the days, which keep on
closing more and more completely,
until all of summer becomes
a room, a room within a dream.

DAME VOR DEM SPIEGEL

Wie in einem Schlaftrunk Spezerein
löst sie leise in dem flüssigklaren
Spiegel ihr ermüdetes Gebaren;
und sie tut ihr Lächeln ganz hinein.

Und sie wartet, daß die Flüssigkeit
davon steigt; dann gießt sie ihre Haare
in den Spiegel und, die wunderbare
Schulter hebend aus dem Abendkleid,

trinkt sie still aus ihrem Bild. Sie trinkt,
was ein Liebender im Taumel tränke,
prüfend, voller Mißtraun; und sie winkt

erst der Zofe, wenn sie auf dem Grunde
ihres Spiegels Lichter findet, Schränke
und das Trübe einer späten Stunde.

As one stirs spices in a soporific:
she gently loosens her wearied features
and dissolves them in the liquid-clear mirror;
then drops her smile inside.

And she waits, while the liquor
rises from it; then pours her hair
into the mirror and, lifting that wondrous
shoulder out of her evening gown,

drinks quietly from her image. What
a lover would drunkenly devour she
tastes slowly, full of mistrust; and only

gestures to her maid when at the bottom
of her mirror she finds candles, cabinets,
and the clouded leavings of a late hour.

Selten reicht ein Schauer feuchter Fäule
aus dem Gartenschatten, wo einander
Tropfen fallen hören und ein Wander-
vogel lautet, zu der Säule,
die in Majoran und Koriander
steht und Sommerstunden zeigt;

nur sobald die Dame (der ein Diener
nachfolgt) in dem hellen Florentiner
über ihren Rand sich neigt,
wird sie schattig und verschweigt—.

Oder wenn ein sommerlicher Regen
aufkommt aus dem wogenden Bewegen
hoher Kronen, hat sie eine Pause;
denn sie weiß die Zeit nicht auszudrücken,
die dann in den Frucht- und Blumenstücken
plötzlich glüht im weißen Gartenhause.

Seldom does a shadow of damp decay
reach from the garden shadows (where the drops
hear one another fall, and a migratory
bird keeps calling) to the column,
which stands in marjoram and coriander
and declares the summer hours;

only when the lady (whom a servant
follows) in the bright wide-brimmed hat
bends down above its edge
does it grow shadowy and secretive——.

Or when a summer rain comes down
from the sudden turbulence
of high treetops, does it grow inactive;
for it can't express the kind of time
which then in fruit-and-flower still lifes
briefly sets the white garden house aglow.

Abseits im Garten blüht der böse Schlaf,
in welchem die, die heimlich eingedrungen,
die Liebe fanden junger Spiegelungen,
die willig waren, offen und konkav,

und Träume, die mit aufgeregten Masken
auftraten, riesiger durch die Kothurne—:
das alles stockt in diesen oben flasken
weichlichen Stengeln, die die Samenurne

(nachdem sie lang, die Knospe abwärts tragend,
zu welken meinten) festverschlossen heben:
gefranste Kelche auseinanderschlagend,
die fieberhaft das Mohngefäß umgeben.

OPIUM POPPY

Off in the garden blooms the evil sleep,
in which those who secretly gained entrance
found the love of young mirror images,
which were all willing, open, and concave,

and dreams which entered in aroused masks,
giantlike amid fantastic backgrounds—:
all this collects in these topmost slender
indolent stems, which (after long expecting,

with their buds weighing downward, to expire)
suddenly lift the tightly shut seed urns:
throwing open disheveled calyxes
that feverishly surround the poppy cup.

DIE FLAMINGOS
Jardin des Plantes, Paris

In Spiegelbildern wie von Fragonard
ist doch von ihrem Weiß und ihrer Röte
nicht mehr gegeben, als dir einer böte,
wenn er von seiner Freundin sagt: sie war

noch sanft von Schlaf. Denn steigen sie ins Grüne
und stehn, auf rosa Stielen leicht gedreht,
beisammen, blühend, wie in einem Beet,
verführen sie verführender als Phryne

sich selber; bis sie ihres Auges Bleiche
hinhalsend bergen in der eignen Weiche,
in welcher Schwarz und Fruchtrot sich versteckt.

Auf einmal kreischt ein Neid durch die Volière;
sie aber haben sich erstaunt gestreckt
und schreiten einzeln ins Imaginäre.

THE FLAMINGOS
Jardin des Plantes, Paris

Such Fragonard-like reflections
can no more convey their white and red
than if someone in love told you
of the friend whose image lingers: she was

still soft with sleep. They stilt into the green
and stand there, turned slightly on pink stems,
together, blooming, as in some garden plot,
seducing themselves, more seductively

than Phryne; until their necks curl down and they
bury their pale eyes in their own softness,
where black and fruit-red lie concealed.

Suddenly an envy shrieks through the great cage;
but they have stretched out in astonishment
and stride, each alone, into the world of dreams.

Phryne: A Greek courtesan famed for her beauty; she is supposed to have modeled for the sculptor Praxiteles.

SCHLAFLIED

Einmal wenn ich dich verlier,
wirst du schlafen können, ohne
daß ich wie eine Lindenkrone
mich verflüstre über dir?

Ohne daß ich hier wache und
Worte, beinah wie Augenlider,
auf deine Brüste, auf deine Glieder
niederlege, auf deinen Mund.

Ohne daß ich dich verschließ
und dich allein mit Deinem lasse
wie einen Garten mit einer Masse
von Melissen und Stern-Anis.

LULLABY

Someday if I lose you,
will you still be able to sleep,
without me to whisper over you
like a crown of linden branches?

Without me to stay awake here
and place words, almost like eyelids,
on your breasts, on your limbs,
down upon your mouth?

Without me to lock you up
and leave you alone with what's yours,
like a garden thickly sown
with mint balm and star anise?

Nein: ein Turm soll sein aus meinem Herzen
und ich selbst an seinen Rand gestellt:
wo sonst nichts mehr ist, noch einmal Schmerzen
und Unsäglichkeit, noch einmal Welt.

Noch ein Ding allein im Übergroßen,
welches dunkel wird und wieder licht,
noch ein letztes, sehnendes Gesicht
in das Nie-zu-Stillende verstoßen,

noch ein äußerstes Gesicht aus Stein,
willig seinen inneren Gewichten,
das die Weiten, die es still vernichten,
zwingen, immer seliger zu sein.

No: my heart shall be a tower,
and I myself set at its highest rim:
where nothing else exists, once again pain
and the unsayable, once again world.

Still one thing alone in immensity,
growing dark then light again,
still one last face full of longing
thrust out into the unappeasable,

still one uttermost face made of stone
heeding only its own inner gravity,
while the distances that silently destroy it
drive it on to an ever deeper bliss.

DER KÄFERSTEIN

Sind nicht Sterne fast in deiner Nähe
und was giebt es, das du nicht umspannst,
da du dieser harten Skarabäe
Karneolkern gar nicht fassen kannst

ohne jenen Raum, der ihre Schilder
niederhält, auf deinem ganzen Blut
mitzutragen; niemals war er milder,
näher, hingegebener. Er ruht

seit Jahrtausenden auf diesen Käfern,
wo ihn keiner braucht und unterbricht;
und die Käfer schließen sich und schläfern
unter seinem wiegenden Gewicht.

Are not stars almost in your vicinity,
and what is there that you don't embrace,
since you can't even close these hard
scarabs' carnelian kernels in your palm

without bearing too, through all your blood,
that space which holds their wing shards down.
Never was space gentler, closer, more
self-surrendered. It rests

for thousands of years upon these beetles,
where no one uses and interrupts it;
and the beetles fold in on themselves
and sleep beneath its gently rocking weight.

Mitte aller Mitten, Kern der Kerne,
Mandel, die sich einschließt und versüßt, —
dieses Alles bis an alle Sterne
ist dein Fruchtfleisch: Sei gegrüßt.

Sieh, du fühlst, wie nichts mehr an dir hängt;
im Unendlichen ist deine Schale,
und dort steht der starke Saft und drängt.
Und von außen hilft ihm ein Gestrahle,

denn ganz oben werden deine Sonnen
voll und glühend umgedreht.
Doch in dir ist schon begonnen,
was die Sonnen übersteht.

Center of all centers, core of cores,
almond, that closes tightly in and sweetens, —
all this world out to the farthest stars
is the flesh around your seed: we greet you.

Look: you can feel how nothing any longer
clings to you; your husk is in infinity,
and the potent juice now stands there pressing.
And from outside a radiance assists it,

for high above, your suns in their full splendor
have wheeled blazingly around.
Yet inside you now, secure and growing:
what lasts beyond the suns.

DUINESER ELEGIEN *(1923)*

DUINO ELEGIES *(1923)*

Wer, wenn ich schriee, hörte mich denn aus der Engel
Ordnungen? und gesetzt selbst, es nähme
einer mich plötzlich ans Herz: ich verginge von seinem
stärkeren Dasein. Denn das Schöne ist nichts
als des Schrecklichen Anfang, den wir noch grade ertragen,
und wir bewundern es so, weil es gelassen verschmäht,
uns zu zerstören. Ein jeder Engel ist schrecklich.
 Und so verhalt ich mich denn und verschlucke den Lockruf
dunkelen Schluchzens. Ach, wen vermögen
wir denn zu brauchen? Engel nicht, Menschen nicht,
und die findigen Tiere merken es schon,
daß wir nicht sehr verläßlich zu Haus sind
in der gedeuteten Welt. Es bleibt uns vielleicht
irgend ein Baum an dem Abhang, daß wir ihn täglich
wiedersähen; es bleibt uns die Straße von gestern
und das verzogene Treusein einer Gewohnheit,
der es bei uns gefiel, und so blieb sie und ging nicht.
 O und die Nacht, die Nacht, wenn der Wind voller Weltraum
uns am Angesicht zehrt—, wem bliebe sie nicht, die ersehnte,
sanft enttäuschende, welche dem einzelnen Herzen
mühsam bevorsteht. Ist sie den Liebenden leichter?
Ach, sie verdecken sich nur mit einander ihr Los.
 Weißt du's *noch* nicht? Wirf aus den Armen die Leere
zu den Räumen hinzu, die wir atmen; vielleicht daß die Vögel
die erweiterte Luft fühlen mit innigerm Flug.

Ja, die Frühlinge brauchten dich wohl. Es muteten manche
Sterne dir zu, daß du sie spürtest. Es hob
sich eine Woge heran im Vergangenen, oder
da du vorüberkamst am geöffneten Fenster,
gab eine Geige sich hin. Das alles war Auftrag.
Aber bewältigtest du's? Warst du nicht immer
noch von Erwartung zerstreut, als kündigte alles
eine Geliebte dir an? (Wo willst du sie bergen,

Who, if I cried out, would hear me among the Angels'
Orders? and even if one of them pressed me
suddenly to his heart: I'd be consumed
in his more potent being. For beauty is nothing
but the beginning of terror, which we can still barely endure,
and while we stand in wonder it coolly disdains
to destroy us. Every Angel is terrifying.
 And so I grip myself and choke down that call note
of dark sobbing. Ah, whom *can* we turn to
in our need? Not Angels, not humans,
and the sly animals see at once
how little at home we are
in the interpreted world. That leaves us
some tree on a slope, to which our eyes returned
day after day; leaves us yesterday's street
and the coddled loyalty of an old habit
that liked it here, lingered, and never left.
 O and the night, the night, when the wind full of worldspace
gnaws at our faces—, for whom *won't* the night be there,
desired, softly disappointing, setting hard tasks
for the single heart. Is it easier on lovers?
Ah, they only use each other to mask their fates.
 You *still* don't see? Fling the emptiness in your arms
out into the spaces we breathe; perhaps the birds
will feel the increase of air with more passionate flight.

Yes, the Springs needed you. Many a star was waiting
for your eyes only. A wave swelled toward you
out of the past, or as you walked by the open window
a violin inside surrendered itself
to pure passion. All that was your charge.
But were you strong enough? Weren't you always distracted
by expectation, as though each such moment
presaged a beloved's coming? (But where would you keep her,

da doch die großen fremden Gedanken bei dir
aus und ein gehn und öfters bleiben bei Nacht.)
Sehnt es dich aber, so singe die Liebenden; lange
noch nicht unsterblich genug ist ihr berühmtes Gefühl.
Jene, du neidest sie fast, Verlassenen, die du
so viel liebender fandst als die Gestillten. Beginn
immer von neuem die nie zu erreichende Preisung;
denk: es erhält sich der Held, selbst der Untergang war ihm
nur ein Vorwand, zu sein: seine letzte Geburt.
Aber die Liebenden nimmt die erschöpfte Natur
in sich zurück, als wären nicht zweimal die Kräfte,
dieses zu leisten. Hast du der Gaspara Stampa
denn genügend gedacht, daß irgend ein Mädchen,
dem der Geliebte entging, am gesteigerten Beispiel
dieser Liebenden fühlt: daß ich würde wie sie?
Sollen nicht endlich uns diese ältesten Schmerzen
fruchtbarer werden? Ist es nicht Zeit, daß wir liebend
uns vom Geliebten befrein und es bebend bestehn:
wie der Pfeil die Sehne besteht, um gesammelt im Absprung
mehr zu sein als er selbst. Denn Bleiben ist nirgends.

Stimmen, Stimmen. Höre, mein Herz, wie sonst nur
Heilige hörten: daß sie der riesige Ruf
aufhob vom Boden; sie aber knieten,
Unmögliche, weiter und achtetens nicht:
So waren sie hörend. Nicht, daß du *Gottes* ertrügest
die Stimme, bei weitem. Aber das Wehende höre,
die ununterbrochene Nachricht, die aus Stille sich bildet.
Es rauscht jetzt von jenen jungen Toten zu dir.
Wo immer du eintratst, redete nicht in Kirchen
zu Rom und Neapel ruhig ihr Schicksal dich an?
Oder es trug eine Inschrift sich erhaben dir auf,

with all those big strange thoughts in you
going and coming and sometimes staying all night?)
No, in the grip of longing sing women who *loved*;
their prodigious feeling still lacks an undying fame.
The abandoned ones you almost envy, since you found them
so much deeper in love than those whom love allayed.
Begin ever anew their impossible praise.
Remember: the hero lives on, even his downfall
was only a pretext for attained existence: his ultimate birth.
But nature, exhausted, takes women in love
back into herself, as though she lacked strength
to create them a second time. Have you praised Gaspara Stampa
intently enough that any girl left by her lover
will be moved by this heightened instance
of a woman's heart to cry out: Let me be as she was!
Isn't it time these most ancient sorrows
at last bore fruit? Time we tenderly detached ourselves
from the loved one and, trembling, stood free:
the way the arrow, suddenly all vector, survives the string
to be *more* than itself. For abiding is nowhere.

Voices, voices. Listen, my heart, the way
only saints have listened till now, as that vast call
lifted them from the ground; while they kept on kneeling
and noticed nothing, those impossible ones:
listeners fully absorbed. Not that you could bear
God's voice—not at all. But listen to the wind's breathing,
the unbroken news that takes shape out of silence.
It's rustling toward you now from all the youthful dead.
When you entered a church in Rome or Naples,
didn't their fate speak quietly to you?
Or an inscription echoed deep within you,

Gaspara Stampa: An Italian noblewoman (1523–54) who fell in love with Count Collatino di
Collalto at the age of twenty-six and was deserted by him three years later. She responded by
recording the story of their love and her experience of solitude and loss in a series of two hun-
dred sonnets.

wie neulich die Tafel in Santa Maria Formosa.
Was sie mir wollen? leise soll ich des Unrechts
Anschein abtun, der ihrer Geister
reine Bewegung manchmal ein wenig behindert.

Freilich ist es seltsam, die Erde nicht mehr zu bewohnen,
kaum erlernte Gebräuche nicht mehr zu üben,
Rosen, und andern eigens versprechenden Dingen
nicht die Bedeutung menschlicher Zukunft zu geben;
das, was man war in unendlich ängstlichen Händen,
nicht mehr zu sein, und selbst den eigenen Namen
wegzulassen wie ein zerbrochenes Spielzeug.
Seltsam, die Wünsche nicht weiterzuwünschen. Seltsam,
alles, was sich bezog, so lose im Raume
flattern zu sehen. Und das Totsein ist mühsam
und voller Nachholn, daß man allmählich ein wenig
Ewigkeit spürt. —Aber Lebendige machen
alle den Fehler, daß sie zu stark unterscheiden.
Engel (sagt man) wüßten oft nicht, ob sie unter
Lebenden gehn oder Toten. Die ewige Strömung
reißt durch beide Bereiche alle Alter
immer mit sich und übertönt sie in beiden.

Schließlich brauchen sie uns nicht mehr, die Früheentrückten,
man entwöhnt sich des Irdischen sanft, wie man den Brüsten
milde der Mutter entwächst. Aber wir, die so große
Geheimnisse brauchen, denen aus Trauer so oft
seliger Fortschritt entspringt—: *könnten* wir sein ohne sie?

as, not long ago, that tablet in Santa Maria Formosa.
Their charge to me? —that I gently dispel
the air of injustice that sometimes
hinders a little their spirits' pure movement.

Granted, it's strange to dwell on earth no more,
to cease observing customs barely learned,
not to give roses and other things of such promise
a meaning in some human future;
to stop being what one was in endlessly anxious hands,
and ignore even one's own name like a broken toy.
Strange, not to go on wishing one's wishes. Strange,
to see all that was once so interconnected
drifting in space. And death exacts a labor,
a long finishing of things half-done, before
one has that first feeling of eternity. —But the living
all make the same mistake: they distinguish too sharply.
Angels (it's said) often don't know whether they're moving among
the living or the dead. The eternal current
sweeps all the ages with it through both kingdoms
forever and drowns their voices in both.

In the end, those torn from us early no longer need us:
slowly one becomes unaccustomed to earthly things,
in the gentle way one leaves a mother's breast. But we, who need
such great mysteries, for whom so often blessed progress
springs from grief—: could *we* exist without *them*?

Santa Maria Formosa: A famous church in Venice, which Rilke visited twice in 1911. The reference is to one of the commemorative tablets on the church walls—it isn't known which one, though there has been much speculation.

Ist die Sage umsonst, daß einst in der Klage um Linos
wagende erste Musik dürre Erstarrung durchdrang;
daß erst im erschrockenen Raum, dem ein beinah göttlicher Jüngling
plötzlich für immer enttrat, das Leere in jene
Schwingung geriet, die uns jetzt hinreißt und tröstet und hilft.

Is it a tale told in vain, that myth of lament for Linos,
in which a daring first music pierced the shell of numbness:
stunned Space, which an almost divine youth
had suddenly left forever; then, in that void, vibrations—
which for us now are rapture and solace and help.

Linos: An obscure figure of Greek myth. Several legends refer to him, always in connection with music, early death, and his relation to Apollo—either as kin (brother, son) or as slain, would-be rival. Some commentaries on "The First Elegy" cite stories in which the void left by Linos's death was so sudden and severe that its trembling amazement was called music. Others make reference to the ritual lament for Linos, supposedly related to music's origin because those who were numbed by his death were revived by the song of Orpheus. Whatever Rilke's sources (and they are fragmentary at best), he conflates the cosmological and the psychological to construct his own elliptical myth of grief: in the beginning full space nurturing an "almost divine" youth; then fullness transformed into emptiness (the void is not originary here; it comes into being as the absence of presence) when the youth inexplicably "steps out of it," "leaves," "is gone" (the word "death" is studiously avoided); then the penetration (equally un-explained) into this absence—characterized not as a realm of lament but as shock petrifying into rigidity, numbness, an almost Golgotha-like aridity of feeling—by a music that is ambigu-ously both "first" and "daring," "adventurous" (the music is already there; no Orphic maker or source is indicated); and with that the desert spell is broken, the void comes alive—not with music per se but with "vibrations," phenomena prior to melodies heard or feelings felt.

Jeder Engel ist schrecklich. Und dennoch, weh mir,
ansing ich euch, fast tödliche Vögel der Seele,
wissend um euch. Wohin sind die Tage Tobiae,
da der Strahlendsten einer stand an der einfachen Haustür,
zur Reise ein wenig verkleidet und schon nicht mehr furchtbar;
(Jüngling dem Jüngling, wie er neugierig hinaussah).
Träte der Erzengel jetzt, der gefährliche, hinter den Sternen
eines Schrittes nur nieder und herwärts: hochauf-
schlagend erschlüg uns das eigene Herz. Wer seid ihr?

Frühe Geglückte, ihr Verwöhnten der Schöpfung,
Höhenzüge, morgenrötliche Grate
aller Erschaffung, —Pollen der blühenden Gottheit,
Gelenke des Lichtes, Gänge, Treppen, Throne,
Räume aus Wesen, Schilde aus Wonne, Tumulte
stürmisch entzückten Gefühls und plötzlich, einzeln,
Spiegel: die die entströmte eigene Schönheit
wiederschöpfen zurück in das eigene Antlitz.

Denn wir, wo wir fühlen, verflüchtigen; ach wir
atmen uns aus und dahin; von Holzglut zu Holzglut
geben wir schwächern Geruch. Da sagt uns wohl einer:
ja, du gehst mir ins Blut, dieses Zimmer, der Frühling
füllt sich mit dir . . . Was hilfts, er kann uns nicht halten,
wir schwinden in ihm und um ihn. Und jene, die schön sind,
o wer hält sie zurück? Unaufhörlich steht Anschein
auf in ihrem Gesicht und geht fort. Wie Tau von dem Frühgras
hebt sich das Unsre von uns, wie die Hitze von einem
heißen Gericht. O Lächeln, wohin? O Aufschaun:

Every Angel is terrifying. And yet, alas,
I still sing to you, almost fatal birds of the soul,
knowing what you bring. Where are the days of Tobias,
when one of your most radiant stood at the simple doorway,
partly disguised for the trip and no longer frightening
(to the youth who peered out curiously, a youth like him).
Were the archangel now to emerge behind the stars
and take just one downward step this way:
our own thundering hearts would slay us. Who *are* you?

Favored first prodigies, creation's darlings,
mountain ranges, peaks, dawn-red ridges
of all genesis, —pollen of a flowering godhead,
links of light, corridors, stairways, thrones,
spaces of being, shields of rapture, torrents
of unchecked ecstatic feeling and then suddenly, singly,
mirrors: scooping their outstreamed beauty back
into their peerless faces.

For our part, when we feel, we evaporate; ah, we breathe
ourselves out and away; from ember to ember
we give off a fainter scent. True, someone may tell us:
You're in my blood, this room, the Spring itself
is full of you . . . But why? He can't hold us,
we vanish in and around him. And the beautiful ones,
ah, who holds *them* back? Appearance ceaselessly
flares in their faces and vanishes. Like dew from the morning grass
what's ours rises from us, the way heat lifts
from a steaming dish. O smile, going where? O upturned look:

Tobias: A figure from the apocryphal Book of Tobit. Ordered by his dying father to travel from
Nineveh to Media to retrieve a sum of money being held there by another man, Tobias looks
for someone who knows the way and encounters a youth his own age who is the archangel
Raphael in disguise. The angel agrees to accompany him, "and so the two went forth, and the
young man's dog went with them."

neue, warme, entgehende Welle des Herzens——;
weh mir: wir *sinds* doch. Schmeckt denn der Weltraum,
in den wir uns lösen, nach uns? Fangen die Engel
wirklich nur Ihriges auf, ihnen Entströmtes,
oder ist manchmal, wie aus Versehen, ein wenig
unseres Wesens dabei? Sind wir in ihre
Züge soviel nur gemischt wie das Vage in die Gesichter
schwangerer Frauen? Sie merken es nicht in dem Wirbel
ihrer Rückkehr zu sich. (Wie sollten sie's merken.)

Liebende könnten, verstünden sie's, in der Nachtluft
wunderlich reden. Denn es scheint, daß uns alles
verheimlicht. Siehe, die Bäume *sind*; die Häuser,
die wir bewohnen, bestehn noch. Wir nur
ziehen allem vorbei wie ein luftiger Austausch.
Und alles ist einig, uns zu verschweigen, halb als
Schande vielleicht und halb als unsägliche Hoffnung.

Liebende, euch, ihr in einander Genügten,
frag ich nach uns. Ihr greift euch. Habt ihr Beweise?
Seht, mir geschiehts, daß meine Hände einander
inne werden oder daß mein gebrauchtes
Gesicht in ihnen sich schont. Das giebt mir ein wenig
Empfindung. Doch wer wagte darum schon zu *sein*?
Ihr aber, die ihr im Entzücken des anderen
zunehmt, bis er euch überwältigt
anfleht: nicht *mehr*——; die ihr unter den Händen
euch reichlicher werdet wie Traubenjahre;
die ihr manchmal vergeht, nur weil der andre
ganz überhand nimmt: euch frag ich nach uns. Ich weiß,
ihr berührt euch so selig, weil die Liebkosung verhält,
weil die Stelle nicht schwindet, die ihr, Zärtliche,
zudeckt; weil ihr darunter das reine
Dauern verspürt. So versprecht ihr euch Ewigkeit fast
von der Umarmung. Und doch, wenn ihr der ersten
Blicke Schrecken besteht und die Sehnsucht am Fenster,
und den ersten gemeinsamen Gang, *ein* Mal durch den Garten:
Liebende, *seid* ihrs dann noch? Wenn ihr einer dem andern

new, warm, departing surge of the heart—;
alas, we *are* the surge. Then does the cosmic space
that we dissolve in taste of us? Do the Angels
recapture only what's theirs, their ceaseless streamings,
or sometimes, as if by accident, does a bit of ours
get mixed in? Are we blended in their features
like the slight vagueness that complicates the looks
of pregnant women? Unnoticed by them as they
swirl back into themselves. (How *could* they notice?)

Lovers, if they only understood, might speak wondrously
in the night air. For everything, it seems,
seeks to conceal us. Look: the trees *exist*; the houses
we dwell in stand there stalwartly. Only we
pass it all by, like a rush of air.
And it all conspires to keep quiet about us,
half out of shame perhaps, half from some secret hope.

Lovers, secure in one another, I ask you
about us. You hold each other. Have you assurances?
It sometimes happens that my hands
grow conscious of each other, or else my weary face
takes refuge in them. That gives me a slight
self-sensation. Yet who, from something so unwarranted,
would dare conclude, "I *am*"? You, though, who keep increasing
through the other's rapture, until, overwhelmed, each
begs the other: "No *more*"—; you who in each other's hands
flourish like vines in vintage years;
you who disappear sometimes only because the other
grows rampant: I ask *you* about *us*. I know
you touch so fervently because the caress protects,
because the place you cover, O tender ones,
doesn't vanish; because, underneath, you feel
pure permanence. Thus your embraces almost promise you
eternity. And yet, when you've passed the terror
of the first look, and the long yearning at the window,
and the first walk—the *one* walk—together through the garden:
lovers, *have* you survived? When you lift yourselves

euch an den Mund hebt und ansetzt——: Getränk an Getränk:
o wie entgeht dann der Trinkende seltsam der Handlung.

Erstaunte euch nicht auf attischen Stelen die Vorsicht
menschlicher Geste? war nicht Liebe und Abschied
so leicht auf die Schultern gelegt, als wär es aus anderm
Stoffe gemacht als bei uns? Gedenkt euch der Hände,
wie sie drucklos beruhen, obwohl in den Torsen die Kraft steht.
Diese Beherrschten wußten damit: so weit sind wirs,
dieses ist unser, uns *so* zu berühren; stärker
stemmen die Götter uns an. Doch dies ist Sache der Götter.

Fänden auch wir ein reines, verhaltenes, schmales
Menschliches, einen unseren Streifen Fruchtlands
zwischen Strom und Gestein. Denn das eigene Herz übersteigt uns
noch immer wie jene. Und wir können ihm nicht mehr
nachschaun in Bilder, die es besänftigen, noch in
göttliche Körper, in denen es größer sich mäßigt.

each to the other's lips and kiss——: drink unto drink:
O how strangely then the drinker slips from the deed.

Remember those Attic stelae, how amazed you were at the caution
of human gestures; at the way love and parting were
so lightly laid on their shoulders, as if made of other stuff
from ours? And their hands, how they touched
without pressure, even though such strength is in the torsos.
Those self-mastered ones knew: *this* far we can go,
this much is *ours*, to touch *this way*; the gods press down
on us more forcefully. But that's for the gods.

If only we too could find a pure, carved-out, narrow
human place, our own small strip of fertile soil
between stream and stone. For even now our heart
transcends us, just as it did those others. And no longer
can we gaze after it into images that soothe it, or
into godlike bodies where it finds a higher restraint.

Attic stelae: Ancient Greek marble tombstones or funerary plaques, often carved with scenes of intimate everyday interaction.

Eines ist, die Geliebte zu singen. Ein anderes, wehe,
jenen verborgenen schuldigen Fluß-Gott des Bluts.
Den sie von weitem erkennt, ihren Jüngling, was weiß er
selbst von dem Herren der Lust, der aus dem Einsamen oft,
ehe das Mädchen noch linderte, oft auch als wäre sie nicht,
ach, von welchem Unkenntlichen triefend, das Gotthaupt
aufhob, aufrufend die Nacht zu unendlichem Aufruhr.
O des Blutes Neptun, o sein furchtbarer Dreizack.
O der dunkele Wind seiner Brust aus gewundener Muschel.
Horch, wie die Nacht sich muldet und höhlt. Ihr Sterne,
stammt nicht von euch des Liebenden Lust zu dem Antlitz
seiner Geliebten? Hat er die innige Einsicht
in ihr reines Gesicht nicht aus dem reinen Gestirn?

Du nicht hast ihm, wehe, nicht seine Mutter
hat ihm die Bogen der Braun so zur Erwartung gespannt.
Nicht an dir, ihn fühlendes Mädchen, an dir nicht
bog seine Lippe sich zum fruchtbarern Ausdruck.
Meinst du wirklich, ihn hätte dein leichter Auftritt
also erschüttert, du, die wandelt wie Frühwind?
Zwar du erschrakst ihm das Herz; doch ältere Schrecken
stürzten in ihn bei dem berührenden Anstoß.
Ruf ihn . . . du rufst ihn nicht ganz aus dunkelem Umgang.
Freilich, er *will*, er entspringt; erleichtert gewöhnt er
sich in dein heimliches Herz und nimmt und beginnt sich.
Aber begann er sich je?
Mutter, *du* machtest ihn klein, du warsts, die ihn anfing;
dir war er neu, du beugtest über die neuen
Augen die freundliche Welt und wehrtest der fremden.
Wo, ach, hin sind die Jahre, da du ihm einfach
mit der schlanken Gestalt wallendes Chaos vertratst?
Vieles verbargst du ihm so; das nächtlich-verdächtige Zimmer
machtest du harmlos, aus deinem Herzen voll Zuflucht
mischtest du menschlichern Raum seinem Nacht-Raum hinzu.

It's one thing to sing the loved one; another, alas,
to sing that hidden guilty river god of the blood.
Her young lover, whom she knows so distantly: what sense has *he*
of that Lord of Lust who often, roused from solitude—
before she could soothe him, and often as though she herself
were nothing—ah, roused from what unsounded depths
lifts his streaming godhead, inciting the night to infinite uproar.
O the blood's Neptune, O his terrible trident!
O the dark wind of his breast from the whorl of the shell.
Listen, as the night becomes tunneled and cavelike. You stars,
does not the lover's delight in his loved one's face
come from you? Does not his passionate oneness with her pure
countenance derive from the pure constellations?

But not for your sight, girl, nor for his mother's,
are his eyebrows arched this taut with expectation.
Not for your mouth, you who hold him now,
have his lips fleshed into these fervent contours.
Do you really think your quiet footsteps
could have convulsed him so, you who move like dawn wind?
True, you startled his heart; but older terrors
rushed into him with that first jolt to his emotions.
Call him . . . you'll never quite retrieve him from those dark consorts.
Yes, he *wants* to, he escapes; relieved, he makes a home
in your familiar heart, takes root there and begins himself again.
But did he *ever* begin himself?
Mother, *you* made him small, it was you who started him;
for you he was new, and over his new eyes you arched
the friendly world, keeping the strange one out.
Where, *where* are those years when with your slender form
you stood calmly between him and his surging chaos?
How much you hid from him that way; everything sinister
in his room at night you made harmless; from your heart full of refuge
you poured a more human space into his own shadowy world.

Nicht in die Finsternis, nein, in dein näheres Dasein
hast du das Nachtlicht gestellt, und es schien wie aus Freundschaft.
Nirgends ein Knistern, das du nicht lächelnd erklärtest,
so als wüßtest du längst, *wann* sich die Diele benimmt . . .
Und er horchte und linderte sich. So vieles vermochte
zärtlich dein Aufstehn; hinter den Schrank trat
hoch im Mantel sein Schicksal, und in die Falten des Vorhangs
paßte, die leicht sich verschob, seine unruhige Zukunft.

Und er selbst, wie er lag, der Erleichterte, unter
schläfernden Lidern deiner leichten Gestaltung
Süße lösend in den gekosteten Vorschlaf—:
schien ein Gehüteter . . . Aber *innen*: wer wehrte,
hinderte innen in ihm die Fluten der Herkunft?
Ach, da *war* keine Vorsicht im Schlafenden; schlafend,
aber träumend, aber in Fiebern: wie er sich ein-ließ.
Er, der Neue, Scheuende, wie er verstrickt war,
mit des innern Geschehns weiterschlagenden Ranken
schon zu Mustern verschlungen, zu würgendem Wachstum, zu tierhaft
jagenden Formen. Wie er sich hingab—. Liebte.
Liebte sein Inneres, seines Inneren Wildnis,
diesen Urwald in ihm, auf dessen stummem Gestürztsein
lichtgrün sein Herz stand. Liebte. Verließ es, ging die
eigenen Wurzeln hinaus in gewaltigen Ursprung,
wo seine kleine Geburt schon überlebt war. Liebend
stieg er hinab in das ältere Blut, in die Schluchten,
wo das Furchtbare lag, noch satt von den Vätern. Und jedes
Schreckliche kannte ihn, blinzelte, war wie verständigt.
Ja, das Entsetzliche lächelte . . . Selten
hast du so zärtlich gelächelt, Mutter. Wie sollte
er es nicht lieben, da es ihm lächelte. *Vor* dir
hat ers geliebt, denn, da du ihn trugst schon,
war es im Wasser gelöst, das den Keimenden leicht macht.

Siehe, wir lieben nicht, wie die Blumen, aus einem
einzigen Jahr; uns steigt, wo wir lieben,
unvordenklicher Saft in die Arme. O Mädchen,
dies: daß wir liebten *in* uns, nicht Eines, ein Künftiges, sondern

You placed the night-light not in the darkness
but in your own nearer being, where it shone like a friend.
The slightest noise—and you explained it, smiling,
as though you'd long known just *when* each floorboard would creak . . .
And he listened and was soothed. Your quiet entrance
had such command; his tall, cloaked destiny
slipped behind the wardrobe, and his unsettled future,
altering slightly, conformed to the curtain's folds.

And he: lying there, relieved, savoring under
drowsy eyelids the sweetness of your gentle presence
as it dissolved into the first hints of sleep—:
he *seemed* well guarded . . . But *within*: who fended *there*,
who checked the floods of origin within him?
Ah, in that sleeper there *was* no caution: sleeping,
but dreaming, and in a kind of fever: what paths he took!
He, so shy, so unwary, how embroiled he became,
with all those spreading tendrils of inner event already
wrought into primitive patterns, into throttling growth, into prowling
animal-like forms. How he surrendered himself—. Loved.
Loved his interior world, his secret jungle, that primeval forest
within him, on whose mute floor of ancient downfall
his heart stood, shimmering green. Loved. Forsook it, followed
his own roots out into that violent source world
where his small birth seemed all but nothing. Loving,
descended into the elder blood, into the ravines
where things hideous lay, still gorged with fathers. And every
terror recognized him, winked, seemed to understand.
Yes, Horror smiled at him . . . So seldom, Mother,
did *you* smile that tenderly. How could he not love
what smiled at him that way? *Before* you
he loved it; for it was there even while you bore him,
dissolved in the fluid that lightens the embryo.

You see, we don't love like flowers, the work
of just one year; sap from time immemorial
mounts in our arms when we love. O girl, it's *this*:
that we've loved, *within* us, not some one, some future person,

das zahllos Brauende; nicht ein einzelnes Kind,
sondern die Väter, die wie Trümmer Gebirgs
uns im Grunde beruhn; sondern das trockene Flußbett
einstiger Mütter—; sondern die ganze
lautlose Landschaft unter dem wolkigen oder
reinen Verhängnis—: *dies* kam dir, Mädchen, zuvor.

Und du selber, was weißt du—, du locktest
Vorzeit empor in dem Liebenden. Welche Gefühle
wühlten herauf aus entwandelten Wesen. Welche
Frauen haßten dich da. Was für finstere Männer
regtest du auf im Geäder des Jünglings? Tote
Kinder wollten zu dir . . . O leise, leise,
tu ein liebes vor ihm, ein verläßliches Tagwerk, —führ ihn
nah an den Garten heran, gieb ihm der Nächte
Übergewicht
 Verhalt ihn

but the whole weltering brood; not a separate child,
but the fathers who lie like mountain ruins
deep within us; and the dried riverbed
of former mothers——; and the whole
soundless landscape beneath our cloudy
or cloudless fate——: all *this*, girl, claimed him first.

And you yourself, unwittingly——: you conjured
primal time in your lover. What feelings
writhed up out of beings long since vanished! What
women within him hated you! Who were those shrouded men
you raised in his youthful veins? Dead children
reached for you . . . O gently, gently,
show him the love in a calm everyday task, ——lead him
close to the garden, give him those nights
that still the scales
 Temper him

O Bäume Lebens, o wann winterlich?
Wir sind nicht einig. Sind nicht wie die Zug-
vögel verständigt. Überholt und spät,
so drängen wir uns plötzlich Winden auf
und fallen ein auf teilnahmslosen Teich.
Blühn und verdorrn ist uns zugleich bewußt.
Und irgendwo gehn Löwen noch und wissen,
solang sie herrlich sind, von keiner Ohnmacht.

Uns aber, wo wir Eines meinen, ganz,
ist schon des andern Aufwand fühlbar. Feindschaft
ist uns das Nächste. Treten Liebende
nicht immerfort an Ränder, eins im andern,
die sich versprachen Weite, Jagd und Heimat.
 Da wird für eines Augenblickes Zeichnung
ein Grund von Gegenteil bereitet, mühsam,
daß wir sie sähen; denn man ist sehr deutlich
mit uns. Wir kennen den Kontur
des Fühlens nicht: nur, was ihn formt von außen.
 Wer saß nicht bang vor seines Herzens Vorhang?
Der schlug sich auf: die Szenerie war Abschied.
Leicht zu verstehen. Der bekannte Garten,
und schwankte leise: dann erst kam der Tänzer.
Nicht *der*. Genug! Und wenn er auch so leicht tut,
er ist verkleidet und er wird ein Bürger
und geht durch seine Küche in die Wohnung.
 Ich will nicht diese halbgefüllten Masken,
lieber die Puppe. Die ist voll. Ich will
den Balg aushalten und den Draht und ihr
Gesicht aus Aussehn. Hier. Ich bin davor.
Wenn auch die Lampen ausgehn, wenn mir auch
gesagt wird: Nichts mehr—, wenn auch von der Bühne
das Leere herkommt mit dem grauen Luftzug,
wenn auch von meinen stillen Vorfahrn keiner

O trees of life, how long till winter?
We lack connection. Aren't in touch
like the migratory birds. Outmoded, late,
we thrust ourselves abruptly on winds
and fall, exhausted, on indifferent waters.
Blooming makes us think: fading.
And somewhere out there lions still roam,
unmindful, in their great splendor, of any weakness.

We, though, even when intent on one thing wholly,
can feel the costs exacted by some other.
Enmity's our next of kin. Aren't lovers always
meeting boundaries, each in the other,
when the promise was of vastness, royal hunting, home?
 Then: for an instant's virtuoso sketch
a ground of contrast is prepared, laboriously,
so we can see it; for they're very clear
with us. We don't know our feelings' contours:
only what molds them from without.
 Who hasn't sat trembling before his heart's curtain?
Up it went: the scenery for *Parting*.
Easy to understand. The familiar garden,
swaying slightly: then—enter the dancer.
Not *him*. Enough! However light he foots it
it's all disguise and he becomes a burgher
who walks through his kitchen into his living room.
 I loathe watching these half-filled masks;
give me the puppet. It's true at least. I can take
the husk of body and the wire and the face
that's pure surface. Right here. I'm out in front.
Even when the lights go out, even when someone
says to me: "It's over—," even when from the stage
a gray gust of emptiness drifts toward me,
even when not one silent ancestor

mehr mit mir dasitzt, keine Frau, sogar
der Knabe nicht mehr mit dem braunen Schielaug:
Ich bleibe dennoch. Es giebt immer Zuschaun.

Hab ich nicht recht? Du, der um mich so bitter
das Leben schmeckte, meines kostend, Vater,
den ersten trüben Aufguß meines Müssens,
da ich heranwuchs, immer wieder kostend
und, mit dem Nachgeschmack so fremder Zukunft
beschäftigt, prüftest mein beschlagnes Aufschaun, —
der du, mein Vater, seit du tot bist, oft
in meiner Hoffnung, innen in mir, Angst hast,
und Gleichmut, wie ihn Tote haben, Reiche
von Gleichmut, aufgiebst für mein bißchen Schicksal,
hab ich nicht recht? Und ihr, hab ich nicht recht,
die ihr mich liebtet für den kleinen Anfang
Liebe zu euch, von dem ich immer abkam,
weil mir der Raum in eurem Angesicht,
da ich ihn liebte, überging in Weltraum,
in dem ihr nicht mehr wart . . . : wenn mir zumut ist,
zu warten vor der Puppenbühne, nein,
so völlig hinzuschaun, daß, um mein Schauen
am Ende aufzuwiegen, dort als Spieler
ein Engel hinmuß, der die Bälge hochreißt.
Engel und Puppe: dann ist endlich Schauspiel.
Dann kommt zusammen, was wir immerfort
entzwein, indem wir da sind. Dann entsteht
aus unsern Jahreszeiten erst der Umkreis
des ganzen Wandelns. Über uns hinüber
spielt dann der Engel. Sieh, die Sterbenden,
sollten sie nicht vermuten, wie voll Vorwand
das alles ist, was wir hier leisten. Alles
ist nicht es selbst. O Stunden in der Kindheit,
da hinter den Figuren mehr als nur
Vergangnes war und vor uns nicht die Zukunft.

sits beside me anymore—not a woman, not even
the boy with the brown squint-eye:
I'll sit here still. One can always watch.

Am I not right? You, Father, for whom life
became so bitter when you tasted mine—
that first murky influx of what would feed my needs—
who, as I grew older, continued sampling,
and, perplexed by the aftertaste of so strange a future,
tried searching my vague clouded gaze, —
you, Father, who, now that you're dead, often
lodge in my deepest hopes, full of fear,
forfeiting that equanimity the dead have, entire
kingdoms of equanimity, for my bit of fate—
am I not right? And you women—am I not right?—
who loved me for that small, hesitating
love for you I always veered away from,
because I felt the space in your faces, even
as I loved it, changing into worldspace
where you were absent . . . : what if I do choose
to wait in front of the puppet stage—no,
to *stare* with so much force that finally, to counteract
my look, an Angel will arrive as puppeteer,
and jerk life into these hard husks.
Angel and Puppet: at last the play begins.
Then what we wedge apart, simply by
our being here, unites. Then from the separate
seasons of our life that one great wheel
of transformation mounts. Above and out beyond us
the Angel plays. The dying—surely *they*
must see how all the things that we achieve here
are full of pretext. Nothing
is what it is. O childhood hours,
when behind each shape there was more
than the mere past, and before us—not the future.

the boy with the brown squint-eye: Rilke's cousin, Egon von Rilke (1873–80), to whose memory
Sonnet 2.8 of the *Sonnets to Orpheus* is dedicated.

Wir wuchsen freilich und wir drängten manchmal,
bald groß zu werden, denen halb zulieb,
die andres nicht mehr hatten, als das Großsein.
Und waren doch, in unserem Alleingehn,
mit Dauerndem vergnügt und standen da
im Zwischenraume zwischen Welt und Spielzeug,
an einer Stelle, die seit Anbeginn
gegründet war für einen reinen Vorgang.

Wer zeigt ein Kind, so wie es steht? Wer stellt
es ins Gestirn und giebt das Maß des Abstands
ihm in die Hand? Wer macht den Kindertod
aus grauem Brot, das hart wird, —oder läßt
ihn drin im runden Mund, so wie den Gröps
von einem schönen Apfel? Mörder sind
leicht einzusehen. Aber dies: den Tod,
den ganzen Tod, noch *vor* dem Leben so
sanft zu enthalten und nicht bös zu sein,
ist unbeschreiblich.

True, we were growing, and we often spurred ourselves
to grow up faster, half to oblige those
who had nothing of their own *except* adulthood.
And yet, off alone, we were happiest
with what always stayed the same, and we stood there
in the space between world and toy,
on a spot which, from the first beginning,
had been established for a pure event.

Who shows a child just as he is? Who sets him
in a constellation and hands him the measure
of distance and interval? Who makes a child's death
out of gray bread that hardens, —or leaves it
in his round mouth like the core
of a beautiful apple? Murderers are
easily understood. But this: one's death,
the whole reach of death, even before life starts,—
to hold it gently and not feel anger:
is indescribable.

DIE FÜNFTE ELEGIE

Frau Hertha Koenig zugeeignet

Wer aber *sind* sie, sag mir, die Fahrenden, diese ein wenig
Flüchtigern noch als wir selbst, die dringend von früh an
wringt ein *wem, wem* zu Liebe
niemals zufriedener Wille? Sondern er wringt sie,
biegt sie, schlingt sie und schwingt sie,
wirft sie und fängt sie zurück; wie aus geölter,
glatterer Luft kommen sie nieder
auf dem verzehrten, von ihrem ewigen
Aufsprung dünneren Teppich, diesem verlorenen
Teppich im Weltall.
Aufgelegt wie ein Pflaster, als hätte der Vorstadt-
Himmel der Erde dort wehe getan.
 Und kaum dort,
aufrecht, da und gezeigt: des Dastehns
großer Anfangsbuchstab . . . , schon auch, die stärksten
Männer, rollt sie wieder, zum Scherz, der immer

THE FIFTH ELEGY
Dedicated to Frau Hertha Koenig

But tell me, who *are* they, these wanderers
(more rootless even than we ourselves) seized early on
and urgently wrenched—for whose *possible* sake?—
by some never satisfied will. And still it wrings them,
bends them, twists them and slings them,
tosses and catches them; as if through smoother,
frictionless air they drop down
onto the threadbare carpet worn even thinner
by their eternal leaping, this carpet
lost in the universe.
Laid down like a bandage, as if the jagged sky
of city edges had wounded the earth there.
 And scarcely in place,
upright, held for display: that initial letter
from their bodies' alphabet . . . , when already the Grip
returns, rolling them again, even the strongest

Dedication: Frau Hertha Koenig was a lyricist who in December 1914 had purchased, perhaps
at Rilke's suggestion, Picasso's 1905 painting *La famille des saltimbanques*. Rilke subsequently
wrote to her asking permission to reside in her Munich apartment while she was away on her
country vacation. She granted his request, and he spent the summer and early fall of 1915 living
beside "the great Picasso." The human figures who stand quietly, almost abstractedly in Pi-
casso's painting mingle in Rilke's imagination with a troupe of real-life acrobats he observed in
Paris, and about whom he wrote a long account in a notebook entry of 1907.
that initial letter: This passage is usually glossed along the following lines: Rilke, perceiving the
standing figures in the Picasso *Saltimbanques* as forming a large *D*, puns on this visual peculiar-
ity by coining the word *Dastehen* (roughly, "standing-thereness," and strongly echoing
Dasein—"existence," "being-thereness") to register the quality of the acrobats' presence.
Hence the translator's challenge is to find an equivalent word that begins with a capital *D*. But
this line of thought may be fundamentally in error. The elegy visualizes a family of itinerant
acrobats *performing* in the outlying regions of the city before passersby who randomly gather
and disperse. The large initial letter of their *Dastehen*—barely there, only a moment erect and
on show, before "even the strongest" are rolled and crumpled again—likely refers to the figure
they construct in one of their feats of acrobatic balancing (later in the elegy Rilke will employ
the metaphor of a swiftly erected and deconstructed tree). The initial letter they form would
thus be like those in the grotesque alphabets of entwined bodies so popular with late medieval
engravers.

kommende Griff, wie August der Starke bei Tisch
einen zinnenen Teller.

Ach und um diese
Mitte, die Rose des Zuschauns:
blüht und entblättert. Um diesen
Stampfer, den Stempel, den von dem eignen
blühenden Staub getroffnen, zur Scheinfrucht
wieder der Unlust befruchteten, ihrer
niemals bewußten, —glänzend mit dünnster
Oberfläche leicht scheinlächelnden Unlust.

Da: der welke, faltige Stemmer,
der alte, der nur noch trommelt,
eingegangen in seiner gewaltigen Haut, als hätte sie früher
zwei Männer enthalten, und einer
läge nun schon auf dem Kirchhof, und er überlebte den andern,
taub und manchmal ein wenig
wirr, in der verwitweten Haut.

Aber der junge, der Mann, als wär er der Sohn eines Nackens
und einer Nonne: prall und strammig erfüllt
mit Muskeln und Einfalt.

Oh ihr,
die ein Leid, das noch klein war,
einst als Spielzeug bekam, in einer seiner
langen Genesungen

Du, der mit dem Aufschlag,
wie nur Früchte ihn kennen, unreif,
täglich hundertmal abfällt vom Baum der gemeinsam
erbauten Bewegung (der, rascher als Wasser, in wenig
Minuten Lenz, Sommer und Herbst hat)—

ones, as in some jest, like Augustus the Strong at table
crumpling a pewter plate.

Ah, and around this center,
the rose of onlooking—
blooming and shedding petals. Around this
pestle, this pistil dusted
with its own pollen, impregnated once more
to bear the feigned fruit of boredom—
boredom self-concealed
beneath the thinnest glaze of rote smiling.

There: the withered strongman, his skin all folds,
the old one who only drums now,
shriveled inside his great physique, as though
it once held two men, and now one
lies dead in the churchyard, and he survived that other,
deaf and sometimes a bit confused
in his widowed skin.

But there the young one, the full man, who might be the offspring
of a neck and a nun: strapping and stretched taut
with sinews and simpleness.

Oh you all:
given once as a plaything
to a young Grief, something to entertain it
during one of its long convalescences . . .

First you, who with the thud
only unripe fruit know
fall a hundred times daily from that tree
of intermeshed movements (tree swifter than water, traversing
spring, summer, autumn all in a few moments)—

Augustus the Strong: The reference is to August II, king of Poland (1670–1733). He was notori-
ous for his feats of strength, his drinking bouts, and his sexual prowess. According to legend he
fathered more than a hundred children.

abfällt und anprallt ans Grab:
manchmal, in halber Pause, will dir ein liebes
Antlitz entstehn hinüber zu deiner selten
zärtlichen Mutter; doch an deinen Körper verliert sich,
der es flächig verbraucht, das schüchtern
kaum versuchte Gesicht . . . Und wieder
klatscht der Mann in die Hand zu dem Ansprung, und eh dir
jemals ein Schmerz deutlicher wird in der Nähe des immer
trabenden Herzens, kommt das Brennen der Fußsohln
ihm, seinem Ursprung, zuvor mit ein paar dir
rasch in die Augen gejagten leiblichen Tränen.
Und dennoch, blindlings,
das Lächeln

Engel! o nimms, pflücks, das kleinblütige Heilkraut.
Schaff eine Vase, verwahrs! Stells unter jene, uns *noch* nicht
offenen Freuden; in lieblicher Urne
rühms mit blumiger schwungiger Aufschrift: »*Subrisio Saltat.*«

Du dann, Liebliche,
du, von den reizendsten Freuden
stumm Übersprungne. Vielleicht sind
deine Fransen glücklich für dich—,
oder über den jungen
prallen Brüsten die grüne metallene Seide
fühlt sich unendlich verwöhnt und entbehrt nichts.
Du,
immerfort anders auf alle des Gleichgewichts schwankende Waagen
hingelegte Marktfrucht des Gleichmuts,
öffentlich unter den Schultern.

Wo, o *wo* ist der Ort—ich trag ihn im Herzen—,
wo sie noch lange nicht *konnten*, noch von einander
abfieln, wie sich bespringende, nicht recht
paarige Tiere; —
wo die Gewichte noch schwer sind;

fall and rebound from the grave:
sometimes, in the briefest pause, a loving look
tries to rise in you and reach across to your seldom
tender mother; but it disperses over your body,
whose surface quickly absorbs that shy,
scarcely attempted face . . . And again
the man claps his hands for the dismount, and before
a hurt can reach your always galloping heart
to become clear at its origin,
the burning in your foot soles overtakes it,
driving into your eyes mere physical tears.
And nevertheless, blindly,
the smile

Angel! O take it, pluck it, that small-petaled herb of healing!
Create a vase, preserve it! Place it among those joys
not yet open to us; in a delicate urn
let an ornate inscription praise it: *"Subrisio Saltat."*

Then you, my sweetest,
you, whom the most ravishing joys
leapt over soundlessly.
Perhaps your fringes feel happy *for* you—,
or the green metallic silk that covers your firm young breasts
feels endlessly pampered and in need of nothing.
You,
market fruit of equanimity, ever placed differently
on the scales of a wavering equipoise,
a public thing amid shoulders.

Where, *where* is that place—I carry it in my heart—,
where for so long they were still not *able*, still fell away
from each other like mismatched animals
trying to mate, —
where the weights are still heavy;

"Subrisio Saltat.": An abbreviation for *Subrisio Saltatoris*—"acrobat's smile." The passage envisions an apothecary's shelf with small labeled vials on it.

wo noch von ihren vergeblich
wirbelnden Stäben die Teller
torkeln

Und plötzlich in diesem mühsamen Nirgends, plötzlich
die unsägliche Stelle, wo sich das reine Zuwenig
unbegreiflich verwandelt—, umspringt
in jenes leere Zuviel.
Wo die vielstellige Rechnung
zahlenlos aufgeht.

Plätze, o Platz in Paris, unendlicher Schauplatz,
wo die Modistin, *Madame Lamort*,
die ruhlosen Wege der Erde, endlose Bänder,
schlingt und windet und neue aus ihnen
Schleifen erfindet, Rüschen, Blumen, Kokarden, künstliche Früchte—, alle
unwahr gefärbt, —für die billigen
Winterhüte des Schicksals.
.

Engel! : Es wäre ein Platz, den wir nicht wissen, und dorten,
auf unsäglichem Teppich, zeigten die Liebenden, die's hier
bis zum Können nie bringen, ihre kühnen
hohen Figuren des Herzschwungs,
ihre Türme aus Lust, ihre
längst, wo Boden nie war, nur an einander
lehnenden Leitern, bebend, —und *könntens*,
vor den Zuschauern rings, unzähligen lautlosen Toten:
 Würfen die dann ihre letzten, immer ersparten,
immer verborgenen, die wir nicht kennen, ewig
gültigen Münzen des Glücks vor das endlich
wahrhaft lächelnde Paar auf gestilltem
Teppich?

where the plates still topple
from the staves that spin and spin
in vain

And suddenly in this effort-filled nowhere, suddenly
the ineffable point where the pure too-little
mysteriously converts—, flips over
into the empty too-much.
Point where the complex equation
achieves zero.

Squares, O town square in Paris, infinite showplace
where the modiste *Madame Lamort*
loops and binds the restless roads of the earth—
unending ribbons—designing new bows,
faddish frills, flowers, cockades, fake fruit—, all
falsely dyed,—for the cheap
winter hats of fate.
.

Angel! Suppose there's a place we don't know of, and there,
on an indescribable carpet, lovers blazoned all
those feats never mastered here—the bold
high figures of their heartleaps across space,
their towers of pure pleasure, their two ladders
that stand leaning only against each other
with no ground underneath, trembling, —and *performed* them,
before the circle of onlookers, the innumerable silent dead:
 Wouldn't these then throw their last coins
of happiness—hoarded for a lifetime,
kept hidden for a lifetime, unknown to us, eternally
valid—before a pair now *truly* smiling at last on the quieted
carpet?

Feigenbaum, seit wie lange schon ists mir bedeutend,
wie du die Blüte beinah ganz überschlägst
und hinein in die zeitig entschlossene Frucht,
ungerühmt, drängst dein reines Geheimnis.
Wie der Fontäne Rohr treibt dein gebognes Gezweig
abwärts den Saft und hinan: und er springt aus dem Schlaf,
fast nicht erwachend, ins Glück seiner süßesten Leistung.
Sieh: wie der Gott in den Schwan.

.......Wir aber verweilen,
ach, uns rühmt es zu blühn, und ins verspätete Innre
unserer endlichen Frucht gehn wir verraten hinein.
Wenigen steigt so stark der Andrang des Handelns,
daß sie schon anstehn und glühn in der Fülle des Herzens,
wenn die Verführung zum Blühn wie gelinderte Nachtluft
ihnen die Jugend des Munds, ihnen die Lider berührt:
Helden vielleicht und den frühe Hinüberbestimmten,
denen der gärtnernde Tod anders die Adern verbiegt.
Diese stürzen dahin: dem eigenen Lächeln
sind sie voran, wie das Rossegespann in den milden
muldigen Bildern von Karnak dem siegenden König.

Wunderlich nah ist der Held doch den jugendlich Toten. Dauern
ficht ihn nicht an. Sein Aufgang ist Dasein; beständig
nimmt er sich fort und tritt ins veränderte Sternbild
seiner steten Gefahr. Dort fänden ihn wenige. Aber,
das uns finster verschweigt, das plötzlich begeisterte Schicksal
singt ihn hinein in den Sturm seiner aufrauschenden Welt.
Hör ich doch keinen wie *ihn*. Auf einmal durchgeht mich
mit der strömenden Luft sein verdunkelter Ton.

O fig tree, how long I've pondered you—
the way you almost ignore flowering completely
and release, unheralded, your pure secret
into the sprigs of fruit already poised to ripen.
Like a fountain's pipe, your bent boughs drive the sap
downward and up: and it leaps from sleep, almost
without waking, into the joy of its sweetest achievement.
Look: like god into swan.

 But we, for our part, linger,
ah, we exult in flowering; the belated inner place
that is our culminating fruit we enter spent, betrayed.
Only a few feel the sap of action rise so strongly
that they're already fixed and glowing in their heart's fullness
when the allure of flowering touches their eyelids,
touches their lips' youth, like soft night air—
heroes, perhaps, and those destined for an early crossing,
whose veins the gardener Death bends differently.
These plunge on ahead of their own smiles,
the way those teams of chargers precede the conquering king
in the gentle bas-reliefs at Karnak.

The hero's oddly like the youthful dead. Long life
does not concern him. *Ascent* is his existence; over and over
he annuls himself and enters that changed constellation
of changeless danger. Few would find him there. But Fate,
which cloaks us in mute obscurity, grows ecstatic
and sings him into the storm of her tumultuous world.
I hear no one like *him*. But suddenly I'm pierced
by his darkened music, borne swift by the rush of air.

Karnak: The site of the Temple of Amon in southern Egypt, which Rilke visited in 1911. The temple's stone pillars depict battle scenes with the pharaoh-generals in their conquering chariots.

Dann, wie verbärg ich mich gern vor der Sehnsucht: O wär ich,
wär ich ein Knabe und dürft es noch werden und säße
in die künftigen Arme gestützt und läse von Simson,
wie seine Mutter erst nichts und dann alles gebar.

War er nicht Held schon in dir, o Mutter, begann nicht
dort schon, in dir, seine herrische Auswahl?
Tausende brauten im Schooß und wollten *er* sein,
aber sieh: er ergriff und ließ aus—, wählte und konnte.
Und wenn er Säulen zerstieß, so wars, da er ausbrach
aus der Welt deines Leibs in die engere Welt, wo er weiter
wählte und konnte. O Mütter der Helden, o Ursprung
reißender Ströme! Ihr Schluchten, in die sich
hoch von dem Herzrand, klagend,
schon die Mädchen gestürzt, künftig die Opfer dem Sohn.

Denn hinstürmte der Held durch Aufenthalte der Liebe,
jeder hob ihn hinaus, jeder ihn meinende Herzschlag,
abgewendet schon, stand er am Ende der Lächeln,
<div align="right">—anders.</div>

Then how I'd like to hide from the yearning: to be,
to be a boy again with the unknown ahead of me
as I sat propped on the arms of my future, reading about Samson,
how his mother bore nothing at first, then—everything.

Wasn't he always the hero, Mother, even in you?
Didn't it already start there in you, his imperious choosing?
Thousands teemed in the womb, wanting to be *him*.
But look: he seized and excluded—, chose and made good.
If he crushed columns, it was when he burst
from the world of your body into the narrower world,
where he continued to choose and make good. O mothers of heroes,
O source of torrential rivers! You gorges into which,
high on the heart's rim, lamenting virgins
have thrown themselves, lives-to-be sacrificed to the son.

For even as the hero stormed through love's intervals,
each heart that beat for him propelled him upward and on: until
facing elsewhere, he stood at the end of the smiles,
 —someone new.

Werbung nicht mehr, nicht Werbung, entwachsene Stimme,
sei deines Schreies Natur; zwar schrieest du rein wie der Vogel,
wenn ihn die Jahreszeit aufhebt, die steigende, beinah vergessend,
daß er ein kümmerndes Tier und nicht nur ein einzelnes Herz sei,
das sie ins Heitere wirft, in die innigen Himmel. Wie er, so
würbest du wohl, nicht minder—, daß, noch unsichtbar,
dich die Freundin erführ, die stille, in der eine Antwort
langsam erwacht und über dem Hören sich anwärmt, —
deinem erkühnten Gefühl die erglühte Gefühlin.

O und der Frühling begriffe—, da ist keine Stelle,
die nicht trüge den Ton der Verkündigung. Erst jenen kleinen
fragenden Auflaut, den, mit steigernder Stille,
weithin umschweigt ein reiner bejahender Tag.
Dann die Stufen hinan, Ruf-Stufen hinan, zum geträumten
Tempel der Zukunft—; dann den Triller, Fontäne,
die zu dem drängenden Strahl schon das Fallen zuvornimmt
im versprechlichen Spiel Und vor sich, den Sommer.

Nicht nur die Morgen alle des Sommers—, nicht nur
wie sie sich wandeln in Tag und strahlen vor Anfang.
Nicht nur die Tage, die zart sind um Blumen, und oben,
um die gestalteten Bäume, stark und gewaltig.
Nicht nur die Andacht dieser entfalteten Kräfte,
nicht nur die Wege, nicht nur die Wiesen im Abend,
nicht nur, nach spätem Gewitter, das atmende Klarsein,
nicht nur der nahende Schlaf und ein Ahnen, abends . . .
sondern die Nächte! Sondern die hohen, des Sommers,
Nächte, sondern die Sterne, die Sterne der Erde.
O einst tot sein und sie wissen unendlich,
alle die Sterne: denn wie, wie, wie sie vergessen!

Siehe, da rief ich die Liebende. Aber nicht *sie* nur
käme . . . Es kämen aus schwächlichen Gräbern

No longer, voice. No longer let wooing shape your cry.
You're beyond it. Even though you'd call out as clear as a bird
when Spring first bears him aloft, almost forgetting
that he's a cautious creature and not an unsheathed heart
being flung into brightness, into passionate skies.
Like him, with all his art, you'd also woo—: as yet invisible,
so that some silent mate might learn of you thus—
while, in her listening, a reply slowly wakened and warmed:
the heart-cry kindled by your own passionate fire.

O and Spring would understand—, annunciation
would echo everywhere. First those small
questioning notes, which a clear confident day
would surround with heightening silence.
Then up the calls, up their flight of steps, to the dreamt-of
temple of the future—; then the trill, that fountain,
whose jet ascends through its own falling as in a union
of promise and play . . . And up ahead, Summer.

Not just all Summer's dawns—, not just
how they change into day and glisten with genesis.
Not just the days, which are mild around flowers, and above,
around the full-formed trees, forceful and strong.
Not just the calm reverence in these outspread powers,
not just the paths, not just the meadows as evening deepens,
not just, after late thunderstorms, the pulsing clarity,
not just the approach of sleep and, at twilight, a premonition . . .
But the nights! All those towering summer nights!
And the stars, the stars of earth.
O to be dead one day and then know them forever,
all the stars: for how, how, how, to forget them!

And thus: I've called to my lover. But not she alone
would come . . . Other girls would come from weak graves

Mädchen und ständen . . . Denn, wie beschränk ich,
wie, den gerufenen Ruf? Die Versunkenen suchen
immer noch Erde. —Ihr Kinder, ein hiesig
einmal ergriffenes Ding gälte für viele.
Glaubt nicht, Schicksal sei mehr, als das Dichte der Kindheit;
wie überholtet ihr oft den Geliebten, atmend,
atmend nach seligem Lauf, auf nichts zu, ins Freie.

Hiersein ist herrlich. Ihr wußtet es, Mädchen, *ihr* auch,
die ihr scheinbar entbehrtet, versankt—, ihr, in den ärgsten
Gassen der Städte, Schwärende, oder dem Abfall
Offene. Denn eine Stunde war jeder, vielleicht nicht
ganz eine Stunde, ein mit den Maßen der Zeit kaum
Meßliches zwischen zwei Weilen—, da sie ein Dasein
hatte. Alles. Die Adern voll Dasein.
Nur, wir vergessen so leicht, was der lachende Nachbar
uns nicht bestätigt oder beneidet. Sichtbar
wollen wirs heben, wo doch das sichtbarste Glück uns
erst zu erkennen sich giebt, wenn wir es innen verwandeln.

Nirgends, Geliebte, wird Welt sein, als innen. Unser
Leben geht hin mit Verwandlung. Und immer geringer
schwindet das Außen. Wo einmal ein dauerndes Haus war,
schlägt sich erdachtes Gebild vor, quer, zu Erdenklichem
völlig gehörig, als ständ es noch ganz im Gehirne.
Weite Speicher der Kraft schafft sich der Zeitgeist, gestaltlos
wie der spannende Drang, den er aus allem gewinnt.
Tempel kennt er nicht mehr. Diese, des Herzens, Verschwendung
sparen wir heimlicher ein. Ja, wo noch eins übersteht,
ein einst gebetetes Ding, ein gedientes, geknietes—,
hält es sich, so wie es ist, schon ins Unsichtbare hin.
Viele gewahrens nicht mehr, doch ohne den Vorteil,
daß sie's nun *innerlich* baun, mit Pfeilern und Statuen, größer!

Jede dumpfe Umkehr der Welt hat solche Enterbte,
denen das Frühere nicht und noch nicht das Nächste gehört.
Denn auch das Nächste ist weit für die Menschen. *Uns* soll
dies nicht verwirren; es stärke in uns die Bewahrung

and gather . . . For how could I limit the call
once I'd called it? The buried are forever seeking
earth's surface again. —You children:
one *present* thing grasped truly would count for so many!
The whole of destiny crowds into childhood;
how often you would overtake your lover, panting,
panting from the blissful race, out ahead, breaking for freedom.

Life here is magic. Even *you* knew that, you girls
who seemed so deprived of it, whose lives twisted down
into the city's vilest streets, festering, or opened
for the worst debris. There was an hour for each of you,
perhaps not even an hour, but between two intervals
a space scarcely measured by the rules of time—,
when you *existed*. Completely. Veins filled with existence.
But we so easily forget what our laughing neighbor
neither covets nor confirms. We want to lift it up
and show it, even though the most visible happiness
only reveals itself when we've changed it, within.

Nowhere, Love, will World exist but within. Our lives
pass in transformation. And all the while the outer realm
is lessening. Where a solid house once was,
some concocted structure shoots into view, as at ease
among concepts as if it still stood in the brain.
The Zeitgeist is stockpiling vast reservoirs of power, formless
as the tensile urge it pulls out of everything.
It no longer recognizes temples. Furtively we hoard
what the heart once lavished. Where one of them still survives,
a thing once prayed to, knelt before, revered—,
it's already reaching out, secretly, into the invisible.
Many no longer see it, yet forgo the advantage
of building it *within* now, with pillars and statues, greater!

Each dull turn of the world creates its dispossessed
for whom neither the past nor what's taking shape has substance.
Since for humans even what's near is far away.
But this needn't perplex *us*—rather strengthen us in our preserving

der noch erkannten Gestalt. —Dies *stand* einmal unter Menschen,
mitten im Schicksal stands, im vernichtenden, mitten
im Nichtwissen-Wohin stand es, wie seiend, und bog
Sterne zu sich aus gesicherten Himmeln. Engel,
dir noch zeig ich es, *da!* in deinem Anschaun
steh es gerettet zuletzt, nun endlich aufrecht.
Säulen, Pylone, der Sphinx, das strebende Stemmen,
grau aus vergehender Stadt oder aus fremder, des Doms.

War es nicht Wunder? O staune, Engel, denn *wir* sinds,
wir, o du Großer, erzähls, daß wir solches vermochten, mein Atem
reicht für die Rühmung nicht aus. So haben wir dennoch
nicht die Räume versäumt, diese gewährenden, diese
unseren Räume. (Was müssen sie fürchterlich groß sein,
da sie Jahrtausende nicht unseres Fühlns überfülln.)
Aber ein Turm war groß, nicht wahr? O Engel, er war es, —
groß, auch noch neben dir? Chartres war groß—, und Musik
reichte noch weiter hinan und überstieg uns. Doch selbst nur
eine Liebende—, oh, allein am nächtlichen Fenster . . .
reichte sie dir nicht ans Knie—?
 Glaub *nicht*, daß ich werbe.
Engel, und würb ich dich auch! Du kommst nicht. Denn mein
Anruf ist immer voll Hinweg; wider so starke
Strömung kannst du nicht schreiten. Wie ein gestreckter
Arm ist mein Rufen. Und seine zum Greifen
oben offene Hand bleibt vor dir
offen, wie Abwehr und Warnung,
Unfaßlicher, weitauf.

the still-recognized form. —This once *stood* among men,
stood with Fate the Destroyer, stood amid
not knowing why or whereto, as though it *lived* there,
and bent stars closer from secured heavens.
Angel, now you shall see it too—*there!* In your gaze
it finally stands redeemed, erect for eternity.
Pillars, pylons, the Sphinx, the cathedral's strong spire
thrusting up out of a vanishing or strange city.

Miracles! O stand in wonder, Angel, for it was *us*,
us, O great one, tell the others of these things we shaped:
my breath lacks power for that praise. So then
we *haven't* failed these generous spaces—, these spaces
that are *ours*. (How frighteningly vast they must be,
since millennia of our feelings haven't crowded them.)
But one tower was great, was it not? O Angel, it was, —
even beside you. Chartres was great—, and music
reached even higher, soared beyond us. But even
just one woman in love, alone, at night, at her window . . .
didn't she reach to your knee—?

 Don't think I'm wooing.
Angel, and if I were! You wouldn't come. For my call
is always full of "Away!" Against such a powerful
current you can't advance. My call to you
is like a stiff, outstretched arm. And its hand, splayed
and raised for grasping, stays before you
always, as if to warn and ward off,
ungraspable one, —its palm out, wide open.

DIE ACHTE ELEGIE
Rudolf Kassner zugeeignet

Mit allen Augen sieht die Kreatur
das Offene. Nur unsre Augen sind
wie umgekehrt und ganz um sie gestellt
als Fallen, rings um ihren freien Ausgang.
Was draußen *ist,* wir wissens aus des Tiers
Antlitz allein; denn schon das frühe Kind
wenden wir um und zwingens, daß es rückwärts
Gestaltung sehe, nicht das Offne, das
im Tiergesicht so tief ist. Frei von Tod.
Ihn sehen wir allein; das freie Tier
hat seinen Untergang stets hinter sich
und vor sich Gott, und wenn es geht, so gehts
in Ewigkeit, so wie die Brunnen gehen.
 Wir haben nie, nicht einen einzigen Tag,
den reinen Raum vor uns, in den die Blumen
unendlich aufgehn. Immer ist es Welt
und niemals Nirgends ohne Nicht: das Reine,
Unüberwachte, das man atmet und
unendlich *weiß* und nicht begehrt. Als Kind
verliert sich eins im Stilln an dies und wird
gerüttelt. Oder jener stirbt und *ists.*
Denn nah am Tod sieht man den Tod nicht mehr
und starrt *hinaus,* vielleicht mit großem Tierblick.
Liebende, wäre nicht der andre, der
die Sicht verstellt, sind nah daran und staunen . . .
Wie aus Versehn ist ihnen aufgetan
hinter dem andern . . . Aber über ihn
kommt keiner fort, und wieder wird ihm Welt.
Der Schöpfung immer zugewendet, sehn
wir nur auf ihr die Spiegelung des Frein,
von uns verdunkelt. Oder daß ein Tier,
ein stummes, aufschaut, ruhig durch uns durch.
Dieses heißt Schicksal: gegenüber sein
und nichts als das und immer gegenüber.

THE EIGHTH ELEGY
Dedicated to Rudolf Kassner

With all its eyes the animal world
beholds the Open. Only ours
are as if inverted and set all around it
like traps at the doors to freedom.
What's outside we know only from the animal's
countenance: for almost from the first we take a child
and turn him around and force him to gaze
backward and take in structure, not the Open
that lies so deep in an animal's face. Free from death.
Only we see death; the free animal has its demise
perpetually behind it and always before it
God, and when it moves, it moves into eternity,
the way brooks and running springs move.
 We, though: never, not for one day, do we
have that pure space ahead of us into which flowers
endlessly open. What we have is World
and always World and never Nowhere without negation:
that pure unguarded element one breathes
and *knows* endlessly and never craves. As a child
one gets lost there in the quiet, only to be
jostled back. Or someone dying *is* it.
For, close to death, one looks at death no longer
but instead stares *out*, perhaps with the wide gaze of animals.
Lovers (although the other's always there,
obstructing the view) are close to it, and marvel . . .
Out past the beloved, as if by some mistake,
it has opened up to each of them . . . But neither
gets beyond the other, and it changes back to World.
Always turned so fervently toward creation,
we see only the reflection of the Open,
which our own presence darkens. Or sometimes
a mute animal looks up and stares right through us.
That's what destiny is: being opposite
and nothing else and always opposite.

Wäre Bewußtheit unsrer Art in dem
sicheren Tier, das uns entgegenzieht
in anderer Richtung—, riß es uns herum
mit seinem Wandel. Doch sein Sein ist ihm
unendlich, ungefaßt und ohne Blick
auf seinen Zustand, rein, so wie sein Ausblick.
Und wo wir Zukunft sehn, dort sieht es Alles
und sich in Allem und geheilt für immer.

Und doch ist in dem wachsam warmen Tier
Gewicht und Sorge einer großen Schwermut.
Denn ihm auch haftet immer an, was uns
oft überwältigt,—die Erinnerung,
als sei schon einmal das, wonach man drängt,
näher gewesen, treuer und sein Anschluß
unendlich zärtlich. Hier ist alles Abstand,
und dort wars Atem. Nach der ersten Heimat
ist ihm die zweite zwitterig und windig.
 O Seligkeit der *kleinen* Kreatur,
die immer *bleibt* im Schooße, der sie austrug;
o Glück der Mücke, die noch *innen* hüpft,
selbst wenn sie Hochzeit hat: denn Schooß ist Alles.
Und sieh die halbe Sicherheit des Vogels,
der beinah beides weiß aus seinem Ursprung,
als wär er eine Seele der Etrusker,
aus einem Toten, den ein Raum empfing,
doch mit der ruhenden Figur als Deckel.
Und wie bestürzt ist eins, das fliegen muß
und stammt aus einem Schooß. Wie vor sich selbst
erschreckt, durchzuckts die Luft, wie wenn ein Sprung
durch eine Tasse geht. So reißt die Spur
der Fledermaus durchs Porzellan des Abends.

If the assured animal that approaches us
on such a different path had within it consciousness
like ours——, it would wheel us around
and make us change our lives. But its existence
is infinite for it, unclouded, without thought
of its condition——, pure, like its outward gaze.
And where we see Future, it sees Everything
and itself in Everything forever healed.

And yet, in that warm, watchful animal
lives the weight and care of an enormous sadness.
For what sometimes overwhelms us often
clings to it, too——a kind of memory that tells us
that what we're now striving for was once
nearer and truer and attached to us
with infinite tenderness. Here all is distance,
there it was breath. After that first home
the second seems drafty and ambiguous.
 O bliss of the *tiny* creatures, which live
their whole lives in the womb that brought them forth!
O joy of the gnat, still leaping *inside*,
even when it weds: for womb is all!
And look at the half-assurance of the bird,
from the manner of its birth almost knowing both——
as if it were the soul of an Etruscan,
released from a dead man into a space
that has his resting figure for a lid.
And how lost is any womb-born creature
that has to fly! As if afraid
of its own self, it zigzags through the air
like a crack through a teacup. The way a bat's trace
crazes the porcelain of evening.

the soul of an Etruscan: The Etruscans depicted the soul as a bird on the walls of their sarcoph-
agus chambers. The lids of the sarcophagi themselves were often sculpted representations of
the dead person lying in repose.

Und wir: Zuschauer, immer, überall,
dem allen zugewandt und nie hinaus!
Uns überfüllts. Wir ordnens. Es zerfällt.
Wir ordnens wieder und zerfallen selbst.

Wer hat uns also umgedreht, daß wir,
was wir auch tun, in jener Haltung sind
von einem, welcher fortgeht? Wie er auf
dem letzten Hügel, der ihm ganz sein Tal
noch einmal zeigt, sich wendet, anhält, weilt—,
so leben wir und nehmen immer Abschied.

And we, spectators, always, everywhere,
looking at, never out of, everything!
It fills us to overflowing. We arrange it. It falls apart.
We rearrange it, and fall apart ourselves.

Who's turned us around like this, so that
always, no matter what we do, we're in the posture
of someone just departing? As he,
on the last hill that shows him his whole valley
one last time, turns, stops, lingers—,
we live our lives, forever taking leave.

Warum, wenn es angeht, also die Frist des Daseins
hinzubringen, als Lorbeer, ein wenig dunkler als alles
andere Grün, mit kleinen Wellen an jedem
Blattrand (wie eines Windes Lächeln)—: warum dann
Menschliches müssen—und, Schicksal vermeidend,
sich sehnen nach Schicksal? . . .

 Oh, *nicht*, weil Glück *ist*,
dieser voreilige Vorteil eines nahen Verlusts.
Nicht aus Neugier, oder zur Übung des Herzens,
das auch im Lorbeer *wäre*

Aber weil Hiersein viel ist, und weil uns scheinbar
alles das Hiesige braucht, dieses Schwindende, das
seltsam uns angeht. Uns, die Schwindendsten. *Ein* Mal
jedes, nur *ein* Mal. *Ein* Mal und nichtmehr. Und wir auch
ein Mal. Nie wieder. Aber dieses
ein Mal gewesen zu sein, wenn auch nur *ein* Mal:
irdisch gewesen zu sein, scheint nicht widerrufbar.

Und so drängen wir uns und wollen es leisten,
wollens enthalten in unsern einfachen Händen,
im überfüllteren Blick und im sprachlosen Herzen.
Wollen es werden. —Wem es geben? Am liebsten
alles behalten für immer . . . Ach, in den andern Bezug,
wehe, was nimmt man hinüber? Nicht das Anschaun, das hier
langsam erlernte, und kein hier Ereignetes. Keins.
Also die Schmerzen. Also vor allem das Schwersein,
also der Liebe lange Erfahrung, —also
lauter Unsägliches. Aber später,
unter den Sternen, was solls: *die* sind *besser* unsäglich.
Bringt doch der Wanderer auch vom Hange des Bergrands
nicht eine Hand voll Erde ins Tal, die Allen unsägliche, sondern
ein erworbenes Wort, reines, den gelben und blaun

Why, when this span of life might be spent
as laurel, a little darker than every
other green, with tiny waves on the edges
of each leaf (like the smile of a wind)——: why then
have to be human—and, fleeing fate,
long for fate? . . .

 Oh, *not* for some dream of happiness,
that premature profit of an imminent loss.
Not out of curiosity, not to exercise the heart,
all of which would pulse with laurel

But because *life* here compels us, and because everything here
seems to need us, all this fleetingness
that strangely entreats us. Us, the *most* fleeting . . .
Once for each thing, only once. Once and no more. And we, too,
only once. Never again. But to have been
once, even though only once:
this having been *earthly* seems lasting, beyond repeal.

And so we press on and try to achieve it,
try to contain it in our simple hands,
in our brimming look, our voiceless heart.
Try to *become* it. Try to give it—to whom? Best of all,
hold on to it all forever . . . Ah, but what can we carry across
into that other relation? Not the craft of seeing,
learned so slowly here, and no event that happened here. Not one.
The pain, then. Above all, the hard labor of living,
the long experience of love, —all the purely
unsayable things. But later,
among the stars, what then: there the unsayable *reigns*.
The traveler doesn't return to the valley from the mountainside
with a handful of sod, around which all stand mute,
but with a word he's won, a pure word, the yellow and blue

Enzian. Sind wir vielleicht *hier*, um zu sagen: Haus,
Brücke, Brunnen, Tor, Krug, Obstbaum, Fenster,—
höchstens: Säule, Turm . . . aber zu *sagen*, verstehs,
oh zu sagen *so*, wie selber die Dinge niemals
innig meinten zu sein. Ist nicht die heimliche List
dieser verschwiegenen Erde, wenn sie die Liebenden drängt,
daß sich in ihrem Gefühl jedes und jedes entzückt?
Schwelle: was ists für zwei
Liebende, daß sie die eigne ältere Schwelle der Tür
ein wenig verbrauchen, auch sie, nach den vielen vorher
und vor den Künftigen . . . , leicht.

Hier ist des *Säglichen* Zeit, *hier* seine Heimat.
Sprich und bekenn. Mehr als je
fallen die Dinge dahin, die erlebbaren, denn,
was sie verdrängend ersetzt, ist ein Tun ohne Bild.
Tun unter Krusten, die willig zerspringen, sobald
innen das Handeln entwächst und sich anders begrenzt.
Zwischen den Hämmern besteht
unser Herz, wie die Zunge
zwischen den Zähnen, die doch,
dennoch, die preisende bleibt.

Preise dem Engel die Welt, nicht die unsägliche, *ihm*
kannst du nicht großtun mit herrlich Erfühltem; im Weltall,
wo er fühlender fühlt, bist du ein Neuling. Drum zeig
ihm das Einfache, das, von Geschlecht zu Geschlechtern gestaltet,
als ein Unsriges lebt, neben der Hand und im Blick.
Sag ihm die Dinge. Er wird staunender stehn; wie du standest
bei dem Seiler in Rom, oder beim Töpfer am Nil.
Zeig ihm, wie glücklich ein Ding sein kann, wie schuldlos und unser,
wie selbst das klagende Leid rein zur Gestalt sich entschließt,
dient als ein Ding, oder stirbt in ein Ding—, und jenseits
selig der Geige entgeht. —Und diese, von Hingang
lebenden Dinge verstehn, daß du sie rühmst; vergänglich,
traun sie ein Rettendes uns, den Vergänglichsten, zu.
Wollen, wir sollen sie ganz im unsichtbarn Herzen verwandeln
in—o unendlich—in uns! Wer wir am Ende auch seien.

gentian. What if we're only *here* to say: *house,*
bridge, fountain, gate, jug, fruit tree, window,—
at most: *column, tower* . . . but for *saying,* understand,
oh for such saying as the things themselves
never dreamt so intensely to be. Isn't this the secret purpose
of the reticent earth, when it urges lovers on:
that in *their* passion each single thing should know ecstasy?
O Threshold: what must it mean for two lovers
to have you for their own, their own older threshold, and be wearing down
a little your ancient sill—, they too, after the many before,
before the many to come

Here is the time for the sayable, *here* is its home.
Speak and attest. More than ever
the things we can live with are falling away,
and ousting them, filling their place: an act without image.
Act under crusts which promptly crack whenever
the business inside swells and commands new contours.
Between the hammers our heart
lives on—as the tongue,
between the teeth, remains
unceasing in praise.

Praise the world to the Angel, not what's unsayable.
You can't impress *him* with lofty emotions; in the cosmos
where he feels more feelingly, you're a mere novice. Therefore show him
some simple thing, formed by generation after generation
until it's truly our own, living in our hands and in our eyes.
Tell him *things.* He'll stand more amazed; as you stood
beside the ropemaker in Rome or the potter by the Nile.
Show him how happy a thing can be, how innocent and ours,
how even lamenting grief decides finally on form,
serves as a thing or dies into a thing—, and in that blissful beyond
is unmoved even by the violin. —And these things
that live on departure know that you praise them; transient,
they look to us, the *most* transient, to save them.
They want us to change them utterly, in our invisible hearts,
into—O endlessly—*us*! Whoever, finally, we may be.

Erde, ist es nicht dies, was du willst: *unsichtbar*
in uns erstehn?—Ist es dein Traum nicht,
einmal unsichtbar zu sein?—Erde! unsichtbar!
Was, wenn Verwandlung nicht, ist dein drängender Auftrag?
Erde, du liebe, ich will. Oh glaub, es bedürfte
nicht deiner Frühlinge mehr, mich dir zu gewinnen—, *einer*,
ach, ein einziger ist schon dem Blute zu viel.
Namenlos bin ich zu dir entschlossen, von weit her.
Immer warst du im Recht, und dein heiliger Einfall
ist der vertrauliche Tod.

Siehe, ich lebe. Woraus? Weder Kindheit noch Zukunft
werden weniger Überzähliges Dasein
entspringt mir im Herzen.

Earth, isn't this what you want: to arise
in us *invisibly*? Isn't it your dream
to be invisible someday? Earth! Invisible!
What, if not transformation, is your urgent charge?
Earth, my darling, I will! Oh believe me,
you need no more of your Springs to win me—, *one*,
just one, is already too much for my blood.
Namelessly I'm wed to you forever.
You have always been right, and your most sacred tenet
is Death the intimate Friend.

Look, I am living. On what? Neither childhood nor future
grows less Overabundant existence
wells up in my heart.

Daß ich dereinst, an dem Ausgang der grimmigen Einsicht,
Jubel und Ruhm aufsinge zustimmenden Engeln.
Daß von den klar geschlagenen Hämmern des Herzens
keiner versage an weichen, zweifelnden oder
reißenden Saiten. Daß mich mein strömendes Antlitz
glänzender mache; daß das unscheinbare Weinen
blühe. O wie werdet ihr dann, Nächte, mir lieb sein,
gehärmte. Daß ich euch knieender nicht, untröstliche Schwestern,
hinnahm, nicht in euer gelöstes
Haar mich gelöster ergab. Wir, Vergeuder der Schmerzen.
Wie wir sie absehn voraus, in die traurige Dauer,
ob sie nicht enden vielleicht. Sie aber sind ja
unser winterwähriges Laub, unser dunkeles Sinngrün,
eine der Zeiten des heimlichen Jahres—, nicht nur
Zeit—, sind Stelle, Siedelung, Lager, Boden, Wohnort.

Freilich, wehe, wie fremd sind die Gassen der Leid-Stadt,
wo in der falschen, aus Übertönung gemachten
Stille, stark, aus der Gußform des Leeren der Ausguß
prahlt: der vergoldete Lärm, das platzende Denkmal.
O, wie spurlos zerträte ein Engel ihnen den Trostmarkt,
den die Kirche begrenzt, ihre fertig gekaufte:
reinlich und zu und enttäuscht wie ein Postamt am Sonntag.
Draußen aber kräuseln sich immer die Ränder von Jahrmarkt.
Schaukeln der Freiheit! Taucher und Gaukler des Eifers!
Und des behübschten Glücks figürliche Schießstatt,
wo es zappelt von Ziel und sich blechern benimmt,
wenn ein Geschickterer trifft. Von Beifall zu Zufall
taumelt er weiter; denn Buden jeglicher Neugier
werben, trommeln und plärrn. Für Erwachsene aber
ist noch besonders zu sehn, wie das Geld sich vermehrt, anatomisch,
nicht zur Belustigung nur: der Geschlechtsteil des Gelds,
alles, das Ganze, der Vorgang—, das unterrichtet und macht
fruchtbar

One day, at the end of the nightmare of knowing,
may I emerge singing praise and jubilation to assenting Angels.
May I strike my heart's keys clearly, and may none fail
because of slack, uncertain, or fraying strings.
May the tears that stream down my face
make me more radiant: may my hidden weeping
blossom. How I will cherish you then, you grief-torn nights!
Had I only received you, inconsolable sisters,
on more abject knees, only buried myself with more abandon
in your loosened hair. How we waste our afflictions!
We study them, stare out beyond them into bleak continuance,
hoping to glimpse some end. Whereas they're really
our wintering foliage, our dark greens of meaning, *one*
of the seasons of the clandestine year—; not only
season—: they're site, settlement, shelter, soil, abode.

Ah, but the City of Pain: how strange its streets:
the false silence of sound canceling sound,
and there—proud, brazen, effluence from the mold of emptiness—
the gilded hubbub, the swollen monument.
How an Angel would stamp out their market of solaces,
set up alongside that church they bought ready-made:
clean and closed and cheerless as a post office on Sunday.
Outside, though, there's always the billowing edge of the fair.
Swings of Freedom! High-divers and Jugglers of Zeal!
And the shooting gallery with its figures of idiot Happiness
which jump, spin, and fall back with a tinny ring
when a better marksman scores. Onward he lurches
cheered by his luck; for hawkers courting each curious taste
are drumming and barking. And then—for adults only—
something *really* worth seeing: how money breeds, the actual sex of it,
not some charade: money's genitals, everything, the act itself
from beginning to end—instructional and guaranteed
to make you potent

. . . Oh aber gleich darüber hinaus,
hinter der letzten Planke, beklebt mit Plakaten des »Todlos«,
jenes bitteren Biers, das den Trinkenden süß scheint,
wenn sie immer dazu frische Zerstreuungen kaun . . . ,
gleich im Rücken der Planke, gleich dahinter, ists *wirklich*.
Kinder spielen, und Liebende halten einander, —abseits,
ernst, im ärmlichen Gras, und Hunde haben Natur.
Weiter noch zieht es den Jüngling; vielleicht, daß er eine junge
Klage liebt Hinter ihr her kommt er in Wiesen. Sie sagt:
—Weit. Wir wohnen dort draußen . . .

 Wo? Und der Jüngling
folgt. Ihn rührt ihre Haltung. Die Schulter, der Hals—, vielleicht
ist sie von herrlicher Herkunft. Aber er läßt sie, kehrt um,
wendet sich, winkt . . . Was solls? Sie ist eine Klage.

Nur die jungen Toten, im ersten Zustand
zeitlosen Gleichmuts, dem der Entwöhnung,
folgen ihr liebend. Mädchen
wartet sie ab und befreundet sie. Zeigt ihnen leise,
was sie an sich hat. Perlen des Leids und die feinen
Schleier der Duldung. —Mit Jünglingen geht sie
schweigend.

Aber dort, wo sie wohnen, im Tal, der Älteren eine, der Klagen,
nimmt sich des Jünglinges an, wenn er fragt: —Wir waren,
sagt sie, ein Großes Geschlecht, einmal, wir Klagen. Die Väter
trieben den Bergbau dort in dem großen Gebirg; bei Menschen
findest du manchmal ein Stück geschliffenes Ur-Leid
oder, aus altem Vulkan, schlackig versteinerten Zorn.
Ja, das stammte von dort. Einst waren wir reich. —

Und sie leitet ihn leicht durch die weite Landschaft der Klagen,
zeigt ihm die Säulen der Tempel oder die Trümmer
jener Burgen, von wo Klage-Fürsten das Land
einstens weise beherrscht. Zeigt ihm die hohen
Tränenbäume und Felder blühender Wehmut,
(Lebendige kennen sie nur als sanftes Blattwerk);

. . . Oh, but just beyond that,
behind the last of the billboards, plastered with signs for "Deathless,"
that bitter beer which tastes sweet to those who drink it
as long as they have fresh distractions to munch on . . . ,
just beyond those boards, just the other side: the *real* world.
Children play, lovers hold each other, off in the shadows,
pensive, on meager grass, while dogs obey nature.
The youth is drawn farther on; perhaps he's fallen in love
with a young Lament He follows her, enters meadowland. She points:
"It's a long way. We live out there . . ."

> Where? And the youth stares.
He's moved by something in her bearing. Her shoulders, neck—,
perhaps she's of noble descent. Still, he leaves her, turns around,
glances back, waves . . . What's the use? She's a Lament.

Only the young dead, in the first state
of timeless equanimity, the phase of the unburdening,
follow her with loving steps. The girls
she waits for and befriends. Gently lets them see
the things that adorn her. Pearls of grief and the delicate
veils of forbearance. —With the young men
she walks on in silence.

Later, though, in the valley where they live, an older one, one of the elder
 Laments,
draws near the youth when he has questions:
—Long ago, she says, we Laments were a powerful race. Our forefathers
worked the mines in those giant mountains; among humans
you'll sometimes find a shard of primeval grief,
or a slag of petrified wrath from an ancient volcano.
Yes, those came from there. We used to be rich. —

And she guides him quietly through the wide land of Laments,
shows him the columns of temples, or the ruins
of those strongholds from which, long ago, Lament kings
wisely governed the land. Shows him the tall
trees of tears and the fields of flowering melancholy
(the living know them only as tender leaves):

zeigt ihm die Tiere der Trauer, weidend, —und manchmal
schreckt ein Vogel und zieht, flach ihnen fliegend durchs Aufschaun,
weithin das schriftliche Bild seines vereinsamten Schreis. —
Abends führt sie ihn hin zu den Gräbern der Alten
aus dem Klage-Geschlecht, den Sibyllen und Warn-Herrn.
Naht aber Nacht, so wandeln sie leiser, und bald
mondets empor, das über Alles
wachende Grab-Mal. Brüderlich jenem am Nil,
der erhabene Sphinx—: der verschwiegenen Kammer
Antlitz.
Und sie staunen dem krönlichen Haupt, das für immer,
schweigend, der Menschen Gesicht
auf die Waage der Sterne gelegt.

Nicht erfaßt es sein Blick, im Frühtod
schwindelnd. Aber ihr Schaun,
hinter dem Pschent-Rand hervor, scheucht es die Eule. Und sie,
streifend im langsamen Abstrich die Wange entlang,
jene der reifesten Rundung,
zeichnet weich in das neue
Totengehör, über ein doppelt
aufgeschlagenes Blatt, den unbeschreiblichen Umriß.

Und höher, die Sterne. Neue. Die Sterne des Leidlands.
Langsam nennt sie die Klage: —Hier,
siehe: den *Reiter*, den *Stab*, und das vollere Sternbild
nennen sie: *Fruchtkranz*. Dann, weiter, dem Pol zu:
Wiege; *Weg*; *Das Brennende Buch*; *Puppe*; *Fenster*.
Aber im südlichen Himmel, rein wie im Innern
einer gesegneten Hand, das klar erglänzende »*M*«,
das die Mütter bedeutet —

shows him the animals of sadness, grazing, —and from time to time
a startled bird, cutting low through their lifted gazes,
draws into the distance the ancient glyph of its desolate cry.
At evening she leads him out to the ancestral tombs
of the House of Lament, those of the sibyls and dire prophets.
But as night nears, they move more slowly, until
suddenly, rising moonlike before them: the great sepulcher
that watches over everything. Twin brother
to the one on the Nile, the exalted Sphinx—: visage
of the hidden chamber.
And they marvel at that kingly head, which silently,
for all time, has weighed the human face
in the stars' balance.

His sight, still unsteady from recent death,
can't quite grasp it. But their gazing
flushes an owl from behind the corona's rim. And the bird,
gliding with slow downstrokes along the cheek,
the one with the fullest curve,
inscribes faintly in the dead youth's new
sense of hearing, as across a doubly
unfolded page, the indescribable outline.

And higher, the stars. New ones. The stars of the Land of Pain.
Slowly the Lament names them: —There, look:
the *Rider*, the *Staff*, and that constellation with so many stars
that we call: *Calyx*. And then, farther, toward the pole:
Cradle; *Path*; *The Burning Book*; *Puppet*; *Window*.
But in the southern sky, pure as if held in the palm
of a sacred hand: that clear, gleaming *M*
that means Mothers —

the corona's rim: *Pschent* is a form of the ancient Egyptian word for the double crown worn by
the pharaohs to signify the union of Upper and Lower Egypt. But the turn-of-the-century
Egyptologists also used the term to designate the headcloth over which the crown was worn.
Before the restoration of the Sphinx in 1925, an actual owl supposedly nested at the headcloth's
edge.

Doch der Tote muß fort, und schweigend bringt ihn die ältere
Klage bis an die Talschlucht,
wo es schimmert im Mondschein:
die Quelle der Freude. In Ehrfurcht
nennt sie sie, sagt:—Bei den Menschen
ist sie ein tragender Strom. —

Stehn am Fuß des Gebirgs,
Und da umarmt sie ihn, weinend.

Einsam steigt er dahin, in die Berge des Ur-Leids.
Und nicht einmal sein Schritt klingt aus dem tonlosen Los.

Aber erweckten sie uns, die unendlich Toten, ein Gleichnis,
siehe, sie zeigten vielleicht auf die Kätzchen der leeren
Hasel, die hängenden, oder
meinten den Regen, der fällt auf dunkles Erdreich im Frühjahr. —

Und wir, die an *steigendes* Glück
denken, empfänden die Rührung,
die uns beinah bestürzt,
wenn ein Glückliches *fällt*.

But the dead youth must go on, and the elder Lament
leads him in silence as far as the wide ravine,
where they see shimmering in moonlight:
the Font of Joy. She names it
reverently and says:—"Among the living
it becomes a powerful stream." —

They stand at the foot of the range.
And she embraces him there, weeping.

He climbs on alone, into the mountains of primeval grief.
And no step echoes back from that soundless fate.

But suppose the endlessly dead were to waken an image in us:
they might point to the catkins hanging
from the empty hazel trees, or direct us to the rain
spattering black earth in early Spring.

And we, who always think of happiness
rising, would feel the emotion
that almost confounds us
when a happy thing *falls*.

DIE SONETTE AN ORPHEUS *(1923)*

GESCHRIEBEN ALS EIN GRAB-MAL

FÜR WERA OUCKAMA KNOOP

SONNETS TO ORPHEUS *(1923)*

WRITTEN AS A GRAVE MONUMENT

FOR VERA OUCKAMA KNOOP

Erster Teil

First Part

Da stieg ein Baum. O reine Übersteigung!
O Orpheus singt! O hoher Baum im Ohr!
Und alles schwieg. Doch selbst in der Verschweigung
ging neuer Anfang, Wink und Wandlung vor.

Tiere aus Stille drangen aus dem klaren
gelösten Wald von Lager und Genist;
und da ergab sich, daß sie nicht aus List
und nicht aus Angst in sich so leise waren,

sondern aus Hören. Brüllen, Schrei, Geröhr
schien klein in ihren Herzen. Und wo eben
kaum eine Hütte war, dies zu empfangen,

ein Unterschlupf aus dunkelstem Verlangen
mit einem Zugang, dessen Pfosten beben, —
da schufst du ihnen Tempel im Gehör.

A tree arose. O pure transcendence!
O Orpheus sings! O tall tree within the ear!
And all was silent. Yet in that silence
pulsed new genesis, new signaling, new change.

Creatures of stillness thronged out of the clear
disentangled forest, from nest and lair;
and it wasn't cunning, wasn't heed or fright
that put such softness in their step,

but listening. Bellow, shriek, and roar
seemed small inside their hearts. And where once
there'd scarcely been a hut to take this in,

a hidden refuge made of darkest longing
with an entranceway whose braces shook, —
you built temples for them in their hearing.

Und fast ein Mädchen wars und ging hervor
aus diesem einigen Glück von Sang und Leier
und glänzte klar durch ihre Frühlingsschleier
und machte sich ein Bett in meinem Ohr.

Und schlief in mir. Und alles war ihr Schlaf.
Die Bäume, die ich je bewundert, diese
fühlbare Ferne, die gefühlte Wiese
und jedes Staunen, das mich selbst betraf.

Sie schlief die Welt. Singender Gott, wie hast
du sie vollendet, daß sie nicht begehrte,
erst wach zu sein? Sieh, sie erstand und schlief.

Wo ist ihr Tod? O, wirst du dies Motiv
erfinden noch, eh sich dein Lied verzehrte? —
Wo sinkt sie hin aus mir? . . . Ein Mädchen fast . . .

And almost a girl it was and came forth
from this glad unity of song and lyre
and shone brightly through her springtime veils
and made herself a bed within my ear.

And slept in me. And all things were her sleep.
The trees I'd always marveled at, these
palpable distances, the deep-felt meadows,
and an entire life's astonishments.

She slept the world. Singing god, how did you
so perfect her that she never once
had need to be awake? Look, she arose and slept.

Where is her death? Ah, will you introduce
that theme before your song expires? —
I can feel her drifting off . . . to where? . . . A girl almost . . .

Ein Gott vermags. Wie aber, sag mir, soll
ein Mann ihm folgen durch die schmale Leier?
Sein Sinn ist Zwiespalt. An der Kreuzung zweier
Herzwege steht kein Tempel für Apoll.

Gesang, wie du ihn lehrst, ist nicht Begehr,
nicht Werbung um ein endlich noch Erreichtes;
Gesang ist Dasein. Für den Gott ein Leichtes.
Wann aber *sind* wir? Und wann wendet *er*

an unser Sein die Erde und die Sterne?
Dies *ists* nicht, Jüngling, daß du liebst, wenn auch
die Stimme dann den Mund dir aufstößt, —lerne

vergessen daß du aufsangst. Das verrinnt.
In Wahrheit singen, ist ein andrer Hauch.
Ein Hauch um nichts. Ein Wehn im Gott. Ein Wind.

3

A god can do it. But how, will you tell me, could
a man follow him through the narrow lyre?
His mind divides. Where two heart roads cross
there can be no temple for Apollo.

Singing, as you teach it, is not desire,
not the courting of some end to be attained.
Singing is being. Easy, for a god.
But for us, when *are* we? And when does *he*

cast all the earth and stars upon our lives?
It's *not*, youth, when you're in love, even
if then your voice forces open your mouth; —

learn to forget those songs. They elapse.
True singing is a different breath.
A breath serving nothing. A gust in the god. A wind.

O ihr Zärtlichen, tretet zuweilen
in den Atem, der euch nicht meint,
laßt ihn an eueren Wangen sich teilen,
hinter euch zittert er, wieder vereint.

O ihr Seligen, o ihr Heilen,
die ihr der Anfang der Herzen scheint.
Bogen der Pfeile und Ziele von Pfeilen,
ewiger glänzt euer Lächeln verweint.

Fürchtet euch nicht zu leiden, die Schwere,
gebt sie zurück an der Esde Gewicht;
schwer sind die Berge, schwer sind die Meere.

Selbst die als Kinder ihr pflanztet, die Bäume,
wurden zu schwer längst; ihr trüget sie nicht.
Aber die Lüfte . . . aber die Räume . . .

4

O you tender ones, step now and then
into the breath that takes no heed of you:
it will part as it brushes your cheeks
and then tremble behind you, united again.

O you who are blissful, you who are whole,
you who seem the beginnings of hearts.
Bows for arrows and arrows' aim, through tears
your smile will glow more eternal.

Don't be afraid to suffer—take your heaviness
and give it back to the earth's own weight;
the mountains are heavy, the oceans are heavy.

Even the trees you planted as a child
have long grown too heavy; you couldn't bear them.
But the breezes . . . and the spaces . . .

Errichtet keinen Denkstein. Laßt die Rose
nur jedes Jahr zu seinen Gunsten blühn.
Denn Orpheus ists. Seine Metamorphose
in dem und dem. Wir sollen uns nicht mühn

um andre Namen. Ein für alle Male
ists Orpheus, wenn es singt. Er kommt und geht.
Ists nicht schon viel, wenn er die Rosenschale
um ein paar Tage manchmal übersteht?

O wie er schwinden muß, daß ihrs begrifft!
Und wenn ihm selbst auch bangte, daß er schwände.
Indem sein Wort das Hiersein übertrifft,

ist er schon dort, wohin ihrs nicht begleitet.
Der Leier Gitter zwängt ihm nicht die Hände.
Und er gehorcht, indem er überschreitet.

Erect no monument. Allow the rose
to unfurl each year on his behalf.
For it's Orpheus. His metamorphosis
in this, in that. We needn't bother

with other names. Once and forever
it's Orpheus, when there's song. He comes and goes.
Isn't it grace enough when now and then
he stays on a few days, outlasting the bowl of roses?

But he must disappear for you to grasp it!
Though he himself feared vanishing.
Even as his word transforms the here and now,

he's already in that other realm, where you can't follow.
The lyre's snare doesn't trap his hands.
And he obeys, even as he overreaches.

6

Ist er ein Hiesiger? Nein, aus beiden
Reichen erwuchs seine weite Natur.
Kundiger böge die Zweige der Weiden,
wer die Wurzeln der Weiden erfuhr.

Geht ihr zu Bette, so laßt auf dem Tische
Brot nicht und Milch nicht; die Toten ziehts—.
Aber er, des Beschwörende, mische
unter der Milde des Augenlids

ihre Erscheinung in alles Geschaute;
und der Zauber von Erdrauch und Raute
sei ihm so wahr wie der klarste Bezug.

Nichts kann das gültige Bild ihm verschlimmern;
sei es aus Gräbern, sei es aus Zimmern,
rühme er Fingerring, Spange und Krug.

6

Is he native to this realm? No,
his wide nature grew out of both worlds.
They more adeptly bend the willow's branches
who have experience of the willow's roots.

When you go to bed, don't leave bread or milk
on the table: it attracts the dead—.
But may he, this quiet conjurer, may he
beneath the mildness of the eyelid

mix their bright traces into every seen thing;
and may the magic of earthsmoke and rue
be as real for him as the clearest connection.

Nothing can mar for him the authentic image;
whether he wanders through houses or graves,
let him praise signet ring, gold necklace, jar.

earthsmoke and rue: Herbs, supposedly with the power to summon the dead.

Rühmen, das ists! Ein zum Rühmen Bestellter,
ging er hervor wie das Erz aus des Steins
Schweigen. Sein Herz, o vergängliche Kelter
eines den Menschen unendlichen Weins.

Nie versagt ihm die Stimme am Staube,
wenn ihn das göttliche Beispiel ergreift.
Alles wird Weinberg, alles wird Traube,
in seinem fühlenden Süden gereift.

Nicht in den Grüften der Könige Moder
straft ihm die Rühmung Lügen, oder
daß von den Göttern ein Schatten fällt.

Er ist einer der bleibenden Boten,
der noch weit in die Türen der Toten
Schalen mit rühmlichen Früchten hält.

Praising, that's it! One appointed to praise,
he came forth like ore out of the stone's
silence. His heart, O ephemeral winepress
for a vintage eternal to man.

Never does his voice die or turn to dust
when the divine moment seizes him.
All becomes vineyard, all becomes grape,
ripened in his sentient South.

Not mold in the vaults of kings
nor any shadow falling from the gods
can give his songs the lie.

He is one of the messengers who stay,
holding far into the doors of the dead
bowls heaped with fruit to be praised.

Nur im Raum der Rühmung darf die Klage
gehn, die Nymphe des geweinten Quells,
wachend über unserm Niederschlage,
daß er klar sei an demselben Fels,

der die Tore trägt und die Altäre. —
Sieh, um ihre stillen Schultern früht
das Gefühl, daß sie die jüngste wäre
unter den Geschwistern im Gemüt.

Jubel *weiß*, und Sehnsucht ist geständig, —
nur die Klage lernt noch; mädchenhändig
zählt sie nächtelang das alte Schlimme.

Aber plötzlich, schräg und ungeübt,
hält sie doch ein Sternbild unsrer Stimme
in den Himmel, den ihr Hauch nicht trübt.

8

Only in the realm of Praise may Lament
range, the nymph of the tear-fed stream,
watching over our cascade to ensure
that it strikes clearly on the same rock

that supports the gates and altars. —
Look, around her quiet shoulders dawns
the feeling that among the siblings
of the heart, she must be the youngest.

Jubilation *knows*, and Longing has admitted, —
only Lament still learns; with slender hands
she counts for nights on end the ancient curse.

Yet suddenly, unpracticed though she is,
she lifts a constellation of our voice
into skies not clouded by her breath.

Nur wer die Leier schon hob
auch unter Schatten,
darf das unendliche Lob
ahnend erstatten.

Nur wer mit Toten vom Mohn
aß, von dem ihren,
wird nicht den leisesten Ton
wieder verlieren.

Mag auch die Spieglung im Teich
oft uns verschwimmen:
Wisse das Bild.

Erst in dem Doppelbereich
werden die Stimmen
ewig und mild.

9

Only he who has also raised
his lyre among shadows
may find his way back
to infinite praise.

Only he who has eaten with the dead
from their stores of poppy
will never lose again
the softest chord.

And though the pool's reflection
often blurs before us:
Know the image.

Only in the double realm
do the voices become
eternal and mild.

Euch, die ihr nie mein Gefühl verließt,
grüß ich, antikische Sarkophage,
die das fröhliche Wasser römischer Tage
als ein wandelndes Lied durchfließt.

Oder jene so offenen, wie das Aug
eines frohen erwachenden Hirten,
—innen voll Stille und Bienensaug—
denen entzückte Falter entschwirrten;

alle, die man dem Zweifel entreißt,
grüß ich, die wiedergeöffneten Munde,
die schon wußten, was schweigen heißt.

Wissen wirs, Freunde, wissen wirs nicht?
Beides bildet die zögernde Stunde
in dem menschlichen Angesicht.

You, who have never left my feelings,
I greet you, antique sarcophagi,
through which the cheerful water of Roman days
flows like a meandering song.

Or you others so open, like the eye
of a happy wakening shepherd,
—full of silence and flowering bee balm—
from which flit ecstatic butterflies;

all that's been wrested from doubt
I greet, the mouths opened again
after knowing well what silence means.

Do we know, friends, do we not know?
Both mold the hour of hesitation
into the contours of the human face.

antique sarcophagi: The ancient stone coffins are often used as troughs or basins in Italian towns and the surrounding countryside; see Rilke's "Roman Sarcophagi" in *New Poems* (1907).
you others so open: "The second stanza refers to the graves in the famous old cemetery of the Alyscamps near Arles, which are also mentioned in The Notebooks of Malte Laurids Brigge."
—Rilke's handwritten note. The latter passage has Malte imagining the prodigal son as a solitary young shepherd standing "in the spirit-populated shadows of the Alyscamps, his gaze following the flight of a dragonfly among the tombs that stand open like the graves of the resurrected."

Sieh den Himmel. Heißt kein Sternbild "Reiter"?
Denn dies ist uns seltsam eingeprägt:
dieser Stolz aus Erde. Und ein Zweiter,
der ihn treibt und hält und den er trägt.

Ist nicht so, gejagt und dann gebändigt,
diese sehnige Natur des Seins?
Weg und Wendung. Doch ein Druck verständigt.
Neue Weite. Und die zwei sind eins.

Aber *sind* sie's? Oder meinen beide
nicht den Weg, den sie zusammen tun?
Namenlos schon trennt sie Tisch und Weide.

Auch die sternische Verbindung trügt.
Doch uns freue eine Weile nun,
der Figur zu glauben. Das genügt.

Scan the sky. Is no constellation named "Horseman"?
For this is strangely imprinted in us:
this earthly pride. And another
who spurs and reins it and whom it bears.

Isn't it thus, pursued and then broken in,
this sinewy nature of our being?
Path and pivot. At a touch: understanding.
New distances. And the two are one.

But *are* they? Or does neither want
the path they trace together? Table and trough
ineffably divide them from the start.

Even the starry union can deceive.
Yet for now let's allow ourselves
to believe in the figure. That suffices.

Heil dem Geist, der uns verbinden mag;
denn wir leben wahrhaft in Figuren.
Und mit kleinen Schritten gehn die Uhren
neben unserm eigentlichen Tag.

Ohne unsern wahren Platz zu kennen,
handeln wir aus wirklichem Bezug.
Die Antennen fühlen die Antennen,
und die leere Ferne trug . . .

Reine Spannung. O Musik der Kräfte!
Ist nicht durch die läßlichen Geschäfte
jede Störung von dir abgelenkt?

Selbst wenn sich der Bauer sorgt und handelt,
wo die Saat in Sommer sich verwandelt,
reicht er niemals hin. Die Erde *schenkt*.

Hail to the spirit that can connect us;
for truly we live our lives in figures.
And with tiny paces the clocks march along
beside our own, individual day.

Without knowing our true place,
we somehow act in genuine rapport.
Antennae feel antennae,
and the empty distance fills with . . .

Pure tension. Music of the Powers!
Does not our endless commerce
deflect from you each interruption?

However much the farmer frets and labors,
he never reaches where the seed
turns into summer. The earth *bestows*.

Voller Apfel, Birne und Banane,
Stachelbeere . . . Alles dieses spricht
Tod und Leben in den Mund . . . Ich ahne . . .
Lest es einem Kind vom Angesicht,

wenn es sie erschmeckt. Dies kommt von weit.
Wird euch langsam namenlos im Munde?
Wo sonst Worte waren, fließen Funde,
aus dem Fruchtfleisch überrascht befreit.

Wagt zu sagen, was ihr Apfel nennt.
Diese Süße, die sich erst verdichtet,
um, im Schmecken leise aufgerichtet,

klar zu werden, wach und transparent,
doppeldeutig, sonnig, erdig, hiesig—:
O Erfahrung, Fühlung, Freude—, riesig!

Ripe apple, blackberry and banana,
nectarine . . . These all speak
death and life into the mouth . . . I feel . . .
Read it in the features of a child

who's tasting them. This comes from far.
Does all grow slowly nameless in your mouth?
Where words once were, discoveries flow,
set free from the fruit's flesh, amazed.

Dare to say what you call "apple."
This sweetness that first condenses, thickens,
 and then, finely sublimed in the taste,

grows clear, awake, transparent,
double-sided, sunny, earthly, native—:
O knowing, feeling, happiness—, immense!

Wir gehen um mit Blume, Weinblatt, Frucht.
Sie sprechen nicht die Sprache nur des Jahres.
Aus Dunkel steigt ein buntes Offenbares
und hat vielleicht den Glanz der Eifersucht

der Toten an sich, die die Erde stärken.
Was wissen wir von ihrem Teil an dem?
Es ist seit lange ihre Art, den Lehm
mit ihrem freien Marke zu durchmärken.

Nun fragt sich nur: tun sie es gern? . . .
Drängt diese Frucht, ein Werk von schweren Sklaven,
geballt zu uns empor, zu ihren Herrn?

Sind *sie* die Herrn, die bei den Wurzeln schlafen,
und gönnen uns aus ihren Überflüssen
dies Zwischending aus stummer Kraft und Küssen?

I 4

We puzzle over flower, vine-leaf, fruit.
They speak not just the language of the year.
A thing of succor rises from the dark
and its hues may gleam with the jealousy

of the dead, those who strengthen the earth.
What do we know of their share in it?
It has long been their practice to enrich
the loam with their own free marrow.

The question is: do they do it willingly? . . .
Does this fruit, a work of sullen slaves,
push through clenched to us, to their masters?

Or are *they* the masters, sleeping among
the roots and granting us from their profusion
this hybrid of mute strength and kisses?

15

Wartet . . . , das schmeckt . . . Schon ists auf der Flucht.
. . . Wenig Musik nur, ein Stampfen, ein Summen—:
Mädchen, ihr warmen, Mädchen, ihr stummen,
tanzt den Geschmack der erfahrenen Frucht!

Tanzt die Orange. Wer kann sie vergessen,
wie sie, ertrinkend in sich, sich wehrt
wider ihr Süßsein. Ihr habt sie besessen.
Sie hat sich köstlich zu euch bekehrt.

Tanzt die Orange. Die wärmere Landschaft,
werft sie aus euch, daß die reife erstrahle
in Lüften der Heimat! Erglühte, enthüllt

Düfte um Düfte! Schafft die Verwandtschaft
mit der reinen, sich weigernden Schale,
mit dem Saft, der die Glückliche füllt!

footer_navigation378/footer_navigation

Wait . . . , this taste . . . Already it's escaping.
. . . A bit of music, feet tapping, a hum—:
You girls, with your silences, your warmth,
dance the knowledge of the tasted fruit.

Dance the orange. Who can forget it,
the way it fights, drowning in itself,
against its sweetness. You've possessed it.
Its deliciousness has entered you.

Dance the orange. Fling the warmer landscape
out from you, so the ripe fruit may glow
in its native breezes! Aglow yourselves, peel

perfume from perfume! Create a kinship
with the pure, reluctant rind,
with the juice that fills the happy fruit!

Du, mein Freund, bist einsam, weil . . .
Wir machen mit Worten und Fingerzeigen
uns allmählich die Welt zu eigen,
vielleicht ihren schwächsten, gefährlichsten Teil.

Wer zeigt mit Fingern auf einen Geruch?—
Doch von den Kräften, die uns bedrohten,
fühlst du viele . . . Du kennst die Toten,
und du erschrickst vor dem Zauberspruch.

Sieh, nun heißt es zusammen ertragen
Stückwerk und Teile, als sei es das Ganze.
Dir helfen, wird schwer sein. Vor allem: pflanze

mich nicht in dein Herz. Ich wüchse zu schnell.
Doch *meines* Herrn Hand will ich führen und sagen:
Hier. Das ist Esau in seinem Fell.

You, my friend, are alone, because . . .
We, with words and pointing fingers,
gradually make the world our own—
perhaps its weakest, most hazardous part.

Who points fingers at a smell?
Yet you feel so many of those forces
that threaten us . . . You recognize the dead,
and you cower before the magic spell.

Look, now we together must manage
with piecework and parts, as if they were the whole.
Helping you will be hard. Above all:

don't plant me in your heart. I'd grow too fast.
But I will guide *my* master's hand and say:
Here. Here is Esau in his pelt.

Zu unterst der Alte, verworrn,
all der Erbauten
Wurzel, verborgener Born,
den sie nie schauten.

Sturmhelm und Jägerhorn,
Spruch von Ergrauten,
Männer im Bruderzorn,
Frauen wie Lauten . . .

Drängender Zweig an Zweig,
nirgends ein freier . . .
Einer! o steig . . . o steig . . .

Aber sie brechen noch.
Dieser erst oben doch
biegt sich zur Leier.

Deepest down: the age-old,
gnarled root
of all erected things,
hidden source they've never seen.

Battle helmet, hunter's horn,
sayings of the elders,
men in their brother-wrath,
women like lutes . . .

Branch crowding branch,
none of them free . . .
Yes one! climb . . . O climb . . .

But still they break.
Until at last that highest one
arcs into a lyre.

Hörst du das Neue, Herr,
dröhnen und beben?
Kommen Verkündiger,
die es erheben.

Zwar ist kein Hören heil
in dem Durchtobtsein,
doch der Maschinenteil
will jetzt gelobt sein.

Sieh, die Maschine:
wie sie sich wälzt und rächt
und uns entstellt und schwächt.

Hat sie aus uns auch Kraft,
sie, ohne Leidenschaft,
treibe und diene.

Master, do you hear the New,
rumbling and quaking?
Harbingers arrive
to proclaim its reign.

Surely no hearing can be whole
in this incessant clamor,
yet every part of the machine
wants its praise.

Behold the machine:
how it rolls and wreaks vengeance
and drains and deforms us.

Yet since it has its strength from us,
let it without vehemence
drive and serve.

Wandelt sich rasch auch die Welt
wie Wolkengestalten,
alles Vollendete fällt
heim zum Uralten.

Über dem Wandel und Gang,
weiter und freier,
währt noch dein Vor-Gesang,
Gott mit der Leier.

Nicht sind die Leiden erkannt,
nicht ist die Liebe gelernt,
und was im Tod uns entfernt,

ist nicht entschleiert.
Einzig das Lied überm Land
heiligt und feiert.

Though the world change swiftly
as the forms in clouds,
all perfected things fall back
to age-old ground.

Over what changes and passes,
wider and freer,
your deep song still hovers,
O god with the lyre.

Pain has not been understood,
love has not been learned,
and what in death removes us

remains undisclosed.
Alone over the land
song hallows and heals.

Dir aber, Herr, o was weih ich dir, sag,
der das Ohr den Geschöpfen gelehrt? —
Mein Erinnern an einen Frühlingstag,
seinen Abend, in Rußland—, ein Pferd . . .

Herüber vom Dorf kam der Schimmel allein,
an der vorderen Fessel den Pflock,
um die Nacht auf den Wiesen allein zu sein;
wie schlug seiner Mähne Gelock

an den Hals im Takte des Übermuts,
bei dem grob gehemmten Galopp.
Wie sprangen die Quellen des Rossebluts!

Der fühlte die Weiten, und ob!
Der sang und der hörte—, dein Sagenkreis
war *in* ihm geschlossen.
 Sein Bild: ich weih's.

20

But what, Master, might I dedicate to you,
O tell me, you who taught the animals their ear. —
My memory of one Spring day
toward evening, in Russia—, a horse . . .

Out from the village came that one white horse,
a hobble trailing from its front fetlock,
to pass the night all alone in the meadows;
how the shock of mane slapped his neck

in time with the sovereign gaiety
in that awkward, hampered gallop.
How the sources of stallion blood leapt!

He felt the distances, and oh!
He sang and heard—: *in* him your legend cycle
rounded to its close.

His image: receive it.

The episode with the white horse occurred in May 1900 during Rilke's second Russian trip with Lou Andreas-Salomé. Writing her in May 1922 about the *Elegies* and *Sonnets*, he marvels: "And imagine, . . . I wrote, made, the horse, you remember, that free happy white horse with the hobble on his foreleg who once, at approach of evening, came galloping over toward us so joyously on a Volga meadow—. . . . I made him, as an *ex voto* for Orpheus!—What is time?—When is Now?—Across so many years he leapt, with his total happiness, into my wide-open feeling."

389

Frühling ist wiedergekommen. Die Erde
ist wie ein Kind, das Gedichte weiß;
viele, o viele . . . Für die Beschwerde
langen Lernens bekommt sie den Preis.

Streng war ihr Lehrer. Wir mochten das Weiße
an dem Barte des alten Manns.
Nun, wie das Grüne, das Blaue heiße,
dürfen wir fragen: sie kanns, sie kanns!

Erde, die frei hat, du glückliche, spiele
nun mit den Kindern. Wir wollen dich fangen,
fröhliche Erde. Dem Frohsten gelingts.

O, was der Lehrer sie lehrte, das Viele,
und was gedruckt steht in Wurzeln und langen
schwierigen Stämmen: sie singts, sie singts!

Spring has come again. The earth
is like a child who knows poems by heart;
many, so many! . . . For the work
of such long learning, she wins the prize.

Her teacher was demanding. We'd grown fond
of the white in the old man's beard.
Now when we ask her what the green and the blue are:
she can tell us, she knows it, she knows!

Earth, lucky earth, on holiday, play
with the children now. We want to catch you,
happy earth. And the luckiest will.

What her teacher taught her! So many things,
and what's imprinted in the roots and on the long
difficult stems: she sings it, she sings!

"This little Spring song seems to me, as it were, an 'interpretation' of a remarkable, dancing music I once heard sung by the convent children at morning Mass in the little cloister church at Ronda (in southern Spain). The children, always to this dance rhythm, sang a text I didn't know, accompanied by triangle and tambourine." —One of only two notes (the other to Sonnet 2.11) that Rilke appended to the published text of the *Sonnets*.

Wir sind die Treibenden.
Aber den Schritt der Zeit,
nehmt ihn als Kleinigkeit
im immer Bleibenden.

Alles das Eilende
wird schon vorüber sein;
denn das Verweilende
erst weiht uns ein.

Knaben, o werft den Mut
nicht in die Schnelligkeit,
nicht in den Flugversuch.

Alles ist ausgeruht:
Dunkel und Helligkeit,
Blume und Buch.

We drive and are driven.
But time's stride—
think of it lost
in the ever remaining.

All that's hurrying
will quickly be past;
only what lingers
grants us credence.

Boys, don't fling your courage
into the thrill of speed
or attempts at flight.

All that is is at rest—
darkness and morning light,
flower and book.

O erst *dann*, wenn der Flug
nicht mehr um seinetwillen
wird in die Himmelsstillen
steigen, sich selber genug,

um in lichten Profilen,
als das Gerät, das gelang,
Liebling der Winde zu spielen,
sicher schwenkend und schlank,—

erst, wenn ein reines Wohin
wachsender Apparate
Knabenstolz überwiegt,

wird, überstürzt von Gewinn,
jener den Fernen Genahte
sein, was er einsam erfliegt.

23

Not till that day when flight
no longer for its own sake
climbs into the silent skies
propelled by sheer bravura,

so that in shining profiles,
as the tool that triumphed,
it can play the wind's favorite,
slender, sure, agile,—

not till a pure "out there"
dispels boyish pride
in the power of instruments,

will one breathless from winning
and closing in on distances
be what his solo flight attains.

Sollen wir unsere uralte Freundschaft, die großen
niemals werbenden Götter, weil sie der harte
Stahl, den wir streng erzogen, nicht kennt, verstoßen
oder sie plötzlich suchen auf einer Karte?

Diese gewaltigen Freunde, die uns die Toten
nehmen, rühren nirgends an unsere Räder.
Unsere Gastmähler haben wir weit——, unsere Bäder,
fortgerückt, und ihre uns lang schon zu langsamen Boten

überholen wir immer. Einsamer nun auf einander
ganz angewiesen, ohne einander zu kennen,
führen wir nicht mehr die Pfade als schöne Mäander,

sondern als Grade. Nur noch in Dampfkesseln brennen
die einstigen Feuer und heben die Hämmer, die immer
größern. Wir aber nehmen an Kraft ab, wie Schwimmer.

Shall we renounce our age-old friendship,
the great undemanding gods, because the hard
steel we raised so fiercely doesn't know them?
Or shall we suddenly search for them on a map?

These potent friends who take the dead from us
nowhere brush against our wheels. We've
moved our baths and banquet places far away,
and their messengers, long too slow for us,

we forever outstrip. More alone now, wholly
dependent on each other, strangers to each other,
we no longer plot beautiful meandering roads

but remorseless thoroughfares. Only in steam boilers
do the old fires burn, driving pistons, ever more gigantic.
While we feel our strength ebb, like swimmers.

Dich aber will ich nun, *Dich,* die ich kannte
wie eine Blume, von der ich den Namen nicht weiß,
noch *ein* Mal erinnern und ihnen zeigen, Entwandte,
schöne Gespielin des unüberwindlichen Schrei's.

Tänzerin erst, die plötzlich, den Körper voll Zögern,
anhielt, als göß man ihr Jungsein in Erz;
trauernd und lauschend—. Da, von den hohen Vermögern
fiel ihr Musik in das veränderte Herz.

Nah war die Krankheit. Schon von den Schatten bemächtigt,
drängte verdunkelt das Blut, doch, wie flüchtig verdächtigt,
trieb es in seinen natürlichen Frühling hervor.

Wieder und wieder, von Dunkel und Sturz unterbrochen,
glänzte es irdisch. Bis es nach schrecklichem Pochen
trat in das trostlos offene Tor.

2 5

But *you* now, O stolen one, whom I knew
like a flower I had no name for, *once* more
will I rehearse you and show you to them,
O beautiful playmate of the unquenchable cry.

Dancer first, whose body, full of hesitation,
suddenly stopped—as if your youth were being cast
in bronze (grieving and listening). Then, from
the powers above, music fell into your altered heart.

Illness was near. Already gripped by shadows,
your blood coursed darker; yet, as if only fleetingly
suspicious, it burst forth into its natural Spring.

Again and again, amid darkness and downfall,
it flared earthly. Until after terrible pounding
it stepped through the hopelessly open gate.

Du aber, Göttlicher, du, bis zuletzt noch Ertöner,
da ihn der Schwarm der verschmähten Mänaden befiel,
hast ihr Geschrei übertönt mit Ordnung, du Schöner,
aus den Zerstörenden stieg dein erbauendes Spiel.

Keine war da, daß sie Haupt dir und Leier zerstör',
wie sie auch rangen und rasten; und alle die scharfen
Steine, die sie nach deinem Herzen warfen,
wurden zu Sanftem an dir und begabt mit Gehör.

Schließlich zerschlugen sie dich, von der Rache gehetzt,
während dein Klang noch in Löwen und Felsen verweilte
und in den Bäumen und Vögeln. Dort singst du noch jetzt.

O du verlorener Gott! Du unendliche Spur!
Nur weil dich reißend zuletzt die Feindschaft verteilte,
sind wir die Hörenden jetzt und ein Mund der Natur.

But you, divine one, intoning to the very end,
when swarmed by the horde of spurned maenads
you drowned their cries with order, sublime one,
up from that mayhem rose your transforming song.

None there could harm your head or lyre,
however they raged and wrestled; all the rough
stones they threw at your heart became soft
when they touched you, and blessed with hearing.

At last, mad for vengeance, they ripped you apart,
but your sound lingered on in lions and rocks
and in the trees and birds. You sing there still.

O you lost god! You neverending trace!
Only because hatred tore and scattered you
are we *hearers* now and a mouth for nature.

Zweiter Teil

Second Part

I

Atmen, du unsichtbares Gedicht!
Immerfort um das eigne
Sein rein eingetauschter Weltraum. Gegengewicht,
in dem ich mich rhythmisch ereigne.

Einzige Welle, deren
allmähliches Meer ich bin;
sparsamstes du von allen möglichen Meeren, —
Raumgewinn.

Wieviele von diesen Stellen der Räume waren schon
innen in mir. Manche Winde
sind wie mein Sohn.

Erkennst du mich, Luft, du, voll noch einst meiniger Orte?
Du, einmal glatte Rinde,
Rundung und Blatt meiner Worte.

Breathing, you invisible poem!
Worldspace in pure continuous interchange
with my own being. Equipoise
in which I rhythmically transpire.

Single wave
whose gradual sea I am;
of all possible seas the most frugal, —
windfall of space.

How many of these places in space were once
in me. Many a breeze
is like my son.

Do you recognize me, air, you, full of places once mine?
You, once the smooth rind,
orb, and leaf of my words.

So wie dem Meister manchmal das eilig
nähere Blatt den *wirklichen* Strich
abnimmt: so nehmen oft Spiegel das heilig
einzige Lächeln der Mädchen in sich,

wenn sie den Morgen erproben, allein, —
oder im Glanze der dienenden Lichter.
Und in das Atmen der echten Gesichter,
später, fällt nur ein Widerschein.

Was haben Augen einst ins umrußte
lange Verglühn der Kamine geschaut:
Blicke des Lebens, für immer verlorne.

Ach, der Erde, wer kennt die Verluste?
Nur, wer mit dennoch preisendem Laut
sänge das Herz, das ins Ganze geborne.

Just as the master's *true* stroke is sometimes
caught by a nearby page that's quickly
seized; so mirrors often take into themselves
that one sacred smile of girls

as they assay the early morning, all alone, —
or in the glimmer of attendant lights.
And later, into the breath of their actual
faces, only a reflection falls.

Those eyes that stare into the charred,
slowly dying glow of hearths: what issues from them?
Life-glimpses, gone forever.

Ah, Earth—who knows her losses?
Only one who, with tones that nonetheless praise,
sings the heart born into the Whole.

Spiegel: noch nie hat man wissend beschrieben,
was ihr in euerem Wesen seid.
Ihr, wie mit lauter Löchern von Sieben
erfüllten Zwischenräume der Zeit.

Ihr, noch des leeren Saales Verschwender—,
wenn es dämmert, wie Wälder weit . . .
Und der Lüster geht wie ein Sechzehn-Ender
durch eure Unbetretbarkeit.

Manchmal seid ihr voll Malerei.
Einige scheinen *in* euch gegangen—,
andere schicktet ihr scheu vorbei.

Aber die Schönste wird bleiben—, bis
drüben in ihre enthaltenen Wangen
eindrang der klare gelöste Narziß.

3

Mirrors: no one who's tried to solve you
has yet unlocked your true being.
You, openings in time, its course filled
as if with endless sieve holes.

You, perpetual spendthrifts of the empty hall—,
when dusk approaches, deep as woods . . .
And there the chandelier, like a sixteen-pointer,
leaps your unbreachable divide.

Sometimes you are full of painting.
A few seem to have passed *into* you—,
others you shyly sent away.

But the one loveliest woman will remain
before you,—till across into her untouched cheeks
the clear released Narcissus penetrates.

sixteen-pointer: A large stag, with sixteen points or branches on its antlers.

O dieses ist das Tier, das es nicht giebt.
Sie wußtens nicht und habens jeden Falls
—sein Wandeln, seine Haltung, seinen Hals,
bis in des stillen Blickes Licht—geliebt.

Zwar *war* es nicht. Doch weil sie's liebten, ward
ein reines Tier. Sie ließen immer Raum.
Und in dem Raume, klar und ausgespart,
erhob es leicht sein Haupt und brauchte kaum

zu sein. Sie nährten es mit keinem Korn,
nur immer mit der Möglichkeit, es sei.
Und die gab solche Stärke an das Tier,

daß es aus sich ein Stirnhorn trieb. Ein Horn.
Zu einer Jungfrau kam es weiß herbei—
und war im Silber-Spiegel und in ihr.

4

O this is the animal that does not exist.
But they didn't know that, and, in any case,
they loved it—loved its gait, its stance,
its neck, loved the light in its quiet gaze.

It never *was*. But since they loved it,
a pure animal *became*. They always left space.
And in that space, unoccupied and bright,
it calmly raised its head and scarcely needed

to exist. They fed it not with grain, —
only with the promise of its being.
And this gave the animal such power

that a horn sprouted from its brow. One horn.
White, it strode up to a virgin—and *was*,
in the mirror's silver and in her.

Blumenmuskel, der der Anemone
Wiesenmorgen nach und nach erschließt,
bis in ihren Schooß das polyphone
Licht der lauten Himmel sich ergießt,

in den stillen Blütenstern gespannter
Muskel des unendlichen Empfangs,
manchmal *so* von Fülle übermannter,
daß der Ruhewink des Untergangs

kaum vermag die weitzurückgeschnellten
Blätterränder dir zurückzugeben:
du, Entschluß und Kraft von *wie*viel Welten!

Wir Gewaltsamen, wir währen länger.
Aber *wann*, in welchem aller Leben,
sind wir endlich offen und Empfänger?

5

Flower-muscle, slowly pulling open
the anemone's vast meadow morning,
until the loud sky's polyphonic light
comes pouring down into its womb,

muscle of infinite reception
flexed in the quiet flower star,
sometimes *so* overwhelmed by fullness
that the sunset's call to rest

is scarcely able to give you back
the wide-sprung petal edges: you,
resolve and strength of *how* many worlds!

We violent ones, we last longer.
But *when*, in which of all these lives,
are we finally open and receivers?

Rose, du thronende, denen im Altertume
warst du ein Kelch mit einfachem Rand.
Uns aber bist du die volle zahllose Blume,
der unerschöpfliche Gegenstand.

In deinem Reichtum scheinst du wie Kleidung um Kleidung
um einen Leib aus nichts als Glanz;
aber dein einzelnes Blatt ist zugleich die Vermeidung
und die Verleugnung jedes Gewands.

Seit Jahrhunderten ruft uns dein Duft
seine süßesten Namen herüber;
plötzlich liegt er wie Ruhm in der Luft.

Dennoch, wir wissen ihn nicht zu nennen, wir raten . . .
Und Erinnerung geht zu ihm über,
die wir von rufbaren Stunden erbaten.

Rose, enthroned there, for the ancients
you were a cup with a simple rim.
But for *us* you are the full multifaceted flower,
the inexhaustible object.

In your opulence you are like garment on garment
round a body made of only light;
yet each single petal is at once the shunning
and the denial of all attire.

For centuries your fragrance has called
its sweetest names across to us;
suddenly it floats in the air like fame.

Still, we can't find the word, we grope . . .
And memory betrays us, goes over
with all we've begged from the responding hours.

Blumen, ihr schließlich den ordnenden Händen verwandte,
(Händen der Mädchen von einst und jetzt),
die auf dem Gartentisch oft von Kante zu Kante
lagen, ermattet und sanft verletzt,

wartend des Wassers, das sie noch einmal erhole
aus dem begonnenen Tod—, und nun
wieder erhobene zwischen die strömenden Pole
fühlender Finger, die wohlzutun

mehr noch vermögen, als ihr ahntet, ihr leichten,
wenn ihr euch wiederfandet im Krug,
langsam erkühlend und Warmes der Mädchen, wie Beichten,

von euch gebend, wie trübe ermüdende Sünden,
die das Gepflückstein beging, als Bezug
wieder zu ihnen, die sich euch blühend verbünden.

You flowers, akin, finally, to the arranging hands
(girls' hands from times before and now),
laid out on the garden table, often end to end,
your strength ebbing, gently wounded,

waiting for the water that might retrieve you
from an encroaching death——, and now
raised up again between the vivifying poles
of feeling fingers, which minister

more potently than you had dreamt, light ones,
as you find yourselves suddenly in the vase,
slowly cooling, and giving off warmth of girls

like confessions, like sad fatiguing sins
incurred in being plucked, and relating you
again to those whose fate, like yours, is blooming.

Wenige ihr, der einstigen Kindheit Gespielen
in den zerstreuten Gärten der Stadt:
wie wir uns fanden und uns zögernd gefielen
und, wie das Lamm mit dem redenden Blatt,

sprachen als Schweigende. Wenn wir uns einmal freuten,
keinem gehörte es. Wessen wars?
Und wie zergings unter allen den gehenden Leuten
und im Bangen des langen Jahrs.

Wagen umrollten uns fremd, vorübergezogen,
Häuser umstanden uns stark, aber unwahr, —und keines
kannte uns je. *Was* war wirklich im All?

Nichts. Nur die Bälle. Ihre herrlichen Bogen.
Auch nicht die Kinder . . . Aber manchmal trat eines,
ach ein vergehendes, unter den fallenden Ball.

(In memoriam Egon von Rilke)

8

O you few, playmates of a former childhood
in the scattered gardens of the city:
how we found each other and slowly grew close
and, like the lamb with the talking scroll,

spoke with our silence. When together we felt happiness,
it belonged to none of us. Whose was it?
And how it seeped away amid the rushing people,
and in the worries of the long year.

Carriages rolled past us, strange and transient,
houses stood around us, strong but false, —and none of it
ever acknowledged us. What in all that was real?

Nothing. Only the balls. Their glorious arcs.
Not even the children . . . But sometimes one stepped—
oh one vanishing—under the plummeting orb.

(In memoriam Egon von Rilke)

the lamb with the talking scroll: "The lamb (in medieval paintings) which speaks only by means of a scroll with an inscription on it." —Rilke's handwritten note.
Dedication, *In memoriam Egon von Rilke*: The poet's cousin, who died while still a child. He is also commemorated in "The Fourth Elegy" and *The Notebooks of Malte Laurids Brigge*.

Rühmt euch, ihr Richtenden, nicht der entbehrlichen Folter
und daß das Eisen nicht länger an Hälsen sperrt.
Keins ist gesteigert, kein Herz—, weil ein gewollter
Krampf der Milde euch zarter verzerrt.

Was es durch Zeiten bekam, das schenkt das Schafott
wieder zurück, wie Kinder ihr Spielzeug vom vorig
alten Geburtstag. Ins reine, ins hohe, ins thorig
offene Herz träte er anders, der Gott

wirklicher Milde. Er käme gewaltig und griffe
strahlender um sich, wie Göttliche sind.
Mehr als ein Wind für die großen gesicherten Schiffe.

Weniger nicht, als die heimliche leise Gewahrung,
die uns im Innern schweigend gewinnt
wie ein still spielendes Kind aus unendlicher Paarung.

9

Don't boast, you men of justice, that the rack is obsolescent
and that iron no longer shackles necks.
No heart's been lightened, not one—, because a willed
spasm of mercy wrenches you more tenderly.

What it's received through the ages, the scaffold
gives back—the way children treat their toys
from past birthdays. Into the pure, the high,
the gatelike open heart, the god of true mercy

would step differently. Gigantic he'd come,
cutting swaths of radiance, as is the wont of gods.
More than a wind for the great confident ships.

Not less than the secret subtle consciousness
that wins us silently inside
like the quietly playing child of an infinite pairing.

Alles Erworbne bedroht die Maschine, solange
sie sich erdreistet, im Geist, statt im Gehorchen, zu sein.
Daß nicht der herrlichen Hand schöneres Zögern mehr prange,
zu dem entschlossenern Bau schneidet sie steifer den Stein.

Nirgends bleibt sie zurück, daß wir ihr *ein* Mal entrönnen
und sie in stiller Fabrik ölend sich selber gehört.
Sie ist das Leben, —sie meint es am besten zu können,
die mit dem gleichen Entschluß ordnet und schafft und zerstört.

Aber noch ist uns das Dasein verzaubert; an hundert
Stellen ist es noch Ursprung. Ein Spielen von reinen
Kräften, die keiner berührt, der nicht kniet und bewundert.

Worte gehen noch zart am Unsäglichen aus . . .
Und die Musik, immer neu, aus den bebendsten Steinen,
baut im unbrauchbaren Raum ihr vergöttlichtes Haus.

All that we've gained the machine threatens, as long
as it dares to exist as Idea, not obedient tool.
To inure us to the hand's more masterful lingerings,
it cuts for rigid buildings starker stone.

Nowhere does it idle, it gives us *no* chance to flee
and leave it self-lubricating in silent factories.
It is life, —believes *it* does everything best,
making, arranging, destroying, all the same.

But for us existence still can enchant; in a hundred
places it's still Origin. A play of pure forces,
which no one touches without kneeling in awe.

Words still softly give way before the unsayable . . .
And music, forever new, out of the most tremulous stones
builds in unusable space her house fit for gods.

Manche, des Todes, entstand ruhig geordnete Regel,
weiterbezwingender Mensch, seit du im Jagen beharrst;
mehr doch als Falle und Netz, weiß ich dich, Streifen von Segel,
den man hinuntergehängt in den höhligen Karst.

Leise ließ man dich ein, als wärst du ein Zeichen,
Frieden zu feiern. Doch dann: rang dich am Rande der Knecht,
—und, aus den Höhlen, die Nacht warf eine Handvoll von bleichen
taumelnden Tauben ins Licht . . .
 Aber auch *das* ist im Recht.

Fern von dem Schauenden sei jeglicher Hauch des Bedauerns,
nicht nur vom Jäger allein, der, was sich zeitig erweist,
wachsam und handelnd vollzieht.

Töten ist eine Gestalt unseres wandernden Trauerns . . .
Rein ist im heiteren Geist,
was an uns selber geschieht.

Many calmly weighed rules entered Death's canon
as we, creatures of conquest, pursued hunting;
more, though, than trap and net, I remember *you*, strip of sail,
which they would hang down into the caverns of Karst.

Gently they lowered you, as though you were a banner
signaling peace. But then: the boy flicked and twisted you,
—and, out of the caves, Darkness cast a handful of pale
tumbling pigeons into the light . . .

 But even *this* is just.

Let every breath of pity be as far from witness
as hunter, —who, when the moment comes,
is quick to do what he does.

Killing is one form of our wandering sorrow . . .
At the serene core
all that befalls us is pure.

"Refers to the way in which, according to an ancient hunting custom in certain regions of
Karst, the strangely pale grotto doves are killed. Hunters carefully lower large pieces of cloth
into the caverns and then suddenly shake them in a special way. The doves, startled out of their
subterranean abodes, are shot during their terrified escape." —Rilke's note.
Karst: A region along the Dalmatian coast known for its limestone caverns.

Wolle die Wandlung. O sei für die Flamme begeistert,
drin sich ein Ding dir entzieht, das mit Verwandlungen prunkt;
jener entwerfende Geist, welcher das Irdische meistert,
liebt in dem Schwung der Figur nichts wie den wendenden Punkt.

Was sich ins Bleiben verschließt, schon *ists* das Erstarrte;
wähnt es sich sicher im Schutz des unscheinbaren Grau's?
Warte, ein Härtestes warnt aus der Ferne das Harte.
Wehe—: abwesender Hammer holt aus!

Wer sich als Quelle ergießt, den erkennt die Erkennung;
und sie führt ihn entzückt durch das heiter Geschaffne,
das mit Anfang oft schließt und mit Ende beginnt.

Jeder glückliche Raum ist Kind oder Enkel von Trennung,
den sie staunend durchgehn. Und die verwandelte Daphne
will, seit sie lorbeern fühlt, daß du dich wandelst in Wind.

Will transformation. O be ravenous for the fire
in which a thing boastful with change forever eludes you;
that designing Spirit which plots earth's flourishes,—
it loves most in the figure's élan the moment of turning.

What shackles itself in survival already *is* rigidity;
does it feel itself safe in the shelter of nondescript gray?
Beware, from afar the hardest is warning the hard.
And woe—: an absent hammer is lifting!

Whoever pours forth as wellspring, Recognition greets;
and she guides him enthralled through the serene Creation
that often ends with beginning and in ending begins.

Every happy space through which they walk marveling
is child or grandchild of Separation. And the transformed Daphne,
feeling so laurel-like, wants *you* to change into wind.

Daphne: A nymph pursued by Apollo and transformed into a laurel tree.

Sei allem Abschied voran, als wäre er hinter
dir, wie der Winter, der eben geht.
Denn unter Wintern ist einer so endlos Winter,
daß, überwinternd, dein Herz überhaupt übersteht.

Sei immer tot in Eurydike—, singender steige,
preisender steige zurück in den reinen Bezug.
Hier, unter Schwindenden, sei, im Reiche der Neige,
sei ein klingendes Glas, das sich im Klang schon zerschlug.

Sei—und wisse zugleich des Nicht-Seins Bedingung,
den unendlichen Grund deiner innigen Schwingung,
daß du sie völlig vollziehst dieses einzige Mal.

Zu dem gebrauchten sowohl, wie zum dumpfen und stummen
Vorrat der vollen Natur, den unsäglichen Summen,
zähle dich jubelnd hinzu und vernichte die Zahl.

Be in advance of all parting, as if it were
behind you like the winter just now going by.
For among winters there's one so endlessly winter
that, wintering, your heart will win through.

Be forever dead in Eurydice——, and climb more singingly,
climb more praisingly, back into the pure relation.
Here, among the vanishing, *be*, in the realm of decline
be a ringing glass that shatters even as it rings.

Be——and know as well the terms of nonbeing,
the infinite ground of your inmost vibration,
so that, this once, you may wholly fulfill them.

To the used, as well as the mute and muffled
stock of nature's fullness, to the inexpressible sums,
add yourself jubilantly, and nullify the score.

Siehe die Blumen, diese dem Irdischen treuen,
denen wir Schicksal vom Rande des Schicksals leihn, —
aber wer weiß es! Wenn sie ihr Welken bereuen,
ist es an uns, ihre Reue zu sein.

Alles will schweben. Da gehn wir umher wie Beschwerer,
legen auf alles uns selbst, vom Gewichte entzückt;
o was sind wir den Dingen für zehrende Lehrer,
weil ihnen ewige Kindheit glückt.

Nähme sie einer ins innige Schlafen und schliefe
tief mit den Dingen—: o wie käme er leicht,
anders zum anderen Tag, aus der gemeinsamen Tiefe.

Oder er bliebe vielleicht; und sie blühten und priesen
ihn, den Bekehrten, der nun den Ihrigen gleicht,
allen den stillen Geschwistern im Winde der Wiesen.

Behold the flowers, those true to the earthly,
to whom we lend fate from the edge of fate, —
Yet who can say? If they regret their fading,
it is for us to *be* their regret.

Everything wants to float. And yet we move about like weights,
attaching ourselves to everything, in thrall to gravity;
O what wearisome teachers we are for things,
while in them eternal childhood prospers.

If someone were to take them into his inmost sleep
and sleep deeply with them—: O how light he'd emerge,
changed, to a changed day, from the mutual depth.

Or perhaps he'd stay; and they'd bloom and praise him,
the convert, become now like one of their own,
all the quiet brothers and sisters in the meadow's wind.

O Brunnen-Mund, du gebender, du Mund,
der unerschöpflich Eines, Reines, spricht, —
du, vor des Wassers fließendem Gesicht,
marmorne Maske. Und im Hintergrund

der Aquädukte Herkunft. Weither an
Gräbern vorbei, vom Hang des Apennins
tragen sie dir dein Sagen zu, das dann
am schwarzen Altern deines Kinns

vorüberfällt in das Gefäß davor.
Dies ist das schlafend hingelegte Ohr,
das Marmorohr, in das du immer sprichst.

Ein Ohr der Erde. Nur mit sich allein
redet sie also. Schiebt ein Krug sich ein,
so scheint es ihr, daß du sie unterbrichst.

O fountain mouth, you giving one, you lips
speaking inexhaustibly one single, one clear thing, —
you marble mask held up before the water's
flowing face. And in the background

origin of aqueducts. From far away,
past graves, down from the Apennine slopes
they bring you the stream of your saying,
which spills past your blackened, aging chin

into the basin opened there before it.
This is the close and sleeping ear,
the marble ear in which you always speak.

An ear of Earth. So that she's talking
with herself alone. Slip a pitcher in,
she'll think you're interrupting.

Immer wieder von uns aufgerissen,
ist der Gott die Stelle, welche heilt.
Wir sind Scharfe, denn wir wollen wissen,
aber er ist heiter und verteilt.

Selbst die reine, die geweihte Spende
nimmt er anders nicht in seine Welt,
als indem er sich dem freien Ende
unbewegt entgegenstellt.

Nur der Tote trinkt
aus der hier von uns *gehörten* Quelle,
wenn der Gott ihm schweigend winkt, dem Toten.

Uns wird nur das Lärmen angeboten.
Und das Lamm erbittet seine Schelle
aus dem stilleren Instinkt.

Torn open by us again and again,
the god is the place that heals.
We're jagged, because we want to know,
but he is scattered and serene.

Even the pure, the consecrated gift
he takes into his world no other way
than this: standing unmoved
opposite the open end.

Only the dead drink
from the spring *heard* here by us, —
when the god signals to them silently, the dead.

To *us* just the noise is given.
And out of quieter instinct
the lamb begs for its bell.

Wo, in welchen immer selig bewässerten Gärten, an welchen
Bäumen, aus welchen zärtlich entblätterten Blüten-Kelchen
reifen die fremdartigen Früchte der Tröstung? Diese
köstlichen, deren du eine vielleicht in der zertretenen Wiese

deiner Armut findest. Von einem zum anderen Male
wunderst du dich über die Größe der Frucht,
über ihr Heilsein, über die Sanftheit der Schale,
und daß sie der Leichtsinn des Vogels dir nicht vorwegnahm und nicht die
 Eifersucht

unten des Wurms. Giebt es denn Bäume, von Engeln beflogen,
und von verborgenen langsamen Gärtnern so seltsam gezogen,
daß sie uns tragen, ohne uns zu gehören?

Haben wir niemals vermocht, wir Schatten und Schemen,
durch unser voreilig reifes und wieder welkes Benehmen
jener gelassenen Sommer Gleichmut zu stören?

Where, in what ever-blissfully watered gardens, on what
branches, out of what tenderly un-petaled flower cups,
do the exotic fruits of consolation ripen? These exquisite
fruits, which sometimes lie there in the trampled

meadow of your losses. Each time you come upon one,
you marvel at the size of the fruit, at its perfect fullness,
at the tenderness of its skin, at how it has escaped
the wantonness of the bird and the jealousy

of the worm below. Are there trees, then, visited by angels,
and so strangely tended by slow occult gardeners
that they bear for us without being ours?

Have we never been able, we shadows and phantoms,
as we go on prematurely ripening and then withering again,
to disturb the equanimity of these serene summers?

Tänzerin: o du Verlegung
alles Vergehens in Gang: wie brachtest du's dar.
Und der Wirbel am Schluß, dieser Baum aus Bewegung,
nahm er nicht ganz in Besitz das erschwungene Jahr?

Blühte nicht, daß ihn dein Schwingen von vorhin umschwärme,
plötzlich sein Wipfel von Stille? Und über ihr,
war sie nicht Sonne, war sie nicht Sommer, die Wärme,
diese unzählige Wärme aus dir?

Aber er trug auch, er trug, dein Baum der Ekstase.
Sind sie nicht seine ruhigen Früchte: der Krug,
reifend gestreift, und die gereiftere Vase?

Und in den Bildern: ist nicht die Zeichnung geblieben,
die deiner Braue dunkler Zug
rasch an die Wandung der eigenen Wendung geschrieben?

O dancer: your steps translating
all vanishing into act: what lines they traced!
and the final spin, that tree of motion,
did it not whirl into itself the fleeting year?

Did it not put forth its crown of stillness—so that
your earlier figures might swarm within it? And up above
was it not summer, was it not sun—all that heat
from you, that measureless radiant warmth?

But it bore too, it bore, your tree of ecstasy.
Are not these its quiet fruits: the jug,
with its ripening stripes, and the fully ripened vase?

And in the pictures: does not the drawing remain,
those dark strokes of your eyebrows
sketched swiftly on the wall of their turning?

Irgendwo wohnt das Gold in der verwöhnenden Bank
und mit Tausenden tut es vertraulich. Doch jener
Blinde, der Bettler, ist selbst dem kupfernen Zehner
wie ein verlorener Ort, wie das staubige Eck unterm Schrank.

In den Geschäften entlang ist das Geld wie zuhause
und verkleidet sich scheinbar in Seide, Nelken und Pelz.
Er, der Schweigende, steht in der Atempause
alles des wach oder schlafend atmenden Gelds.

O wie mag sie sich schließen bei Nacht, diese immer offene Hand.
Morgen holt sie das Schicksal wieder, und täglich
hält es sie hin: hell, elend, unendlich zerstörbar.

Daß doch einer, ein Schauender, endlich ihren langen Bestand
staunend begriffe und rühmte. Nur dem Aufsingenden säglich.
Nur dem Göttlichen hörbar.

Somewhere gold dwells in an indulgent bank
and is intimate with thousands. But to the copper coin
the blind man, that beggar standing there, is like
a lost place, like the dusty corner behind the cupboard.

All along the shops money feels at home,
and parades by dressed in silk, carnations, furs.
He, the silent one, stands in the pauses
money's breathing makes, sleeping or awake.

O how does it close at night, that ever open hand?
Tomorrow morning Fate will fetch it again and hold it out,
day after day: bright, wretched, endlessly fragile.

Till finally some astonished onlooker understands
and praises its long endurance. Sayable only by the singer.
Audible only by the god.

Zwischen den Sternen, wie weit; und doch, um wievieles noch weiter,
was man am Hiesigen lernt.
Einer, zum Beispiel, ein Kind . . . und ein Nächster, ein Zweiter—,
o wie unfaßlich entfernt.

Schicksal, es mißt uns vielleicht mit des Seienden Spanne,
daß es uns fremd erscheint;
denk, wieviel Spannen allein vom Mädchen zum Manne,
wenn es ihn meidet und meint.

Alles ist weit—, und nirgends schließt sich der Kreis.
Sieh in der Schüssel, auf heiter bereitetem Tische,
seltsam der Fische Gesicht.

Fische sind stumm . . . , meinte man einmal. Wer weiß?
Aber ist nicht am Ende ein Ort, wo man das, was der Fische
Sprache wäre, *ohne* sie spricht?

Between the stars, such distances; and yet how much vaster
are the distances we learn of here.
Take a child . . . and next to him, place another—,
O how ineffably far.

Could it be that Fate measures us in spans of being,
and *hence* seems to us so alien?
Think how many such spans stretch from a woman
to the man she longs for and avoids.

All is distance—, and nowhere does the circle close.
See the plate on the gaily laid table:
those fish, their strange expressions.

Fish are mute . . . , one used to think. Who knows?
But is there not finally a place where what fish language
would be is spoken *without* them?

Singe die Gärten, mein Herz, die du nicht kennst; wie in Glas
eingegossene Gärten, klar, unerreichbar.
Wasser und Rosen von Ispahan oder Schiras,
singe sie selig, preise sie, keinem vergleichbar.

Zeige, mein Herz, daß du sie niemals entbehrst.
Daß sie dich meinen, ihre reifenden Feigen.
Daß du mit ihren, zwischen den blühenden Zweigen
wie zum Gesicht gesteigerten Lüften verkehrst.

Meide den Irrtum, daß es Entbehrungen gebe
für den geschehnen Entschluß, diesen: zu sein!
Seidener Faden, kamst du hinein ins Gewebe.

Welchem der Bilder du auch im Innern geeint bist
(sei es selbst ein Moment aus dem Leben der Pein),
fühl, daß der ganze, der rühmliche Teppich gemeint ist.

Sing the gardens, my heart, those you never knew; gardens
as if poured into glass: bright, unattainable.
Waters and roses of Isfahan or Shiraz,
sing them blissfully, praise them, beyond compare.

Show, my heart, that you *aren't* without them.
That when their figs ripen, they have *you* in mind.
That when their winds grow almost visible
amid the flowering branches, it's *you* they embrace.

Avoid this error: that so many chances die
when the one choice is made: to be!
Silk thread, you were drawn into the fabric.

Whatever single image you made yourself part of
(be it even a scene from a life of torment),
feel how the whole carpet is meant, its glorious weave.

O trotz Schicksal: die herrlichen Überflüsse
unseres Daseins, in Parken übergeschäumt, —
oder als steinerne Männer neben die Schlüsse
hoher Portale, unter Balkone gebäumt!

O die eherne Glocke, die ihre Keule
täglich wider den stumpfen Alltag hebt.
Oder die *eine*, in Karnak, die Säule, die Säule,
die fast ewige Tempel überlebt.

Heute stürzen die Überschüsse, dieselben,
nur noch als Eile vorbei, aus dem waagrechten gelben
Tag in die blendend mit Licht übertriebene Nacht.

Aber das Rasen zergeht und läßt keine Spuren.
Kurven des Flugs durch die Luft und die, die sie fuhren,
keine vielleicht ist umsonst. Doch nur wie gedacht.

O in spite of Fate: the magnificent overflows
of our existence, spilling over into parks, —
or taking shape as stone men shouldering
tall portals, rearing up under balconies!

O the bronze bell, that daily lifts its cudgel
against the dull quotidian.
Or at Karnak that *one* column, that column
outliving temples almost eternal.

Today the abundances plunge by, the same ones,
but only as haste, out of the horizontal
yellow day into the dazzlingly exaggerated night.

But the frenzy passes and leaves no trace.
Arcs of flight through the air and those who made them:
perhaps all live on. But only as thought.

Karnak: A site of ancient ruins in Egypt, which Rilke visited in early 1911: "This inconceivable temple-world of Karnak, at which, on the very first evening, and again yesterday, in the moon just starting to wane, I gazed, gazed, gazed,—my God, one gathers oneself, looks with all one's power of belief through both totally focused eyes—and yet it begins beyond them, stretches everywhere far beyond them (only a god can command such a field of view)—and there stands a lotus-bud column, solitary, surviving, and one cannot grasp it, so purely does it stand there, out beyond one's life . . ." (letter to Clara Rilke, January 18, 1911).

Rufe mich zu jener deiner Stunden,
die dir unaufhörlich widersteht:
flehend nah wie das Gesicht von Hunden,
aber immer wieder weggedreht,

wenn du meinst, sie endlich zu erfassen.
so Entzognes ist am meisten dein.
Wir sind frei. Wir wurden dort entlassen,
wo wir meinten, erst begrüßt zu sein.

Bang verlangen wir nach einem Halte,
wir zu Jungen manchmal für das Alte
und zu alt für das, was niemals war.

Wir, gerecht nur, wo wir dennoch preisen,
weil wir, ach, der Ast sind und das Eisen
und das Süße reifender Gefahr.

Call me to that one among your hours
that incessantly resists you:
beseechingly near like a dog's face,
yet ever again turned away

just when you think to grasp it.
What's thus withdrawn is most your own.
We are free. We were dismissed
at the very place where we expected welcome.

Afraid, we yearn for some handhold,
often too young for what's ancient
and too old for what has never been.

And yet: only *just* when we praise,
since, ah, we are the branch and the axe
and the nectar of ripening risk.

O diese Lust, immer neu, aus gelockertem Lehm!
Niemand beinah hat den frühesten Wagern geholfen.
Städte entstanden trotzdem an beseligten Golfen,
Wasser und Öl füllten die Krüge trotzdem.

Götter, wir planen sie erst in erkühnten Entwürfen,
die uns das mürrische Schicksal wieder zerstört.
Aber sie sind die Unsterblichen. Sehet, wir dürfen
jenen erhorchen, der uns am Ende erhört.

Wir, ein Geschlecht durch Jahrtausende: Mütter und Väter,
immer erfüllter von dem künftigen Kind,
daß es uns einst, übersteigend, erschüttere, später.

Wir, wir unendlich Gewagten, was haben wir Zeit!
Und nur der schweigsame Tod, der weiß, was wir sind
und was er immer gewinnt, wenn er uns leiht.

O this delight, ever new, born of loosened clay!
The first to venture had almost no one's help.
Nevertheless, cities sprang up by blissful harbors,
water and oil filled the jugs.

Gods—we plot them first in emboldened sketches,
which Fate then sullenly destroys.
Yet they are the Immortals. Should we not heed them,
since in the end they will hear us?

We, a race thousands of years old, mothers and fathers
ever more pregnant with the future child
destined to surpass us and then destroy us.

We, the endlessly ventured, what time we have!
And only close-lipped Death knows what we really are,
and how he always profits when he lends us out.

Schon, horch, hörst du der ersten Harken
Arbeit; wieder den menschlichen Takt
in der verhaltenen Stille der starken
Vorfrühlingserde. Unabgeschmackt

scheint dir das Kommende. Jenes so oft
dir schon Gekommene scheint dir zu kommen
wieder wie Neues. Immer erhofft,
nahmst du es niemals. Es hat dich genommen.

Selbst die Blätter durchwinterter Eichen
scheinen im Abend ein künftiges Braun.
Manchmal geben sich Lüfte ein Zeichen.

Schwarz sind die Sträucher. Doch Haufen von Dünger
lagern als satteres Schwarz in den Aun.
Jede Stunde, die hingeht, wird jünger.

2 5

Listen: already you can hear the first hoes
working: the human rhythm again
in the taut stillness of the hard
pre-vernal earth. What's fast approaching

seems not stale to you. What has come
to you so often seems coming now
as something new. Always poised for it,
you never seized it. It seized you.

In the light of dusk even the leaves
of wintered oaks appear a future brown.
Sometimes the winds exchange a sign.

The shrubs are black. But heaps of dung
lie scattered in the fields, a richer black.
Each passing hour grows younger.

Wie ergreift uns der Vogelschrei . . .
Irgend ein einmal erschaffenes Schreien.
Aber die Kinder schon, spielend im Freien,
schreien an wirklichen Schreien vorbei.

Schreien den Zufall. In Zwischenräume
dieses, des Weltraums, (in welchen der heile
Vogelschrei eingeht, wie Menschen in Träume—)
treiben sie ihre, des Kreischens, Keile.

Wehe, wo sind wir? Immer noch freier,
wie die losgerissenen Drachen
jagen wir halbhoch, mit Rändern von Lachen,

windig zerfetzten. —Ordne die Schreier,
singender Gott! daß sie rauschend erwachen,
tragend als Strömung das Haupt und die Leier.

How the cry of a bird can move us . . .
Any shaped, created cry.
But children, playing out in the open,
cry beyond real cries.

Cry hazard. Into the narrow crevices
of this worldspace (through which the uncaught
bird cry slips, the way we enter dreams—)
they drive their shrieking's wedges.

Alas, where are we? Drifting freer and freer,
like kites torn loose from their strings
we lurch about in midair, frayed by laughter,

ripped by winds. —Oh array the criers,
singing god! Let them awake as a roaring,
one deep current carrying head and lyre.

Giebt es wirklich die Zeit, die zerstörende?
Wann, auf dem ruhenden Berg, zerbricht sie die Burg?
Dieses Herz, das unendlich den Göttern gehörende,
wann vergewaltigts der Demiurg?

Sind wir wirklich so ängstlich Zerbrechliche,
wie das Schicksal uns wahr machen will?
Ist die Kindheit, die tiefe, versprechliche,
in den Wurzeln—später—still?

Ach, das Gespenst des Vergänglichen,
durch den arglos Empfänglichen
geht es, als wär es ein Rauch.

Als die, die wir sind, als die Treibenden,
gelten wir doch bei bleibenden
Kräften als göttlicher Brauch.

Does it really exist, Time the Destroyer?
When, on the peaceful mountain, does it crush the fortress?
And this heart, always the gods' possession,
when does the Demiurge pillage it?

Are we really so anxiously brittle
as Fate would have us believe?
Is childhood, so deep, so rich with promise,
in the roots—later on—stilled?

Ah, the spectre of transience,
through the guilelessly receptive
it passes like wisps of smoke.

And we, with our driving, our striving, —
the abiding Strengths assume
that the gods have some need for us.

Demiurge: In Gnostic tradition, a lower deity who created the world of time.

O komm und geh. Du, fast noch Kind, ergänze
für einen Augenblick die Tanzfigur
zum reinen Sternbild eines jener Tänze,
darin wir die dumpf ordnende Natur

vergänglich übertreffen. Denn sie regte
sich völlig hörend nur, da Orpheus sang.
Du warst noch die von damals her Bewegte
und leicht befremdet, wenn ein Baum sich lang

besann, mit dir nach dem Gehör zu gehn.
Du wußtest noch die Stelle, wo die Leier
sich tönend hob—; die unerhörte Mitte.

Für sie versuchtest du die schönen Schritte
und hofftest, einmal zu der heilen Feier
des Freundes Gang und Antlitz hinzudrehn.

O come and go. You, still almost a child,
with your spell transform for an instant
the dance figure, make it one of those pure
constellations in which we fleetingly

transcend dull ordering Nature. For she was roused
to full hearing only when Orpheus sang.
You were still swayed by those ancient chords
and a bit annoyed if a tree took stock

before it followed where your hearing led.
You still knew the place where the lyre
rose resounding——: the undreamt-of center.

For it you practiced those beautiful steps
and hoped one day to turn toward
pure happiness your friend's face and stride.

Stiller Freund der vielen Fernen, fühle,
wie dein Atem noch den Raum vermehrt.
Im Gebälk der finstern Glockenstühle
laß dich läuten. Das, was an dir zehrt,

wird ein Starkes über dieser Nahrung.
Geh in der Verwandlung aus und ein.
Was ist deine leidendste Erfahrung?
Ist dir Trinken bitter, werde Wein.

Sei in dieser Nacht aus Übermaß
Zauberkraft am Kreuzweg deiner Sinne,
ihrer seltsamen Begegnung Sinn.

Und wenn dich das Irdische vergaß,
zu der stillen Erde sag: Ich rinne.
Zu dem raschen Wasser sprich: Ich bin.

Silent friend of the many distances,
feel how your every breath enlarges space.
Amid the rafters of dark belfries
let yourself peal. Whatever feeds on you

is taking strength from such fare.
Know every path through transformation.
What one memory holds your deepest grief?
If you find drinking bitter, become wine.

Now in this night of fire and excess
be magic power at your senses' crossroads,
the meaning of their strange encounter.

And if the earthly should forget you,
say to the silent loam: I flow.
To the rushing water speak: I am.

UNCOLLECTED POEMS *(1909–1926)*

Vergiß, vergiß und laß uns jetzt nur dies
erleben, wie die Sterne durch geklärten
Nachthimmel dringen; wie der Mond die Gärten
voll übersteigt. Wir fühlten längst schon, wies
spiegelnder wird im Dunkel; wie ein Schein
entsteht, ein weißer Schatten in dem Glanz
der Dunkelheit. Nun aber laß uns ganz
hinübertreten in die Welt hinein
die monden ist—

∾

Forget, forget, and let us live now
only this: how the stars pierce the cleared
nocturnal sky; how the moon's full disk
surmounts the gardens. We've sensed so long
how the darkness breeds many mirrors; how a gleam
takes shape, a white shadow in the radiance
of night. But now let us cross over
and invest this world where
everything is lunar—

Paris, early summer 1909

Sag weißt du Liebesnächte? Treiben nicht
auf deinem Blut Kelchblätter weicher Worte?
Sind nicht an deinem lieben Leibe Orte,
die sich entsinnen wie ein Angesicht?

～

You don't know nights of love? No
petals of soft words float on your blood?
No secret places on your body
throb with memories, like eyes?

Paris, summer 1909

Weg in den Garten, tief wie ein langes Getränke,
leise im weichen Gezweig ein entgehender Schwung.
Oh und der Mond, der Mond, fast blühen die Bänke
von seiner zögernden Näherung.

Stille, wie drängt sie. Bist du jetzt oben erwacht?
Sternig und fühlend steht dir das Fenster entgegen.
Hände der Winde verlegen
an dein nahes Gesicht die entlegenste Nacht.

MOONLIT NIGHT

Path through the garden, deep as a long drink,
gently in soft branches gathering force then gone.
Oh and the moon, the moon, the benches
almost blooming from its slow approach.

The silence—how it throngs. Are you awake up there?
Starry and full of feeling the window faces you.
Hands of the wind transpose to your near countenance
remotest night.

Paris, beginning of July 1911

Schläfer, schwarz ist das Naß noch an meinen Füßen, ungenau. Tau sagen sie. / Ach, daß ich Judith bin, herkomme von ihm, aus dem Zelt aus dem Bett, austriefend sein Haupt, dreifach trunkenes Blut. Weintrunken, trunken vom Räucherwerk, trunken von mir—und jetzt nüchtern wie Tau. / Niedrig gehaltenes Haupt über dem Morgengras; ich aber oben auf meinem Gang, ich Erhobene. / Plötzlich leeres Gehirn, abfließende Bilder ins Erdreich; mir aber quillend ins Herz alle Breite der Nach-Tat. / Liebende, die ich bin. / Schrecken trieben in mir alle Wonnen zusamm, an mir sind alle Stellen. / Herz, mein berühmtes Herz, schlag an den Gegenwind:

wie ich geh, wie ich geh / und schneller die Stimme in mir, meine, die rufen wird, Vogelruf, vor der Not-Stadt.

Sleepers, the damp on my feet is black still, indistinct. Dew, they say. / Ah, that I am Judith, am coming from him, out of the tent out of the bed, out-trickling his head, three-times drunken blood. Wine-drunk, drunk with incense work, drunk with me—and now sober as dew. / Head held low over the morning grass; but I on my way high above, exalted. / Suddenly empty brain, images draining away into the soil; but gushing into my heart all the breadth of the after-deed. / Woman in love that I am. / Terrors have chased all raptures into me, on me all places find their spot. / Heart, famed heart, beat on the countering wind:

how I stride, stride / and swifter the voice in me, mine that will call, bird-call, before the locked-in city of fear.

Paris, July 1911

[AN LOU ANDREAS-SALOMÉ]

I

Ich hielt mich überoffen, ich vergaß,
daß draußen nicht nur Dinge sind und voll
in sich gewohnte Tiere, deren Aug
aus ihres Lebens Rundung anders nicht
hinausreicht als ein eingerahmtes Bild;
daß ich in mich mit allem immerfort
Blicke hineinriß: Blicke, Meinung, Neugier.
 Wer weiß, es bilden Augen sich im Raum
und wohnen bei. Ach nur zu dir gestürzt,
ist mein Gesicht nicht ausgestellt, verwächst
in dich und setzt sich dunkel
unendlich fort in dein geschütztes Herz.

II

Wie man ein Tuch vor angehäuften Atem,
nein: wie man es an eine Wunde preßt,
aus der das Leben ganz, in einem Zug,
hinauswill, hielt ich dich an mich: ich sah,
du wurdest rot von mir. Wer spricht es aus,
was uns geschah? Wir holten jedes nach,
wozu die Zeit nie war. Ich reifte seltsam
in jedem Antrieb übersprungner Jugend,
und du, Geliebte, hattest irgendeine
wildeste Kindheit über meinem Herzen.

III

Entsinnen ist da nicht genug, es muß
von jenen Augenblicken pures Dasein
auf meinem Grunde sein, ein Niederschlag
der unermeßlich überfüllten Lösung.
Denn ich *gedenke* nicht, das, was ich *bin*
rührt mich um deinetwillen. Ich erfinde
dich nicht an traurig ausgekühlten Stellen,

472

I

I held myself too open, I forgot
that outside not just things exist and animals
fully at ease in themselves, whose eyes
reach from their lives' roundedness no differently
than portraits do from frames; forgot that I
with all I did incessantly crammed
looks into myself: looks, opinion, curiosity.
 Who knows: perhaps eyes take shape in space
and watch intently. Ah, only as it plunges down to you
does my face cease being on display—grows
into you and twines on darkly,
endlessly, into your sheltered heart.

II

As one puts a handkerchief before held-in breath—
no: as one presses it against a wound
out of which the whole of life, in a single gush,
wants to stream, I held you to me: I saw
you turn red from me. How could anyone express
what took place between us? We made up for everything
there was never time for. I matured strangely
in every impulse of unperformed youth,
and you, love, somehow had
wildest childhood over my heart.

III

Memory won't suffice here: from those moments
there must be layers of pure existence
on my being's floor, a precipitate
from that immensely overfilled solution.
For I don't *think back*; all that I *am*
moves me because of you. I don't invent you
in sadly cooled-off places from which

von wo du wegkamst; selbst, daß du nicht da bist,
ist warm von dir und wirklicher und mehr
als ein Entbehren. Sehnsucht geht zu oft
ins Ungenaue. Warum soll ich mich
auswerfen, während mir vielleicht dein Einfluß
leicht ist, wie Mondschein einem Platz am Fenster.

you've gone away; even your not being there
is warm with you and more real and more
than a privation. Too often longing arcs out
into vagueness. Why should I fling myself,
when, for all I know, your influence falls on me,
gently, like moonlight on a window seat.

Duino, late autumn 1911

O die Kurven meiner Sehnsucht durch das Weltall,
und auf jedem Streifen: meines Wesens
hingeschleudert. Manches nicht vor tausend
Jahren auf der wehn Ellipse seines
Schwunges wiederkommend und vorüber.
Eilend durch die einst gewesne Zukunft,
sich erkennend in den Jahreszeiten
oder luftig, als genauer Einfluß
beinah sternisch in den überwachen
Apparaten eine Weile bebend

O the curves of my longing through the cosmos,
and in every streak: my being's
flung-outness. Many of them returning
only after a thousand years on the sad ellipse
of their momentum and passing on.
Hastening through the once-existent future,
knowing themselves in the seasons
or airily, as a precisely timed influence
almost starlike in the overwakeful
apparatus for a brief moment trembling

Venice, mid-July 1912

ᥫ

Ich Wissender: oh der ich eingeweiht
in alles Handeln bin und mich nicht rühre,
fortwährend tritt der Held aus meiner Türe
hinausentschlossen, wie mit mir entzweit.

I, knower: possessing the secrets
of all action and not stirring,
while the hero strides out my door
outwardly resolved, as if breaking off with me.

Ronda, beginning of January 1913

479

Die Mandelbäume in Blüte: alles, was wir hier leisten können, ist, sich ohne Rest erkennen in der irdischen Erscheinung.

Unendlich staun ich euch an, ihr Seligen, euer Benehmen,
wie ihr die schwindliche Zier traget in ewigem Sinn.
Ach wers verstünde zu blühn: dem wär das Herz über alle
schwachen Gefahren hinaus und in der großen getrost.

*The almond trees in bloom: the most we can achieve here is to know ourselves un-
reservedly in our earthly appearance.*

Always I marvel at you, blessed ones, —at your demeanor,
the way you wear transient jewels with eternal ease.
Ah, if we knew how to blossom: our hearts would be out beyond
all lesser dangers, secure in the single great one.

Ronda, December 1912–January 1913

[I]
Aus dieser Wolke, siehe: die den Stern
so wild verdeckt, der eben war–(und mir),
aus diesem Bergland drüben, das jetzt Nacht,
Nachtwinde hat für eine Zeit—(und mir),
aus diesem Fluß im Talgrund, der den Schein
zerrissner Himmels-Lichtung fängt—(und mir);
aus mir und alledem ein einzig Ding
zu machen, Herr: aus mir und dem Gefühl,
mit dem die Herde, eingekehrt im Pferch,
das große dunkle Nichtmehrsein der Welt
ausatmend hinnimmt—, mir und jedem Licht
im Finstersein der vielen Häuser, Herr:
ein Ding zu machen; aus den Fremden, denn
nicht Einen kenn ich, Herr, und mir und mir
ein Ding zu machen; aus den Schlafenden,
den fremden alten Männern im Hospiz,
die wichtig in den Betten husten, aus
schlaftrunknen Kindern an so fremder Brust,
aus vielen Ungenaun und immer mir,
aus nichts als mir und dem, was ich nicht kenn,
das Ding zu machen, Herr Herr Herr, das Ding,
das welthaft-irdisch wie ein Meteor
in seiner Schwere nur die Summe Flugs
zusammennimmt: nichts wiegend als die Ankunft.

[II]
Warum muß einer gehn und fremde Dinge
so auf sich nehmen, wie vielleicht der Träger
den fremdlings mehr und mehr gefüllten Marktkorb
von Stand zu Stand hebt und beladen nachgeht
und kann nicht sagen: Herr, wozu das Gastmahl?
Warum muß einer dastehn wie ein Hirt,
so ausgesetzt dem Übermaß von Einfluß,

I

From this cloud—look: that so wildly covers
the star that was just shining—(and from me),
from this handful of hills, which now holds
night and its winds a while—(and from me),
from this stream on the valley's floor, which catches
the gleam of torn sky clearings—(and from me);
from me and from all of this, Lord, to make
a single thing: from me and that night-breathing
with which the herd, put up in the fold,
waits out the great dark cessation
of the world—, from me and from every light
amid the darkness of the many houses, Lord:
to make one thing; from the strangers, for
I know no one, Lord, and from me and from me
to make *one* thing; from those sleeping,
the strange old men in the hospice
who cough out importantly in their beds,
from sleep-drunk children on such a foreign breast,
from many vaguenesses and always from me,
from me alone and all that I don't know,
to make the thing, Lord Lord Lord, the thing
that, cosmic-terrestrial, like a meteor
gathers in its gravity only the sum of flight:
weighing nothing finally but arrival.

II

Why must a man go about and take unknown things
so much upon himself—the way perhaps a porter
hefts from stall to stall the market basket
that keeps on filling up while he, weighed down,
must follow and can never ask: Master, why this feast?
Why must a man stand here like a shepherd—
so exposed to excess of influence,

beteiligt so an diesem Raum voll Vorgang,
daß er gelehnt an einen Baum der Landschaft
sein Schicksal hätte, ohne mehr zu handeln.
Und hat doch nicht im viel zu großen Blick
die stille Milderung der Herde. Hat
nichts als Welt, hat Welt in jedem Aufschaun,
in jeder Neigung Welt. Ihm dringt, was andern
gerne gehört, unwirtlich wie Musik
und blind ins Blut und wandelt sich vorüber.

Da steht er nächtens auf und hat den Ruf
des Vogels draußen schon in seinem Dasein
und fühlt sich kühn, weil er die ganzen Sterne
in sein Gesicht nimmt, schwer—, o nicht wie einer,
der der Geliebten diese Nacht bereitet
und sie verwöhnt mit den gefühlten Himmeln.

[I I I]

Daß mir doch, wenn ich wieder der Städte Gedräng
und verwickelten Lärmknäul und die
Wirrsal des Fahrzeugs um mich habe, einzeln,
daß mir doch über das dichte Getrieb
Himmel erinnerte und der erdige Bergrand,
den von drüben heimwärts die Herde betrat.
Steinig sei mir zu Mut
und das Tagwerk des Hirten scheine mir möglich,
wie er einhergeht und bräunt und mit messendem Steinwurf
seine Herde besäumt, wo sie sich ausfranst.
Langsamen Schrittes, nicht leicht, nachdenklichen Körpers,
aber im Stehn ist er herrlich. Noch immer dürfte ein Gott
heimlich in diese Gestalt und würde nicht minder.
Abwechselnd weilt er und zieht, wie selber der Tag,
und Schatten der Wolken
durchgehn ihn, als dächte der Raum
langsam Gedanken für ihn.

Sei er wer immer für euch. Wie das wehende Nachtlicht
in den Mantel der Lampe stell ich mich innen in ihn.

involved so in this space full of happening
that, merely leaning against a tree in the landscape,
he'd have his fate, nothing else to do.
And yet lacks in his always too open gaze
the quiet solace of the herd. Has
only world, world in each upward glance,
world each time his eyes look down. What in others
gladly takes up residence shoots through his blood like music—
blindly, inhospitably, changing and passing on.

At night then he gets up and has the call
of birds from outside deep within him
and feels bold, since he takes all the stars
into his sight, gravely—, O not like one
who shapes this night for his beloved
so he can gladden her with heart-filled skies.

III

But may I, when alone again I have the city's crush
and tangled noise-skein and the furor
of its traffic all around me,
may I above that mindless swirl
recall sky and the gentle mountain rim
on which that far-off herd curved homeward.
May my spirit be hard as rock
and the shepherd's life to me seem possible—
the way he drifts and turns brown in the sun and with a practiced
stone-throw mends his flock, whenever it frays.
Steps slow, not light, his body pensive,
but in his standing there, majestic. Even now a god
might enter this form and not be lessened.
He lingers for a while, then moves on, like the day itself,
and shadows of the clouds
pass through him, as though space were slowly
thinking thoughts for him.

Make of him what you will. Like a wind-whipped nightflame
in the lamp's mantle I place myself in him.

Ein Schein wird ruhig. Der Tod
fände sich reiner zurecht.

A flare grows steady. May Death
less darkly find its way.

Ronda, early January 1913

Also, das tat not für den und den,
weil sie Zeichen brauchten, welche schrieen.
Doch er träumte, Marthen und Marieen
müßte es genügen, einzusehn,
daß er *könne.* Aber keiner glaubte,
alle sprachen: Herr, was kommst du *nun?*
Und da ging er hin, das Unerlaubte
an der ruhigen Natur zu tun.
Zürnender. Die Augen fast geschlossen,
fragte er sie nach dem Grab. Er litt.
Ihnen schien es, seine Tränen flossen,
und sie drängten voller Neugier mit.
Noch im Gehen wars ihm ungeheuer,
ein entsetzlich spielender Versuch,
aber plötzlich brach ein hohes Feuer
in ihm aus, ein solcher Widerspruch
gegen alle ihre Unterschiede,
ihr Gestorben-, ihr Lebendigsein,
daß er Feindschaft war in jedem Gliede,
als er heiser angab: Hebt den Stein!
Eine Stimme rief, daß er schon stinke,
(denn er lag den vierten Tag)—doch Er
stand gestrafft, ganz voll von jenem Winke,
welcher stieg in ihm und schwer, sehr schwer
ihm die Hand hob—(niemals hob sich eine
langsamer als diese Hand und mehr)
bis sie dastand, scheinend in der Luft;
und dort oben zog sie sich zur Kralle:
denn ihn graute jetzt, es möchten alle
Toten durch die angesaugte Gruft
wiederkommen, wo es sich herauf
raffte, larvig, aus der graden Lage—
doch dann stand nur Eines schief im Tage,

Yes, it was necessary for the rabble,
since they required signs, signs that screamed.
Yet he dreamt how for Martha and Mary
it would be enough simply to see
that he *could*. But none of these believed,
they all said: Lord, why come *now*?
And so he went, to do what was forbidden
to peaceful Nature.
In anger. His eyes almost shut,
he asked where the grave was. Bore it.
They thought his tears streamed,
so they all thronged behind him, full of curiosity.
Even on the way he thought it monstrous,
an appalling, frivolous experiment,
but suddenly a great fire broke out in him,
such an argument
against their prized distinctions,
their death and life, their here and there,
that he was enmity in every limb
when he ordered hoarsely: Lift the stone!
A voice called out that he must stink by now
(for he'd been lying there four days)—but
He stood tensed, entirely filled with that gesture
that rose in him and heavily, so heavily
lifted his hand—(no hand ever raised itself
this slowly, with this much weight)
until it stood there, shining in the air—
and clenched into an upraised fist;
for he dreaded now that all the dead might
come rushing back through the suction
of that tomb, where the thing had started
writhing, larva-like, out of its stiff reclining—
but then just a simple figure stood there,

und man sah: das ungenaue vage
Leben nahm es wieder mit in Kauf.

crooked in the daylight, and one witnessed:
indiscriminate vague Life accept it.

Ronda, January 1913

DER GEIST ARIEL

(Nach der Lesung von Shakespeares Sturm)

Man hat ihn einmal irgendwo befreit
mit jenem Ruck, mit dem man sich als Jüngling
ans Große hinriß, weg von jeder Rücksicht.
Da ward er willens, sieh: und seither dient er,
nach jeder Tat gefaßt auf seine Freiheit.
Und halb sehr herrisch, halb beinah verschämt,
bringt mans ihm vor, daß man für dies und dies
ihn weiter brauche, ach, und muß es sagen,
was man ihm half. Und dennoch fühlt man selbst,
wie alles das, was man mit ihm zurückhält,
fehlt in der Luft. Verführend fast und süß:
ihn hinzulassen—, um dann, nicht mehr zaubernd,
ins Schicksal eingelassen wie die andern,
zu wissen, daß sich seine leichte Freundschaft,
jetzt ohne Spannung, nirgends mehr verpflichtet,
ein Überschuß zu dieses Atmens Raum,
gedankenlos im Element beschäftigt.
Abhängig fürder, länger nicht begabt,
den dumpfen Mund zu jenem Ruf zu formen,
auf den er stürzte. Machtlos, alternd, arm
und doch *ihn* atmend wie unfaßlich weit
verteilten Duft, der erst das Unsichtbare
vollzählig macht. Auflächelnd, daß man dem
so winken durfte, in so großen Umgang
so leicht gewöhnt. Aufweinend vielleicht auch,
wenn man bedenkt, wie's einen liebte und
fortwollte, beides, immer ganz in Einem.

(Ließ ich es schon? Nun schreckt mich dieser Mann,
der wieder Herzog wird. Wie er sich sanft
den Draht ins Haupt zieht und sich zu den andern
Figuren hängt und künftighin das Spiel
um Milde bittet . . . Welcher Epilog

THE SPIRIT ARIEL

(After reading Shakespeare's Tempest*)*

Once long ago somewhere you freed him
with that same jolt with which as a young man
you tore yourself toward greatness, away from all regard.
He became willing, and ever since he serves,
poised for freedom after every deed.
And half imperiously, half almost ashamed,
you inform him that for this and that
you still require him, and, ah, must tell again
that story of how you helped him. And yet you feel, yourself,
how everything that you keep back through him
is missing from the air. How sweet and almost tempting:
to let him go—, and then, no longer conjuring,
enrolled in fate like all the others,
to know that his light friendship now,
without any strain, nowhere any obligation,
an adjunct to this breathing's space,
is at work in the element, unthinkingly.
Henceforth dependent, no longer with that gift
to shape the dull mouth into the call
at which he came. Powerless, aging, poor,
yet breathing *him* like incomprehensibly far-flung
scattered fragrance by which alone the invisible
is made complete. Smiling, that you could
summon him this way, in such great dealings
so easily at home. Perhaps weeping too,
when you remember how it loved and longed
to leave you, both, always the same desire.

(Have I let it go? Now this man frightens me,
who's becoming Duke again. How gently
he draws the cord through his head and hangs
himself up with the other figures and begs
henceforth the play's indulgence . . . What an epilogue

vollbrachter Herrschaft. Abtun, bloßes Dastehn
mit nichts als eigner Kraft: »und das ist wenig.«)

to mastery achieved. Mere naked standing-there
with nothing but his strength: "which is most faint.")

Ronda, January–February 1913

So angestrengt wider die starke Nacht
werfen sie ihre Stimmen ins Gelächter,
das schlecht verbrennt O aufgelehnte Welt
voll Weigerung. Und atmet doch den Raum,
in dem die Sterne gehen. Siehe, dies
bedürfte nicht und könnte, der Entfernung
fremd hingegeben, in dem Übermaß
von Fernen sich ergehen, fort von uns.
Und nun geruhts und reicht uns ans Gesicht
wie der Geliebten Aufblick; schlägt sich auf
uns gegenüber und zerstreut vielleicht
an uns sein Dasein. Und wir sinds nicht wert.
Vielleicht entziehts den Engeln etwas Kraft,
daß nach uns her der Sternenhimmel nachgiebt
und uns hereinhängt ins getrübte Schicksal.
Umsonst. Denn wer gewahrts? Und wo es einer
gewärtig wird: wer darf noch an den Nacht-Raum
die Stirne lehnen wie ans eigne Fenster?
Wer hat dies nicht verleugnet? Wer hat nicht
in dieses eingeborne Element
gefälschte, schlechte, nachgemachte Nächte
hereingeschleppt und sich daran begnügt?
Wir lassen Götter stehn um gohren Abfall,
denn Götter locken nicht. Sie haben Dasein
und nichts als Dasein, Überfluß von Dasein,
doch nicht Geruch, nicht Wink. Nichts ist so stumm
wie eines Gottes Mund. Schön wie ein Schwan
auf seiner Ewigkeit grundlosen Fläche:
so zieht der Gott und taucht und schont sein Weiß.

Alles verführt. Der kleine Vogel selbst
tut Zwang an uns aus seinem reinen Laubwerk,
die Blume hat nicht Raum und drängt herüber;
was will der Wind nicht alles? Nur der Gott,

Straining so hard against the strength of night
they cast their voices into that laughter
that will not burn. O obstinate world
full of refusal. Yet breathing the same space
in which the stars move. Look, all this
needs nothing and could, having pledged itself
to distance, roam through the deepest
regions of remoteness, far from us.
And deigns now instead to touch our faces
as does the loved one's glance; opens
before us and perhaps scatters us
with its being. And we're not worth it.
Perhaps it subtracts some power from the angels
so that the starry sky will bend to us
and suspend itself inside our murky fate.
In vain. For who takes note? And even where
someone does: who dares lean his brow
against night-space as against his own window?
Who hasn't disavowed all this? Who hasn't
hauled counterfeited, third-rate, mimic nights
into this inborn element of ours
and been content with that?
We pass gods by and fix on rotting refuse,
for gods do not entice. They have being
and only being, enormous stores of being,
but not scent, not gesture. Nothing is so silent
as a god's mouth. Serenely, like a swan
on its eternity of unplumbed surface:
the god glides and dives and saves his whiteness.

Everything tempts. Even the small bird,
deep in its realm of pure foliage, compels us;
the flower has no space and crowds over into ours;
what would the wind *not* have? Only the god,

wie eine Säule, läßt vorbei, verteilend
hoch oben, wo er trägt, nach beiden Seiten
die leichte Wölbung seines Gleichmuts.

like a column, lets pass, distributing
far above, where he holds up, on either side
the light arch of his equanimity.

Paris, end of February 1913

∾

Wir wissen nicht, was wir verbringen: siehe,
Benanntes ist vorbei und jedes Sein
erfindet sich im letzten Augenblick
und will nichts hören / Wink von Zeichen, kaum
ein Blatt verkehrts: wir aber sind schon anders,
verleugnen, lächeln, kennen schon nicht mehr,
was gestern Glück war. Und die Göttin selbst
schwankt über uns.

&

We don't know what we spend:
all that is named is past and each being
invents itself at the last second
and will hear nothing / Hint of signals,
barely a leaf turns: but by now we've changed,
we disavow, smile, already lack all sense
of yesterday's good fortune. And the goddess herself
sways above us.

Paris, beginning of March 1913

~

Lange mußt du leiden, kennend nicht was,
bis plötzlich aus gehässig erbissener Frucht
deines Leidens Geschmack eintritt in dir.
Und da liebst du schon fast das Gekostete. Keiner
redet dirs wieder aus

~

You must suffer long, not knowing what,
until suddenly out of bitterly chewed fruit
your suffering's taste comes forth in you.
Then almost instantly you'll love what's tasted. No one
will ever talk you out of it

Paris, March 1913

~

Unwissend vor dem Himmel meines Lebens,
anstaunend steh ich. O die großen Sterne.
Aufgehendes und Niederstieg. Wie still.
Als wär ich nicht. Nehm ich denn Teil? Entriet ich
dem reinen Einfluß? Wechselt Flut und Ebbe
in meinem Blut nach dieser Ordnung? Abtun
will ich die Wünsche, jeden andern Anschluß,
mein Herz gewöhnen an sein Fernstes. Besser
es lebt im Schrecken seiner Sterne, als
zum Schein beschützt, von einer Näh beschwichtigt.

~

Unknowing before the heavens of my life
I stand in wonder. O the great stars.
The rising and going down. How quiet.
As if I didn't exist. *Am* I a part? Did I abjure
the pure influence? Do high and low tide
alternate in my blood according to this order?
I'll cast off all wishes, all other links,
accustom my heart to its remotest space. Better
it live in the terror of its stars than in
a dream of refuge, soothed by something near.

Paris, early 1913

CHRISTI HÖLLENFAHRT

Endlich verlitten, entging sein Wesen dem schrecklichen
Leibe der Leiden. Oben. Ließ ihn.
Und die Finsternis fürchtete sich allein
und warf an das Bleiche
Fledermäuse heran, —immer noch schwankt abends
in ihrem Flattern die Angst vor dem Anprall
an die erkaltete Qual. Dunkle ruhlose Luft
entmutigte sich an dem Leichnam; und in den starken
wachsamen Tieren der Nacht war Dumpfheit und Unlust.
Sein entlassener Geist gedachte vielleicht in der Landschaft
anzustehen, unhandelnd. Denn seiner Leidung Ereignis
war noch genug. Maßvoll
schien ihm der Dinge nächtliches Dastehn,
und wie ein trauriger Raum griff er darüber um sich.
Aber die Erde, vertrocknet im Durst seiner Wunden,
aber die Erde riß auf, und es rufte im Abgrund.
Er, Kenner der Martern, hörte die Hölle
herheulend, begehrend Bewußtsein
seiner vollendeten Not: daß über dem Ende der seinen
(unendlichen) ihre, während Pein erschrecke, ahne.
Und er stürzte, der Geist, mit der völligen Schwere
seiner Erschöpfung herein: schritt als ein Eilender
durch das befremdete Nachschaun weidender Schatten,
hob zu Adam den Aufblick, eilig,
eilte hinab, schwand, schien und verging in dem Stürzen
wilderer Tiefen. Plötzlich (höher höher) über der Mitte
aufschäumender Schreie, auf dem langen
Turm seines Duldens trat er hervor: ohne Atem,
stand, ohne Geländer, Eigentümer der Schmerzen. Schwieg.

Finally suffered out, his being exited the terrible
body of pain. Up there. Deserted it.
And the darkness, abandoned, took fright,
and against the pallor cast bats
(even now their nightfall swervings
preserve the fear of impact
with that chilled anguish). Dark restless air
grew despondent near the corpse; and in the strong
watchful animals of the night there was dullness and torpor.
His expelled spirit thought perhaps to bide its time
in the landscape, inactive. For the extremes of his suffering
were still all too sharp. There was measure, it felt,
in the nocturnal standing there of things,
and like a saddened space began thinning, coalescing.
But the earth, parched in the thirst of his wounds,
the earth ripped open, and there were calls in its chasm.
He, expert in agony, heard hell
howling toward him, craving confirmation
of his completed pain: imagining in the end of his
torment (infinite) that of its own, ongoing.
And he, the spirit, sank into it with the full
weight of his exhaustion: strode as one hurrying
through the puzzled backward stare of pasturing shades,
raised his glance toward Adam, hastily,
hurried down, glimmered in the distance and vanished in the plunging
wilder depths. Suddenly (higher higher) over the center
of foaming cries, he stepped out onto the tall
tower of his endurance: without breathing,
stood, with no railing, suffering's sole heir. Was silent.

Paris, April 1913

Nun wachen wir mit den Erinnerungen
und halten das Gesicht an das, was war;
flüsternde Süße, die uns einst durchdrungen,
sitzt schweigend neben mit gelöstem Haar

ॐ

Now we wake with our memory
and fix our gazes on what once was;
whispering sweetness, which once coursed through us,
sits silently beside us with disheveled hair

Paris, May 1913

Bestürz mich, Musik, mit rhythmischem Zürnen!
Hoher Vorwurf, dicht vor dem Herzen erhoben,
das nicht so wogend empfand, das sich schonte. Mein Herz: *da*:
sieh deine Herrlichkeit. Hast du fast immer Genüge,
minder zu schwingen? Aber die Wölbungen warten,
die obersten, daß du sie füllst mit orgelndem Andrang.
Was ersehnst du der fremden Geliebten verhaltenes Antlitz?—
Hat deine Sehnsucht nicht Atem, aus der Posaune des Engels,
der das Weltgericht anbricht, tönende Stürme zu stoßen:
oh, so *ist* sie auch nicht, nirgends, wird nicht geboren,
die du verdorrend entbehrst . . .

\sim

Assault me, music, with rhythmic fury!
Lofty reproach, hurled high before the heart
that didn't feel with such surges, that spared itself. My heart: *there*:
behold your glory. You can almost always make do
with lesser pulsings? Yes, but the arches wait,
the uppermost, to be filled with thundering onrush.
Why do you pine for the unknown loved one's withheld face?—
Does your craving lack breath to blast echoing storms
from that angel's trumpet who proclaims the world's judgment:
then she does not exist, *is* nowhere, will not be born,
she whose absence you parchingly endure . . .

Paris, May 1913

Wie das Gestirn, der Mond, erhaben, voll Anlaß,
plötzlich die Höhn übertritt, die entworfene Nacht
gelassen vollendend: siehe: so steigt mir
rein die Stimme hervor aus Gebirgen des Nichtmehr.
Und die Stellen, erstaunt, an denen du dawarst und fortkamst,
schmerzen klarer dir nach.

꩜

The way that bright planet, the moon, exalted, full of purpose,
all at once surmounts the peaks, serenely filling in
the outlined night: look: just so my voice
rises purely from the mountains of No Longer.
And the places—awestruck—that you occupied and left
ache more clearly for you.

Autumn 1913

Tränen, Tränen, die aus mir brechen.
Mein Tod, Mohr, Träger
meines Herzens, halte mich schräger,
daß sie abfließen. Ich will sprechen.

Schwarzer, riesiger Herzhalter.
Wenn ich auch spräche,
glaubst du denn, daß das Schweigen bräche?

Wiege mich, Alter.

Tears, tears that break out of me.
My death, great Moor, bearer
of my heart, hold me at a slant
so they'll run off. I want to speak.

Black, gigantic heart holder.
Even if I were to speak,
do you think the silence would break?

Cradle me, old man.

Paris, late autumn 1913

Einmal nahm ich zwischen meine Hände
dein Gesicht. Der Mond fiel darauf ein.
Unbegreiflichster der Gegenstände
unter überfließendem Gewein.

Wie ein williges, das still besteht,
beinah war es wie ein Ding zu halten.
Und doch war kein Wesen in der kalten
Nacht, das mir unendlicher entgeht.

O da strömen wir zu diesen Stellen,
drängen in die kleine Oberfläche
alle Wellen unsres Herzens,
Lust und Schwäche,
und wem halten wir sie schließlich hin?

Ach dem Fremden, der uns mißverstanden,
ach dem andern, den wir niemals fanden,
denen Knechten, die uns banden,
Frühlingswinden, die damit entschwanden,
und der Stille, der Verliererin.

～

Once I took your face into
my hands. Moonlight fell on it.
Most incomprehensible object
under overflowing tears.

Like something docile, that quietly endures,
it felt almost the way a thing feels.
And yet there was no being in that chill
night, which endlessly eludes.

O those places that we surge toward,
thrusting into their scant surfaces
all the waves of our heart,
our pleasures and weaknesses,
and to whom finally do we hold them out?

To the stranger, who misunderstood us,
to the other, whom we never found,
to those slaves, who held us captive,
to the Spring winds, which promptly vanished,
and to that spendthrift, silence.

Paris, end of 1913

Oft anstaunt ich dich, stand an gestern begonnenem Fenster,
stand und staunte dich an. Noch war mir die neue
Stadt wie verwehrt, und die unüberredete Landschaft
finsterte hin, als wäre ich nicht. Nicht gaben die nächsten
Dinge sich Müh, mir verständlich zu sein. An der Laterne
drängte die Gasse herauf: ich sah, daß sie fremd war.
Drüben—ein Zimmer, mitfühlbar, geklärt in der Lampe—,
schon nahm ich teil; sie empfandens, schlossen die Läden.
Stand. Und dann weinte ein Kind. Ich wußte die Mütter
rings in den Häusern, was sie vermögen—, und wußte
alles Weinens zugleich die untröstlichen Gründe.
Oder es sang eine Stimme und reichte ein Stück weit
aus der Erwartung heraus, oder es hustete unten
voller Vorwurf ein Alter, als ob sein Körper im Recht sei
wider die mildere Welt. Dann schlug eine Stunde—,
aber ich zählte zu spät, sie fiel mir vorüber. —
Wie ein Knabe, ein fremder, wenn man endlich ihn zuläßt,
doch den Ball nicht fängt und keines der Spiele
kann, die die andern so leicht an einander betreiben,
dasteht und wegschaut, —wohin—?: stand ich und plötzlich,
daß *du* umgehst mit mir, spielest, begriff ich, erwachsene
Nacht, und staunte dich an. Wo die Türme
zürnten, wo abgewendeten Schicksals
eine Stadt mich umstand und nicht zu erratende Berge
wider mich lagen, und im genäherten Umkreis
hungernde Fremdheit umzog das zufällige Flackern
meiner Gefühle—: da war es, du Hohe,
keine Schande für dich, daß du mich kanntest. Dein Atem
ging über mich. Dein auf weite Ernste verteiltes
Lächeln trat in mich ein.

Once I stared at you, stood at the window begun yesterday,
stood and stared at you in wonder. As yet the new
city seemed denied to me, and the unpersuaded landscape
darkened as if I didn't exist. Even the nearest things
cared not the least if I understood them. At the lamppost
the street thrust up into view: I saw it was foreign.
Across the way—a room, inviting, clear in its lamplight—,
already I was taking part; they sensed it, pulled the shutters closed.
I stood. And then a child cried. I thought of the mothers
all around in the houses, what power they had—, and thought
at the same time of all crying's inconsolable ground.
Or a voice sang and reached a bit beyond
expectation, or down below an old man coughed
full of reproach, as though his body were in the right
and the gentler world self-deceived. Then an hour struck—,
but I started counting too late, it tumbled past me. —
The way a boy, the new one, when he's finally chosen,
drops the first ball and gets lost in those games
the others pursue together with such ease
and stands and looks off—where?—: I stood and suddenly
felt *you* befriending me, *you* playing, adult
night, and I stared at you in wonder. Where the towers
raged, where a city surrounded me
with an averted fate and inscrutable mountains
camped against me, and hungering
strangeness prowled in narrowing circles
around the chance fires
of my feeling—: it was then that you, great Night,
with no trace of shame, acknowledged me. Your breath
passed over me. Your smile, spanning vast
solemnities, entered me.

Paris, January 1914

〜

Hebend die Blicke vom Buch, von den nahen zählbaren Zeilen,
in die vollendete Nacht hinaus:
O wie sich sternegemäß die gedrängten Gefühle verteilen,
so als bände man auf
einen Bauernstrauß:

Jugend der leichten und neigendes Schwanken der schweren
und der zärtlichen zögernder Bug—.
Überall Lust zu Bezug und nirgends Begehren;
Welt zu viel und Erde genug.

Looking up from my book, from the close countable lines
into the finished-full night outside:
how in starry measure my packed feelings scatter,
as though a bouquet of wildflowers
were being untied:

youth of the light and bending sway of the heavy
and these tender ones' hesitant curve—.
Everywhere joy in relation and no craving anywhere;
world in excess and earth sufficient.

Paris, February 1914

Du im Voraus
verlorne Geliebte, Nimmergekommene,
nicht weiß ich, welche Töne dir lieb sind.
Nicht mehr versuch ich, dich, wenn das Kommende wogt,
zu erkennen. Alle die großen
Bilder in mir, im Fernen erfahrene Landschaft,
Städte und Türme und Brücken und un-
vermutete Wendung der Wege
und das Gewaltige jener von Göttern
einst durchwachsenen Länder:
steigt zur Bedeutung in mir
deiner, Entgehende, an.

Ach, die Gärten bist du,
ach, ich sah sie mit solcher
Hoffnung. Ein offenes Fenster
im Landhaus—, und du tratest beinahe
mir nachdenklich heran. Gassen fand ich, —
du warst sie gerade gegangen,
und die Spiegel manchmal der Läden der Händler
waren noch schwindlich von dir und gaben erschrocken
mein zu plötzliches Bild. —Wer weiß, ob derselbe
Vogel nicht hinklang durch uns
gestern, einzeln, im Abend?

You, the loved one lost
in advance, you who never arrived,
I don't even know what sounds you like best.
No longer, when the future crests toward the present,
do I try to discern you. All the great
images in me—the landscape widening far off,
cities and towers and bridges and un-
suspected turns in the path
and the forcefulness of those lands
once intertwined with gods:
they all mount up in me to signify
you, forever not here.

You are the gardens.
With such hope
I saw them. An open window
in the country house—, and you almost
stepped out pensively to meet me. I found streets, —
you had just walked down them,
and sometimes the mirrors in the merchants' shops
were still drunk with you and with a start
reflected my too-sudden image. —Who knows
if the same birdsong did not ring through both of us
yesterday, each of us alone, at evening?

Paris, winter 1913–14

WENDUNG

Der Weg von der Innigkeit zur Größe
geht durch das Opfer.—Kassner

Lange errang ers im Anschaun.
Sterne brachen ins Knie
unter dem ringenden Aufblick.
Oder er anschaute knieend,
und seines Instands Duft
machte ein Göttliches müd,
daß es ihm lächelte schlafend.

Türme schaute er so,
daß sie erschraken:
wieder sie bauend, hinan, plötzlich, in Einem!
Aber wie oft, die vom Tag
überladene Landschaft
ruhete hin in sein stilles Gewahren, abends.

Tiere traten getrost
in den offenen Blick, weidende,
und die gefangenen Löwen
starrten hinein wie in unbegreifliche Freiheit;
Vögel durchflogen ihn grad,
den gemütigen; Blumen
wiederschauten in ihn
groß wie in Kinder.

Und das Gerücht, daß ein Schauender sei,
rührte die minder,
fraglicher Sichtbaren,
rührte die Frauen.

TURNING

*The path from inner intensity to greatness
leads through sacrifice. —Kassner*

He had long prevailed through gazing.
Stars fell to their knees
in the grip of his powerful up-glance.
Or *he* gazed kneeling,
and the scent of his urgency
overcame an Immortal,
until it smiled on him from sleep.

Towers he stared at with such force
that they were startled:
building them up again, abruptly, as One!
But how often the landscape,
overburdened by the day,
came at evening to rest in his quiet watching.

Animals stepped trustingly
into his open gaze where they pastured,
and the caged lions
stared in, as into inconceivable freedom;
birds flew straight through it,
feeling its welcome; flowers
gazed back into it
greatly, as they do with children.

And the rumor that a *gazer* existed
stirred the less clearly,
more questionably visible ones,
stirred women.

Kassner: Rudolf Kassner (1873–1959), Austrian writer and cultural philosopher and Rilke's close friend (the eighth Duino elegy is dedicated to him). The epigraph is one of Kassner's "Sayings of the Yogi" (1911), altered by Rilke's strong misremembering of it. Its actual wording is: "He who wants to proceed from inner intensity [*Innigkeit*] to greatness must sacrifice himself."

Schauend wie lang?
Seit wie lange schon innig entbehrend,
flehend im Grunde des Blicks?

Wenn er, ein Wartender, saß in der Fremde; des Gasthofs
zerstreutes, abgewendetes Zimmer
mürrisch um sich, und im vermiedenen Spiegel
wieder das Zimmer
und später vom quälenden Bett aus
wieder:
da beriets in der Luft,
unfaßbar beriet es
über sein fühlbares Herz,
über sein durch den schmerzhaft verschütteten Körper
dennoch fühlbares Herz
beriet es und richtete:
daß es der Liebe nicht habe.

(Und verwehrte ihm weitere Weihen.)

Denn des Anschauns, siehe, ist eine Grenze.
Und die geschautere Welt
will in der Liebe gedeihn.

Werk des Gesichts ist getan,
tue nun Herz-Werk
an den Bildern in dir, jenen gefangenen; denn du
überwältigtest sie: aber nun kennst du sie nicht.
Siehe, innerer Mann, dein inneres Mädchen,
dieses errungene aus
tausend Naturen, dieses
erst nur errungene, nie
noch geliebte Geschöpf.

Gazing how long?
For how long inwardly starving,
beseeching in the very depths of his glance?

When he, forever waiting, sat in foreign places; the hotel's
averted, preoccupied room
sullen around him, and in the avoided mirror
again the room
and later on from the tormenting bed
again:
there was argument in the air,
incomprehensibly voices conferred
about his still feelable heart,
about his heart which through the painfully buried body
could nevertheless be felt,
they conferred and reached judgment:
that it had no love.

(And denied him further ordination.)

For gazing, you see, sets limits.
And the more truly gazed-at world
wants to grow boundless in love.

Work of the eyes is done,
begin heart-work now
on those images in you, those captive ones;
for you overpowered them: but you don't yet know them.
Behold, inner man, your inner woman,
she who was won
from a thousand natures, she
the till now *only* won,
as yet never loved creation.

Paris, June 20, 1914

527

Fast wie am Jüngsten Tag die Toten sich reißen
aus der Umarmung der Erde, und der erleichterte Ball
hinter ihnen empor sich in die Himmel verliert—:
so fast stürzen sich jetzt diese, die leben, ins Erdreich,
und die beladene sinkt, die Erde, zum Weltgrund
in der Jahrtausende Tang, wo die Schicksale noch—
stumme mit stumpfem Fischblick—
kalte Begegnungen haben. Wo aus Röhren hervor,
wie See-Anemonen,
prachtvoll die Wunden erblühn, und dem furchtbaren Pulp
selber die Strömung den Tast-Arm
an das zu Fassende trägt. Da bildet
aus dem gebeinernen Kalk sich die blasse Koralle
starrlebendigen Grauns, die sich schweigend verzweigt.

A black ornamental flourish (swash symbol) appears at the top.

Almost as on the last day when the dead will tear themselves
from the earth's embrace and, the unburdened ball
racing after them, vanish into the sky—:
thus almost now these, the living, plunge into the soil,
and that soil, the earth, sinks laden toward the watery world-bed
into millennial weed, where destinies as yet—
mutely with blank fish eyes—
have cold encounters. Where out of tubes,
as with sea anemones,
wounds bloom resplendent, and the terrible pulp's
waving slime-arm is borne by the current
toward that thing to be seized. On the floor
out of skeletal lime the pale coral's
stiff-living horror evolves, and branches in silence.

Irschenhausen, early September 1914

Ausgesetzt auf den Bergen des Herzens. Siehe, wie klein dort,
siehe: die letzte Ortschaft der Worte, und höher,
aber wie klein auch, noch ein letztes
Gehöft von Gefühl. Erkennst du's?
Ausgesetzt auf den Bergen des Herzens. Steingrund
unter den Händen. Hier blüht wohl
einiges auf; aus stummem Absturz
blüht ein unwissendes Kraut singend hervor.
Aber der Wissende? Ach, der zu wissen begann
und schweigt nun, ausgesetzt auf den Bergen des Herzens.
Da geht wohl, heilen Bewußtseins,
manches umher, manches gesicherte Bergtier,
wechselt und weilt. Und der große geborgene Vogel
kreist um der Gipfel reine Verweigerung. —Aber
ungeborgen, hier auf den Bergen des Herzens . . .

Abandoned on the mountains of the heart. Look, how small there,
look: the last village of words, and higher,
but how small too, still one last
farmstead of feeling. Do you see it?
Abandoned on the mountains of the heart. Rockground
under the hands. Here, granted,
some things do flourish; out of mute downthrust
an unknowing herb breaks forth singing.
But the one who knows? Ah, who began knowing
and now keeps silent, abandoned on the mountains of the heart.
True, many an unhurt consciousness roams here,
many, so many sure mountain animals
change fields and stay. And the great sheltered bird
circles the peaks' pure refusal. —But
unsheltered, here on the mountains of the heart . . .

Irschenhausen, September 20, 1914

Immer wieder, ob wir der Liebe Landschaft auch kennen
und den kleinen Kirchhof mit seinen klagenden Namen
und die furchtbar verschweigende Schlucht, in welcher die andern
enden: immer wieder gehn wir zu zweien hinaus
unter die alten Bäume, lagern uns immer wieder
zwischen die Blumen, gegenüber dem Himmel.

Again and again, even though we know love's landscape
and the little churchyard with its lamenting names
and the terrible reticent gorge in which the others
end: again and again the two of us walk out together
under the ancient trees, lay ourselves down again and again
among the flowers, and look up into the sky.

Munich(?), end of 1914

Keiner, der finstere nur gefallene Engel
wollte; nahm Waffen, trat tödlich
den Gebotenen an. Aber schon wieder
klirrte er hin rückwärts, aufwärts,
schrie in die Himmel: Ich kann nicht!

Denn gelassen durch die dickichte Braue
hatte ihn Moses gewahrt und weitergeschrieben:
Worte des Segens und den unendlichen Namen.
Und sein Auge war rein bis zum Grunde der Kräfte.

Also der Herr, mitreißend die Hälfte der Himmel,
drang herab und bettete selber den Berg auf;
legte den Alten. Aus der geordneten Wohnung
rief er die Seele; die, auf! und erzählte
vieles Gemeinsame, eine unzählige Freundschaft.

Aber am Ende wars ihr genug. Daß es genug sei,
gab die vollendete zu. Da beugte der alte
Gott zu dem Alten langsam sein altes
Antlitz. Nahm ihn im Kusse aus ihm
in sein Alter, das ältere. Und mit Händen der Schöpfung
grub er den Berg zu. Daß es nur einer,
ein wiedergeschaffener, sei unter den Bergen der Erde,
Menschen nicht kenntlich.

THE DEATH OF MOSES

None of them, only the dark, fallen angel
was willing; took weapons, stepped with deadly aim
toward the commanded one. But already
he was clanging backward, upward,
and shouting out into the heavens: I can't!

For calmly through his brow's thicket
Moses had noticed him and continued writing:
words of blessing and the infinite name.
And his eye was pure to the very depth of his powers.

So the Lord, tearing half the heavens with him,
swooped down and made the mountain bed ready himself;
laid the old man in it. From her ordered dwelling
he called the soul; up she sped, and recounted
so many things in common, an inexpressible friendship.

But finally she was convinced. Fulfilled, she
admitted it was time. Then the old god
slowly bowed his old countenance
to the old man. With a kiss extracted him
into his own older age. And with hands of creation
closed up the mountain tomb. So it would be merely one,
a re-created one, among the mountains of the earth,
indistinguishable to men.

Lines 1–14, Paris, summer 1914; lines 15–22, Munich, October 1915

Da steht der Tod, ein bläulicher Absud
in einer Tasse ohne Untersatz.
Ein wunderlicher Platz für eine Tasse:
steht auf dem Rücken einer Hand. Ganz gut
erkennt man noch an dem glasierten Schwung
den Bruch des Henkels. Staubig. Und: »*Hoff-nung*«
an ihrem Bug in aufgebrauchter Schrift.

Das hat der Trinker, den der Trank betrifft,
bei einem fernen Frühstück ab-gelesen.

Was sind denn das für Wesen,
die man zuletzt wegschrecken muß mit Gift?

Blieben sie sonst? Sind sie denn hier vernarrt
in dieses Essen voller Hindernis?
Man muß ihnen die harte Gegenwart
ausnehmen, wie ein künstliches Gebiß.
Dann lallen sie. Gelall, Gelall
. .

O Sternenfall,
von einer Brücke einmal eingesehn—:
Dich nicht vergessen. Stehn!

And here is Death, a bluish distillate
in a cup without a saucer.
Such a very strange place for a cup:
balanced on the back of a hand. Quite clearly
you can still see on its glazed side
the break of the handle. Dusty. And *"Hope"*
along its rim in worn-out writing.

That's what the drinker whom the drink was for
read-off at some distant morning meal.

What sort of beings are these, then,
who finally must be driven off with poison?

Otherwise would they remain? Are they so engrossed here
in this meal full of hindrance?
The hard present moment has to be pulled out of them
like a set of false teeth.
Then their tongues blather: bla, blalall
. .

O fall of stars,
once glimpsed while leaning from a bridge—:
Never to forget you. To stay!

Munich, November 9, 1915

DIE WORTE DES HERRN
AN JOHANNES AUF PATMOS

Siehe: (denn kein Baum soll dich zerstreuen)
reinen Raum auf diesem Eiland stehn.
Vögel? Sei gefaßt auf Leuen
welche durch die Lüfte gehn.
Bäume würden scheuen,
und ich will nicht, daß sie sehn.

Aber du, du sieh, gewahre, sei
schauender als je ein Mann gewesen.
Du sollst fassen, nehmen, lesen,
schlingen sollst du, die ich dir entzwei
breche, meines Himmels volle Frucht.
Daß der Saft dir in die Augen tropfe,
sollst du knieen mit erhobnem Kopfe:
dazu hab ich dich gesucht.

Und sollst schreiben, ohne hin zu sehn;
denn auch dieses ist von Nöten: schreibe.
Leg die Rechte rechts und links auf den
Stein die Linke: daß ich beide treibe.

Und nun will ich ganz geschehn.

Jahrmillionen muß ich mich verhalten,
weil die Welten langsamer verleben,
muß den kalten
nach und nach von meinen Gluten geben
statt in allen, alle Glut zu sein.
Und so bin ich niemals im Geschaffnen:
wenn die Menschen eben mich vermuten,
so vergißt mich schon der Stein.

Einmal will ich mich vor dir entwaffnen.
Meine Mäntel, meine Reichsgewänder,

THE WORDS OF THE LORD
TO JOHN ON PATMOS

Behold: (for no tree shall distract you)
pure space stands on this island.
Birds? Be prepared for lions
that run rampant through the air.
Trees would be frightened,
and I choose not to have them see.

But *you, you* shall see, shall perceive, shall
gaze more deeply than anyone before.
You shall seize, take, read,
gulp down what I split open for you,
my heaven's ripe fruit.
You shall kneel with upturned head
so that the juice may pour into your eyes:
it's why I've sought you out.

And you shall write without looking down:
for that also is why you're here: for writing.
Place your left hand on the stone's left
and your right on its right: so I can use them both.

And now I'll utterly unfold.

Over millions of years I must restrain myself
since worlds take such time evolving,
must pierce their coldness with my ardor
bit by bit, instead of becoming fire
in all of them, one giant flame.
And so I'm never completely in creation:
by the time humans start to suspect me,
I've long been forgotten by the stone.

This once I'll divest myself before you.
My robes, my royal attire,

meine Rüstung: alles, was mich schnürt,
abtun, und dem hohen Doppelhänder
den der Engel für mich führt
meiner Rechten Strom entziehn. Doch jetzt
siehe die Bedeutung meiner Trachten.
Da Wir uns so große Kleider machten,
kommt das Unbekleidetsein zuletzt.

Knechte hat der Satan, die mit Knütteln
niederschlagen, was am zärtsten wächst,
und so muß ich Menschen noch zunächst
in dem eingesehnen Bild bestärken;
doch ich will an meinen Tieren rütteln:
denn es ist ein Drang in meinen Werken,
der nach wachsender Verwandlung lechzt.

Menschen heften sich an die Begriffe,
fanden mühsam sich hinein.
Eine Zeit noch sollen Schiffe Schiffe
und ein Haus soll wie die Häuser sein.
Und der Stuhl, der Tisch, der Schrank, die Truhe
und der Hut, der Mantel und die Schuhe
ohne daß man ihnen etwas tue—:
aber diese Formen sind nicht mein.

Manchmal wenn sie heulen daß ich tobe
werf ich liebend meine Feuerprobe
über das besitzende Geschlecht.
Und ich koste eines ihrer Dinge,
ob ich es empfinge—:
wenn es aufbrennt ist es echt.

Wüßten Menschen was der Engel Seele
hinreißt, daß sie wie ein Katarakt
über meine ältesten Befehle
weiterstürzt———. Ich hätte die Kameele
längst zurückgenommen und zerhackt.
An der Bildung ist mir nichts gelegen

my armor that straps me in
I shall cast off, and from the high great sword
that the angel bears before me shall
withdraw my right hand's force. Yet now
behold the meaning of my garb.
Since we've made ourselves such splendid garments,
stripping bare awaits us at the end.

Satan has knaves who with cudgels
beat down whatever grows most tenderly,
so for a while yet I must uphold
humans in clearly outlined images;
but I will set off tremors in my animals:
for there is a thirsting in my works
that craves even greater transformation.

Humans hold fiercely to the terms
in which they've so firmly placed their faith.
So for a time yet ships shall be ships
and houses houses.
And chair, table, cupboard, chest,
hat, coat, and shoes—
all shall stay as they are;
but these forms are none of mine.

Sometimes when they howl that I'm incensed
lovingly I'll cast my trial of fire
over that complacently possessive race.
And I'll taste one of their things,
to see if I'd like it—:
if it ignites it's real.

If humans only knew the transport
that fills an angel's soul—the way like a cataract
it plunges wildly over my oldest
commandments———. Long ago I should have
taken back camels and hacked them into pieces.
Nurturing is no concern of mine

denn ich bin der Feuerregen
und mein Blick ist, wie der Blitz gezackt.

Sieh ich dulde nicht daß einer bleibe.
Schreibe:
denn durch ihres Leibes Staub
werfe ich die Männer nach der Scheibe
nach dem Werke oder nach dem Weibe
und die Weiber will ich, wie das Laub.
Nur im Kinde mach ich eine Pause
daß sich das verbreitete Gebrause
sammele im muscheligen Ohr.
Sieh, in diesem Engen, Hingestellten
ordn ich das Gewühle meiner Welten:
das Vergehende geht in ihm vor.

for I am the rain of fire
and my glance is jagged like the lightning.

I'll not suffer one human to *remain*.
Write:
given their bodies' dust
I turn men out as on a potter's wheel
in the workman's fashion or after woman's way
and I'll have these women as the leaves.
Only in the child sometimes I pause
so that the far-flung outroar
may gather in its conchlike ear.
Behold, within this one small place
I bring order to the tumult of my worlds:
and the perishing proceeds.

Munich, late November 1915

Da wird der Hirsch zum Erdteil. Hebt und trägt
den Winterbaum, sein reines unbelaubtes
verzweigtes Spiel. Der Friede seines Hauptes
reicht nicht soweit, daß er in Blätter schlägt.

Now the stag becomes part of the earth. Lifts and holds
the tree of winter, its pure unfoliated
branched-out play. The peacefulness of its head
stops just short of breaking into leaves.

Munich, September–October 1916

∾

Nur zu Verlierern spricht das Verwandelte. Alle
Haltenden würgen.

∾

The transformed speaks only to relinquishers. All
holders-on are stranglers.

Böckel, early autumn 1917

Musik: Atem der Statuen. Vielleicht:
Stille der Bilder. Du Sprache wo Sprachen
enden. Du Zeit,
die senkrecht steht auf der Richtung vergehender Herzen.

Gefühle zu wem? O du der Gefühle
Wandlung in was? —: in hörbare Landschaft.
Du Fremde: Musik. Du uns entwachsener
Herzraum. Innigstes unser,
das, uns übersteigend, hinausdrängt, —
heiliger Abschied:
da uns das Innre umsteht
als geübteste Ferne, als andre
Seite der Luft:
rein,
riesig,
nicht mehr bewohnbar.

TO MUSIC

Music: breathing of statues. Maybe:
silence of paintings. You language where languages
end. You time
standing straight up on the path of vanishing hearts.

Feelings . . . for whom? O you the mutation
of feelings . . . into what? —: into audible landscape.
You stranger: music. You heartspace
grown up from us. Innermost thing
that, as it exceeds us, crowds its way out, —
sacred farewell:
when the inner surrounds us
as the most practiced distance, as the air's
other side:
pure,
immense,
no longer to be lived in.

Munich, January 11–12, 1918

Gott läßt sich nicht wie leichter Morgen leben.
Wer einfährt in den Schacht, der hat der vollen
Erde Gefühl um Werkschaft aufzugeben:
der steht gebückt und lockert ihn im Stollen.

ω

God won't be lived like some light morning.
Whoever climbs down the shaft must give up
earth's repleteness for the craft of mining:
stand hunched and pry him loose in tunnels.

Munich, mid-March 1919

Dies überstanden haben: auch das Glück
freudig bestanden haben, still und gründlich.
Bald war die Prüfung stumm, bald war sie mündlich.
Wer schaute nicht verwundert her zurück?

Gekonnt hats keiner, denn das Leben währt,
weils keiner konnte. —Aber der Versuche
Unendlichkeit. Das neue Grün der Buche
ist nicht so neu, wie was uns widerfährt.

Waldtaube gurrt. Und wieder scheint dir ach
was du erlittest, wie noch unerlitten.
Der Vogel ruft. Du bist inmitten
des Vogelrufs. Zugleich erwacht und schwach.

To have come through it: to have joyfully
survived even the happiness—quietly, completely.
First the testings were mute, then verbal.
Who could look back unamazed?

No one has *been able*, since life lasts
because no one *could*. —But the infinite
attempts! The new greenness of birch trees
is not so new as what befalls us.

A wood dove coos. And again what you suffered
seems, ah, as if yet unlived-through.
The bird keeps calling. You are in the middle
of the call. Awake and weakened.

Schloss Berg am Irchel, beginning of April 1921

DIE HAND

Siehe die kleine Meise,
hereinverirrte ins Zimmer:
zwanzig Herzschläge lang
lag sie in einer Hand.
Menschenhand. Einer zu schützen entschlossenen.
Unbesitzend beschützenden.
Aber
jetzt auf dem Fensterbrett
frei
bleibt sie noch immer im Schrecken
sich selber
und dem Umgebenden fremd,
dem Weltall, erkennts nicht.
Ach so beirrend ist Hand
selbst noch im Retten.
In der beiständigsten Hand
ist noch Todes genug
und war Geld

THE HAND

See the little titmouse,
lost and bewildered in the room:
twenty heartbeats long
it lay in a hand.
Human hand. One determined to protect.
But
now on the windowsill
free
it remains cut off in its fear
from itself
and what surrounds it,
the cosmos, which it doesn't recognize.
Ah, how perplexing a hand is
even bent on rescue.
Even in the most helping hand
there's still death enough
and was money

Muzot, end of 1921

Solang du Selbstgeworfnes fängst, ist alles
Geschicklichkeit und läßlicher Gewinn—;
erst wenn du plötzlich Fänger wirst des Balles,
den eine ewige Mit-Spielerin
dir zuwarf, deiner Mitte, in genau
gekonntem Schwung, in einem jener Bögen
aus Gottes großem Brücken-Bau:
erst dann ist Fangen-Können ein Vermögen, —
nicht deines, einer Welt. Und wenn du gar
zurückzuwerfen Kraft und Mut besäßest,
nein, wunderbarer: Mut und Kraft vergäßest
und schon geworfen *hättest* (wie das Jahr
die Vögel wirft, die Wandervogelschwärme,
die eine ältre einer jungen Wärme
hinüberschleudert über Meere—) erst
in diesem Wagnis spielst du gültig mit.
Erleichterst dir den Wurf nicht mehr; erschwerst
dir ihn nicht mehr. Aus deinen Händen tritt
das Meteor und rast in seine Räume . . .

As long as you catch self-thrown things
it's all dexterity and venial gain—;
only when suddenly you hold that ball
which she, one of the eternal players,
has tossed to you, to your center, with
a precisely judged throw, in one of those arcs
that exist in God's great bridge system:
only then is catching a proficiency,—
not yours, a world's. And if then you had
the strength and courage to return the throw—
no, more wonderful—forgot strength and courage
and had thrown *already* (the way the year
throws the birds, those migrating bird swarms,
which an older to a younger warmth sends
catapulting across oceans—) only in
that venture would you truly play the game.
No longer making the toss easy; no longer making
it hard. Out of your hands the meteor
would launch itself and flame into its spaces . . .

Muzot, January 31, 1922

~

... Wann wird, wann wird, wann wird es genügen
das Klagen und Sagen? Waren nicht Meister im Fügen
menschlicher Worte gekommen? Warum die neuen Versuche?

Sind nicht, sind nicht, sind nicht vom Buche
die Menschen geschlagen wie von fortwährender Glocke?
Wenn dir, zwischen zwei Büchern, schweigender Himmel erscheint:
 frohlocke ... ,
oder ein Ausschnitt einfacher Erde im Abend.

Mehr als die Stürme, mehr als die Meere haben
die Menschen geschrieen ... Welche Übergewichte von Stille
müssen im Weltraum wohnen, da uns die Grille
hörbar blieb, uns schreienden Menschen. Da uns die Sterne
schweigende scheinen, im angeschrieenen Äther!

Redeten uns die fernsten, die alten und ältesten Väter!
Und wir: Hörende endlich! Die ersten hörenden Menschen.

≈

... When will, when will, when will it be enough,
the saying and lamenting? Have not master practitioners
of human words been here? Why try and try again?

Are not, are not, are not we humans
hammered at by books as by endless bells?
When, between two books, silent sky appears: rejoice . . . ,
or a patch of simple earth at evening.

Louder than storms, louder than oceans, humans
have been crying out . . . What preponderance of quietness
must abide in cosmic space, since the cricket
remains audible to us, for all our screaming. When the star
shines silently for us, in the screamed-at ether!

If the remotest, old and most ancient fathers would talk to us!
And we: listeners at last! The first human listeners.

Muzot, February 1, 1922

In a selection of unpublished poems Rilke copied out for Katharina Kippenberg in June 1926, this poem bears the dedication "from M's belongings," along with the postscript "Written on the evening before the Orpheus sonnets."

Oh, daß ihr hier, Frauen, einhergeht,
hier unter uns, leidvoll,
nicht geschonter als wir und dennoch imstande,
selig zu machen wie Selige.

Woher,
wenn der Geliebte erscheint,
nehmt ihr die Zukunft?
Mehr, als je sein wird.
Wer die Entfernungen weiß
bis zum äußersten Fixstern,
staunt, wenn er diesen gewahrt,
euern herrlichen Herzraum.
Wie, im Gedräng, spart ihr ihn aus?
Ihr, voll Quellen und Nacht.

Seid ihr wirklich die gleichen,
die, da ihr Kind wart,
unwirsch im Schulgang
anstieß der ältere Bruder?
Ihr Heilen.

Wo wir als Kinder uns schon
häßlich für immer verzerrn,
wart ihr wie Brot vor der Wandlung.

Ah, women, that you are here on earth, that you
move here among us, grief-filled,
no more watched over than we and yet able
to bless like the blessed.

From what region,
when the loved one appears,
do you fetch the future?
More than will ever exist.
He who knows distances
out to the outermost fixed star
is amazed to find this,
your magnificent heartspace.
How, in the crush, do you keep it free?
You, filled with sources and night.

Are you really the same
as those girls who on the path
to school were rudely
shoved aside by an older brother?
You whole ones.

> Whereas we, even when children, hatefully
> disfigure ourselves forever,
> you were like bread before the Change.

Rilke originally conceived this poem as the fifth of the *Duino Elegies*; he replaced it with the "Saltimbanques," the last of the elegies to be composed. (It was written on February 14, five days after "Antistrophes" was completed.)

Abbruch der Kindheit
war euch nicht Schaden. Auf einmal
standet ihr da, wie im Gott
plötzlich zum Wunder ergänzt.

Wir, wie gebrochen vom Berg,
oft schon als Knaben scharf
an den Rändern, vielleicht
manchmal glücklich behaun;
wir, wie Stücke Gesteins,
über Blumen gestürzt.

Blumen des tieferen Erdreichs,
von allen Wurzeln geliebte,
ihr, der Eurydike Schwestern,
immer voll heiliger Umkehr
hinter dem steigenden Mann.

Wir, von uns selber gekränkt,
Kränkende gern und gern
Wiedergekränkte aus Not.
Wir, wie Waffen, dem Zorn
neben den Schlaf gelegt.

Ihr, die ihr beinah Schutz seid, wo niemand
schützt. Wie ein schattiger Schlafbaum
ist der Gedanke an euch
für die Schwärme des Einsamen.

Childhood's breaking off
did you no harm. All at once
you stood there, complete,
as if made manifest in the god.

We, as if broken from cliffs,
even as young boys sharp
at the edges, though sometimes
maybe smoothly cut;
we, like big chunks of rock
dumped over flowers.

Flowers of the deeper soil,
loved by all roots,
you, Eurydice's sisters,
always full of sacred turning-back
behind the ascending man.

We, hurt by ourselves, keen
to be hurters and keen
to be hurt back deep inside.
We, like weapons laid
beside anger asleep.

You, who are almost protection where no one
protects. The thought of you
is like a shady sleeptree
for the swarms of the solitary man.

Lines 1–4: Venice, summer 1912; lines 5–46, Muzot, February 9, 1922

563

Wir, in den ringenden Nächten,
wir fallen von Nähe zu Nähe;
und wo die Liebende taut,
sind wir ein stürzender Stein.

∾

We, in the grappling nights,
we drop from nearness to nearness;
and where the woman in love falls like dew,
we're a hurtling stone.

Muzot, February 9, 1922

Erst eine Kindheit, grenzenlos und ohne
Verzicht und Ziel. O unbewußte Lust.
Auf einmal Schrecken, Schranke, Schule, Frohne
und Absturz in Versuchung und Verlust.

Trotz. Der Gebogene wird selber Bieger
und rächt an anderen, daß er erlag.
Geliebt, gefürchtet, Retter, Ringer, Sieger
und Überwinder, Schlag auf Schlag.

Und dann allein im Weiten, Leichten, Kalten.
Doch tief in der errichteten Gestalt
ein Atemholen nach dem Ersten, Alten . . .

Da stürzte Gott aus seinem Hinterhalt.

IMAGINARY CAREER

First a childhood, boundless and without
negation and goal. O unthinking joy.
Suddenly fright, limit, schoolroom, slavery,
and fall into temptation, into loss.

Defiance. The bent becomes the bender now
and seeks revenge on others, makes *them* succumb.
Loved, feared; savior, enemy, victor,
vanquisher, role by role.

And then alone in vastness, lightness, cold.
Yet deep in that erected figure
a breathing toward the First, the Ancient . . .

Then God stepped out of his hiding place.

Schöneck, September 15, 1923

TRÄNENKRÜGLEIN

Andere fassen den Wein, andere fassen die Öle
in dem gehöhlten Gewölb, das ihre Wandung umschrieb.
Ich, als ein kleineres Maß, und als schlankestes, höhle
mich einem andern Bedarf, stürzenden Tränen zulieb.

Wein wird reicher, und Öl klärt sich noch weiter im Kruge.
Was mit den Tränen geschieht? —Sie machten mich schwer,
machten mich blinder und machten mich schillern am Buge,
machten mich brüchig zuletzt und machten mich leer.

LACHRYMATORY

Others carry the wine, others carry the oil
in the hollowed vault their partition circumscribed.
I, as a smaller measure, and as the slimmest vessel, hollow myself
for a different need, for the sake of plummeting tears.

Wine becomes richer, and oil keeps clarifying in the jug.
What happens with tears? —They made me heavy,
made me blinder and made me iridescent where I curve,
made me brittle finally and made me empty.

Schöneck, September 16, 1923

Wir sind nur Mund. Wer singt das ferne Herz,
das heil inmitten aller Dinge weilt?
Sein großer Schlag ist in uns eingeteilt
in kleine Schläge. Und sein großer Schmerz
ist, wie sein großer Jubel, uns zu groß.
So reißen wir uns immer wieder los
und sind nur Mund. Aber auf einmal bricht
der große Herzschlag heimlich in uns ein,
so daß wir schrein . . .
Und sind dann Wesen, Wandlung und Gesicht.

We're only mouth. Who sings the distant heart
that dwells whole at the center of all things?
Its great pulse is distributed among us
in tiny beatings. And its great pain
is, like its great rejoicing, too much for us.
So again and again we tear ourselves loose
and are only mouth. But all at once
the great heartbeat secretly breaks in on us
so that we scream . . .
And then are being, transformation, visage.

Schöneck, end of September 1923

Auch noch Verlieren ist *unser*; und selbst das Vergessen
hat noch Gestalt in dem bleibenden Reich der Verwandlung.
Losgelassenes kreist; und sind wir auch selten die Mitte
einem der Kreise: sie ziehn um uns die heile Figur.

FOR HANS CAROSSA

Losing is also *ours*; and even forgetting
has its shape in the permanent realm of change.
Things we've let go of circle; and though we're rarely at the center
of these circles: they trace around us the unbroken figure.

Muzot, February 7, 1924

Da dich das geflügelte Entzücken
über manchen frühen Abgrund trug,
baue jetzt der unerhörten Brücken
kühn berechenbaren Bug.

Wunder ist nicht nur im unerklärten
Überstehen der Gefahr;
erst in einer klaren reingewährten
Leistung wird das Wunder wunderbar.

Mitzuwirken ist nicht Überhebung
an dem unbeschreiblichen Bezug,
immer inniger wird die Verwebung,
nur Getragensein ist nicht genug.

Deine ausgeübten Kräfte spanne,
bis sie reichen, zwischen zwein
Widersprüchen . . . Denn im Manne
will der Gott beraten sein.

As once the winged energy of delight
carried you over those many first abysses,
now build the unimagined bridges'
sternly calculated arc.

Miracle is not only when some danger
has been incomprehensibly survived;
only in a clear, consummate achievement
is the miracle *defined*.

There's no presumption in joining in
on the indescribable relation;
the interweaving grows ever more ardent;
being borne along is not enough.

Take your most practiced strengths
and stretch them till they reach
between two contradictions . . . For in you
the god is waiting to consult.

Muẓot, mid-February 1924

VORFRÜHLING

Härte schwand. Auf einmal legt sich Schonung
an der Wiesen aufgedecktes Grau.
Kleine Wasser ändern die Betonung.
Zärtlichkeiten, ungenau,

greifen nach der Erde aus dem Raum.
Wege gehen weit ins Land und zeigens.
Unvermutet siehst du seines Steigens
Ausdruck in dem leeren Baum.

Harshness vanished. Suddenly caring
spreads itself over the field's uncovered gray.
Little rivulets change their intonations.
Tendernesses, inexpertly,

reach toward the earth from space.
Roads run far into the land, foretelling it.
Unexpectedly you see its rising's
visage in the empty tree.

Muzot, mid-February 1924

~

Weißt du noch: fallende Sterne, die
quer wie Pferde durch die Himmel sprangen
über plötzlich hingehaltne Stangen
unsrer Wünsche—hatten wir so viele?—
denn es sprangen Sterne, ungezählt;
fast ein jeder Aufblick war vermählt
mit dem raschen Wagnis ihrer Spiele,
und das Herz empfand sich als ein Ganzes
unter diesen Trümmern ihres Glanzes
und war heil, als überstünd es sie!

Do you still remember: falling stars,
how they leapt slantwise through the sky
like horses over suddenly held-out hurdles
of our wishes—did we have *so* many?—
for stars, innumerable, leapt everywhere;
almost every gaze upward became
wedded to the swift hazard of their play,
and our heart felt like a single thing
beneath that vast disintegration of their brilliance—
and was whole, as if it would survive them!

Muzot, June 1924

Wie steht er da vor den Verdunkelungen
des Regenabends, jung und rein;
in seinen Ranken schenkend ausgeschwungen
und doch versunken in sein Rose-sein;

die flachen Blüten, da und dort schon offen,
jegliche ungewollt und ungepflegt:
so, von sich selbst unendlich übertroffen
und unbeschreiblich aus sich selbst erregt,

ruft er dem Wandrer, der in abendlicher
Nachdenklichkeit den Weg vorüberkommt:
Oh sieh mich stehn, sieh her, was bin ich sicher
und unbeschützt und habe was mir frommt.

WILD ROSEBUSH

How it stands out against the darkenings
of the rainy evening, young and pure,
its tendrils arched everywhere in givingness
yet absorbed in its own rose-being;

the shallow flowers, already open here and there,
each unasked for and untended:
thus, immeasurably exceeded by itself
and indescribably self-aroused,

it calls to the wanderer, who in his evening
meditating comes past along the road:
Oh look at me, see, over here, how safe I am
and unprotected and having all I need.

Muzot, June 1, 1924

Durch den sich Vögel werfen, ist nicht der
vertraute Raum, der die Gestalt dir steigert.
(Im Freien, dorten, bist du dir verweigert
und schwindest weiter ohne Wiederkehr.)

Raum greift aus uns und übersetzt die Dinge:
daß dir das Dasein eines Baums gelinge,
wirf Innenraum um ihn, aus jenem Raum,
der in dir west. Umgieb ihn mit Verhaltung.
Er grenzt sich nicht. Erst in der Eingestaltung
in dein Verzichten wird er wirklich Baum.

~

What birds dive through is not that intimate space
in which you feel all forms intensified.
(Out there, in the Open, you'd be denied yourself
and vanish on and on with no return.)

Space juts out from us and translates each thing:
to succeed with a tree's essence
cast innerspace around it, out of that space
that has its life in you. Surround it with restraint.
In itself it has no bounds. Only in the field
of your renouncing does it rise as Tree.

Muzot, June 16, 1924

Welt war in dem Antlitz der Geliebten—,
aber plötzlich ist sie ausgegossen:
Welt ist draußen, Welt ist nicht zu fassen.

Warum trank ich nicht, da ich es aufhob,
aus dem vollen, dem geliebten Antlitz
Welt, die nah war, duftend meinem Munde?

Ach, ich trank. Wie trank ich unerschöpflich.
Doch auch ich war angefüllt mit zuviel
Welt, und trinkend ging ich selber über.

World was in the face of the beloved—,
but suddenly was all poured out.
World is outside. World cannot be grasped.

Why, when I raised to my lips the full,
beloved face, did I not drink in world,
which was so near I tasted its bouquet?

Ah, I drank. Insatiably I drank.
But already I was overbrimming
with too much world, and as I drank I spilled.

Ragaz, mid-July 1924

Unstete Waage des Lebens
immer schwankend, wie selten
wagt ein geschicktes Gewicht
anzusagen die immerfort andre
Last gegenüber.

Drüben, die ruhige
Waage des Todes.
Raum auf den beiden
verschwisterten Schalen.
Gleichviel Raum. Und daneben,
ungebraucht,
alle Gewichte des Gleichmuts,
glänzen, geordnet.

～

Unsteady scales of life
forever swaying, how seldom
a confident weight dares
announce the load of its constantly
altering opposite number.

Across the way, death's
peaceful scales.
Space on the
brother-and-sister pans.
Distinctionless space. And beside it,
unused,
all of equanimity's weights,
gleaming, in order.

Ragaz, mid-July 1924

Ach, im Wind gelöst,
wieviel vergebliche Wiederkehr.
Manches, was uns verstößt,
tut hinterher,
wenn wir vorüber sind,
ratlos die Arme auf.
Denn es giebt keinen Lauf
zurück. Alles hebt uns hinaus,
und das spät offene Haus
bleibt leer.

\sim

Ah, adrift in the air,
how much unfulfilled return.
The things that expel us,
so often, afterward,
once we've gone,
hopelessly spread their arms.
For no course leads back.
Everything lifts us up and away,
and the belatedly open house
stays empty.

Ragaz, mid-July 1924

Innres der Hand. Sohle, die nicht mehr geht
als auf Gefühl. Die sich nach oben hält
und im Spiegel
himmlische Straßen empfängt, die selber
wandelnden.
Die gelernt hat, auf Wasser zu gehn,
wenn sie schöpft,
die auf den Brunnen geht,
aller Wege Verwandlerin.
Die auftritt in anderen Händen,
die ihresgleichen
zur Landschaft macht:
wandert und ankommt in ihnen,
sie anfüllt mit Ankunft.

PALM OF THE HAND

Hand's secret self. Sole, that has ceased to walk
except on feeling. That extends faceup
and in that mirror
receives heavenly streets, themselves
out wandering.
That has learned to walk on water
when it scoops,
that walks on wells,
that changes every path it travels.
That enters other hands,
turns its doubles
into landscape:
wanders and arrives in them,
fills them with arrival.

Muzot, beginning of October 1924

Irgendwo blüht die Blume des Abschieds und streut
immerfort Blütenstaub, den wir atmen, herüber;
auch noch im kommendsten Wind atmen wir Abschied.

℘

Somewhere the flower of farewell blooms and ceaselessly
scatters its pollen, which we breathe;
even in the winds that reach us first we breathe farewell.

Muzot, mid-October 1924

＊

Ach, nicht getrennt sein,
nicht durch so wenig Wandung
ausgeschlossen vom Sternen-Maß.
Innres, was ists?
Wenn nicht gesteigerter Himmel,
durchworfen mit Vögeln und tief
von Winden der Heimkehr.

Ah, not to be cut off,
not by such slight partition
to be excluded from the stars' measure.
What is inwardness?
What if not sky intensified,
flung through with birds and deep
with winds of homecoming.

Paris, summer 1925 (before July 6)

~

Unaufhaltsam, ich will die Bahn vollenden,
mich schreckt es, wenn mich ein Sterbliches hält.
Einmal hielt mich ein Schooß.
Ihm sich entringen, war tödlich:
ich rang mich ins Leben. Aber sind Arme so tief,
sind sie so fruchtbar, um ihnen
durch die beginnliche Not
neuer Geburt zu entgehn?

～

Undeterrable, I'll complete this course,
I'm frightened when something mortal holds me.
Once a womb held me.
Wresting free from it was deadly:
I wrestled into life. But arms—how deep are arms,
how fertile are they, what chance
that *they* through the inaugural agony
of new birth might be escaped?

Paris, early summer 1925

Jetzt wär es Zeit, daß Götter träten aus
bewohnten Dingen . . .
Und daß sie jede Wand in meinem Haus
umschlügen. Neue Seite. Nur der Wind,
den solches Blatt im Wenden würfe, reichte hin,
die Luft, wie eine Scholle, umzuschaufeln:
ein neues Atemfeld. Oh Götter, Götter!
Ihr Oftgekommnen, Schläfer in den Dingen,
die heiter aufstehn, die sich an den Brunnen,
die wir vermuten, Hals und Antlitz waschen
und die ihr Ausgeruhtsein leicht hinzutun
zu dem, was voll scheint, unserm vollen Leben.
Noch einmal sei es euer Morgen, Götter.
Wir wiederholen. Ihr allein seid Ursprung.
Die Welt steht auf mit euch, und Anfang glänzt
an allen Bruchstelln unseres Mißlingens . . .

Now it is time that gods stepped out
of lived-in things . . .
Time they ripped down every wall
in my house. New page. Only the wind
made by such a page turning over
could shovel the air as a spade turns over earth:
new breathfield. Oh gods, gods!
You who came so often, sleepers inside things,
who cheerfully arise, who at wells
that we conjecture wash face and neck
and lightly add your restedness
to that which seems replete, our own full lives.
May it once again be your morning, gods.
We repeat. You alone are source.
The world gets up with you, and Beginning shines
on all the cracks in our failures . . .

Muzot, mid-October 1925

Rose, oh reiner Widerspruch, Lust,
Niemandes Schlaf zu sein unter soviel
Lidern.

ॐ

Rose, O pure contradiction, delight
in being no one's sleep under so many
eyelids.

Muzot, October 27, 1925

Epitaph composed by Rilke and included in his last will and testament. It is inscribed on his
tombstone in the churchyard at Raron, Switzerland.

GONG (I)

Klang, nichtmehr mit Gehör
meßbar. Als wäre der Ton,
der uns rings übertrifft,
eine Reife des Raums.

GONG (I)

Sound, no longer measurable
with the sense of hearing. As if that tone
outstripping us on every side
were space ripening.

Muzot, end of October 1925

Gott oder Göttin des Katzenschlafs,
kostende Gottheit, die in dem dunkeln
Mund reife Augen-Beeren zerdrückt,
süßgewordnen Schauns Traubensaft,
ewiges Licht in der Krypta des Gaumens.
Schlaf-Lied nicht, —Gong! Gong!
Was die anderen Götter beschwört,
entläßt diesen verlisteten Gott
an seine einwärts fallende Macht.

God or goddess of the sleep of cats,
savoring deity, who in the dark
mouth crushes ripe eyeberries,
grape juice of seeing grown sweet,
eternal torchlight in the palate's crypt.
Not lullaby, —Gong! Gong!
What conjures all the other gods
lets this god of ancient wiles slip back
into its inwardly collapsing might.

Line 1, Paris, summer 1925; lines 2–9, Muzot, November 1925

Nicht mehr für Ohren . . . : Klang,
der, wie ein tieferes Ohr,
uns, scheinbar Hörende, hört.
Umkehr der Räume. Entwurf
innerer Welten im Frein . . . ,
Tempel vor ihrer Geburt,
Lösung, gesättigt mit schwer
löslichen Göttern . . . : Gong!

Summe des Schweigenden, das
sich zu sich selber bekennt,
brausende Einkehr in sich
dessen, das an sich verstummt,
Dauer, aus Ablauf gepreßt,
umgegossener Stern . . . : Gong!

Du, die man niemals vergißt,
die sich gebar im Verlust,
nichtmehr begriffenes Fest,
Wein an unsichtbarem Mund,
Sturm in der Säule, die trägt,
Wanderers Sturz in den Weg,
unser, an Alles, Verrat . . . : Gong!

GONG (II)

Not for ears anymore . . . :
sound which, as if a deeper ear,
hears us, apparent listeners.
Spaces reversing. Design
for inner worlds out in the Open . . . ,
temple before their birth,
solution oversaturated with gods
difficult to dissolve . . . : Gong!

Sum of all things silent, which
acknowledges itself alone,
thunderous inturn of something
in itself struck dumb,
duration pressed from transience,
star repoured . . . : Gong!

You, whom one never forgets,
who gave birth to yourself in loss,
festival no longer understood,
wine on invisible lips,
storm in the column that upholds,
wanderer's fall onto the path,
our treason—to everything . . . : Gong!

Muzot, November 1925

Die Vogelrufe fangen an zu rühmen.
Und sind im Recht. Wir hören lange hin.
(Wir hinter Masken, ach, und in Kostümen!)
Was rufen sie? ein wenig Eigensinn,

ein wenig Wehmut und sehr viel Versprechen,
das an der halbverschlossnen Zukunft feilt.
Und zwischendurch in unserm Horchen heilt
das schöne Schweigen, das sie brechen.

The birdcalls start their praise.
And rightly so. We listen long.
(We behind masks, in costumes!)
What do we hear? a little willfulness,

a little sadness, and tremendous promise,
sawing away at the half-locked future.
And in between, healing in our listening:
the beautiful silence they break.

Val-Mont, mid-March 1926

ॐ

Bruder Körper ist arm . . . : da heißt es, reich sein für ihn.
Oft war *er* der Reiche: so sei ihm verziehn
das Armsein seiner argen Momente.
Wenn er dann tut, als ob er uns kaum noch kennte,
darf man ihn leise erinnern an alles Gemeinsame.

Freilich wir sind nicht Eines, sondern zwei Einsame:
unser Bewußtsein und Er;
aber wie vieles, das wir einander weither
verdanken,
wie Freunde es tun! Und man erfährt im Erkranken:
Freunde haben es schwer!

Brother body is poor . . . : then we'll have to be rich for him.
Often *he* was the rich one: so may he be pardoned
the meanness of his worst moments.
And if he behaves as though he scarcely knows us,
let us gently remind him of all we've shared.

Granted, we're not one, but a solitary two:
our consciousness and he;
but how much we owe each other
past conceiving,
the way it is with friends! And one learns in illness:
friendship is hard!

Val-Mont, May 1, 1926

ELEGIE
An Marina Zwetajewa-Efron

O die Verluste ins All, Marina, die stürzenden Sterne!
Wir vermehren es nicht, wohin wir uns werfen, zu welchem
Sterne hinzu! Im Ganzen ist immer schon alles gezählt.
So auch, wer fällt, vermindert die heilige Zahl nicht.
Jeder verzichtende Sturz stürzt in den Ursprung und heilt.
Wäre denn alles ein Spiel, Wechsel des Gleichen, Verschiebung,
nirgends ein Name und kaum irgendwo heimisch Gewinn?
Wellen, Marina, wir Meer! Tiefen, Marina, wir Himmel.
Erde, Marina, wir Erde, wir tausendmal Frühling, wie Lerchen,
die ein ausbrechendes Lied in die Unsichtbarkeit wirft.
Wir beginnens als Jubel, schon übertrifft es uns völlig;
plötzlich, unser Gewicht dreht zur Klage abwärts den Sang.
Aber auch so: Klage? Wäre sie nicht: jüngerer Jubel nach unten.
Auch die unteren Götter wollen gelobt sein, Marina.
So unschuldig sind Götter, sie warten auf Lob wie die Schüler.
Loben, du Liebe, laß uns verschwenden mit Lob.
Nichts gehört uns. Wir legen ein wenig die Hand um die Hälse
ungebrochener Blumen. Ich sah es am Nil in Kôm-Ombo.
So, Marina, die Spende, selber verzichtend, opfern die Könige.
Wie die Engel gehen und die Türen bezeichnen jener zu Rettenden,
also rühren wir dieses und dies, scheinbar Zärtliche, an.
Ach wie weit schon Entrückte, ach, wie Zerstreute, Marina,
auch noch beim innigsten Vorwand. Zeichengeber, sonst nichts.

ELEGY

To Marina Tsvetayeva-Efron

O the losses into the All, Marina, the falling stars!
We don't add to it, no matter where we fling ourselves, out
to whatever star! In the Whole everything has already
been summed. Nor does falling lessen the sacred count.
Each renouncing plunge falls to the source and heals.
Is it all a game then—displacement, exchanging of sameness,
nowhere a name and scarcely anywhere indigenous gain?
Waves, Marina, we're ocean! Depths, Marina, we're sky!
Earth, Marina, we're earth, we're a thousand times Spring, like larks
which an outburst of song flings toward the Invisible.
We begin it as jubilation, from the first it wildly exceeds us;
suddenly our weight bends the song toward lament.
But why "lament"? Why not "younger jubilation coursing downward"?
Even the gods below want to be praised, Marina.
Gods are so guileless, they wait for praise like schoolchildren.
Praising, dearest, let us be lavish with praise.
Nothing is ours. We curl our hand lightly around the necks
of flowers we leave unplucked. I saw it on the Nile, in Kom Ombo.
Just so, Marina, kings make the sacrifice a self-renouncing.
As angels walk and mark doors of those to be saved,
so we, seemingly sensitive, pause to touch this and this.
Ah, how far removed already, how distracted, Marina,
even in our most fervent pretext. Sign givers, nothing more.

Marina Tsvetayeva (1892–1941): One of the great modern Russian poets. Without ever meet-
ing, she and Rilke carried on a passionate correspondence (which she initiated) during the
spring and summer of 1926. Her long poem "Novogodnee," written in early January 1927, ad-
dresses a loved Rilke with wild directness, as in a phantasmic refusal to grieve.

Kom Ombo: Probably a stop on Rilke's trip to Egypt in 1911. What he "saw" there remains ob-
scure, as does the elliptical formulation of a renunciation or self-withholding in the poem's next
line. Something of what Rilke has in mind may be illuminated by a passage from a letter to
Katharina Kippenberg of May 28, 1924: "[Instead of picking flowers from my garden and send-
ing them to you for your birthday on a journey they could never survive,] I will offer them in
the manner of the sacrificers on the Egyptian reliefs, who dedicated and presented their flowers
to the gods not by picking them, but by holding their hands for a time quietly and intently
around the living, growing stems."

Dieses leise Geschäft, wo es der Unsrigen einer
nicht mehr erträgt und sich zum Zugriff entschließt,
rächt sich und tötet. Denn daß es tödliche Macht hat,
merkten wir alle an seiner Verhaltung und Zartheit
und an der seltsamen Kraft, die uns aus Lebenden zu
Überlebenden macht. Nicht-Sein. Weißt du's, wie oft
trug uns ein blinder Befehl durch den eisigen Vorraum
neuer Geburt . . . Trug: *uns?* Einen Körper aus Augen
unter zahllosen Lidern sich weigernd. Trug das in uns
niedergeworfene Herz eines ganzen Geschlechts. An ein Zugvogelziel
trug er die Gruppe, das Bild unserer schwebenden Wandlung.
Liebende dürften, Marina, dürfen soviel nicht
von dem Untergang wissen. Müssen wie neu sein.
Erst ihr Grab ist alt, erst ihr Grab besinnt sich, verdunkelt
unter dem schluchzenden Baum, besinnt sich auf Jeher.
Erst ihr Grab bricht ein; sie selber sind biegsam wie Ruten;
was übermäßig sie biegt, ründet sie reichlich zum Kranz.
Wie sie verwehen im Maiwind! Von der Mitte des Immer,
drin du atmest und ahnst, schließt sie der Augenblick aus.
(O wie begreif ich dich, weibliche Blüte am gleichen
unvergänglichen Strauch. Wie streu ich mich stark in die Nachtluft,
die dich nächstens bestreift.) Frühe erlernten die Götter
Hälften zu heucheln. Wir in das Kreisen bezogen
füllten zum Ganzen uns an wie die Scheibe des Monds.
Auch in abnehmender Frist, auch in den Wochen der Wendung
niemand verhülfe uns je wieder zum Vollsein, als der
einsame eigene Gang über der schlaflosen Landschaft.

This delicate business, should one on our side,
no longer able to bear it, tense himself for the grasp,
strikes first and kills. For that it has death-dealing strength
we could see in its restraint and tenderness
and in the strange power that turns us from living beings
into survivors. Not-being. Remember how often
a blind command bore us through the icy antechamber
of new birth? . . . Bore: *us?* Bore a body of eyes
balking under myriad eyelids. Bore in us the hurled-down
heart of an entire race. Bore the group as to a goal
of migrating birds, that figure of our soaring transformation.
Lovers ought not, Marina, lovers *may* not know
so deeply of decline. Must be as new.
Only their grave is old, only their grave ponders, grows dark
under the sobbing tree, thinking back on everything.
Only their grave collapses; they themselves grow supple like reeds:
what bends them violently rounds them richly into wreaths.
How they blow about in the May wind! From the midst of Ever,
in which you breathe and surmise, the Moment bars them.
(O how I feel you, female blossom on the same
undying shrub. How I scatter myself strongly into the night breeze
that soon will brush you.) Early on, the gods learned
to simulate halves. We, lured into the circle,
filled ourselves out to a whole like the moon's disk.
Even in the waning phase, even in the weeks of the turning,
no one could ever help us again to fullness—there's only
our own solitary course over the sleepless landscape.

Muzot, June 8, 1926

VOLLMACHT

Ach entzögen wir uns Zählern und Stundenschlägern.
Einen Morgen hinaus, heißes Jungsein mit Jägern,
 Rufen im Hundegekläff.
Daß im durchdrängten Gebüsch Kühle uns fröhlich besprühe,
und wir im Neuen und Frein—in den Lüften der Frühe
 fühlten den graden Betreff!

Solches war uns bestimmt. Leichte beschwingte Erscheinung.
Nicht, im starren Gelaß, nach einer Nacht voll Verneinung,
 ein verneinender Tag.
Diese sind ewig im Recht: dringend dem Leben Genahte;
weil sie Lebendige sind, tritt das unendlich bejahte
 Tier in den tödlichen Schlag.

FULL POWER

Ah, could we escape counters and strikers of hours.
One morning eagerly outside, hot youthfulness with hunters,
 shouts in the clamor of hounds.
Thrashing through bushes, coolness joyfully spraying us,
and we in the new and the free—feeling in the earliest breezes
 the exact connection!

This we were meant for. Lighthearted exhilarated appearance.
Not, in the rigid room, after a night of negation,
 one more negation-filled day.
These are eternally in the right, these pressed so close to life;
because they are the living, the infinitely affirmed
 animal steps up to the mortal blow.

Muzot, June 9, 1926

Komm du, du letzter, den ich anerkenne,
heilloser Schmerz im leiblichen Geweb:
wie ich im Geiste brannte, sieh, ich brenne
in dir; das Holz hat lange widerstrebt,
der Flamme, die du loderst, zuzustimmen,
nun aber nähr' ich dich und brenn in dir.
Mein hiesig Mildsein wird in deinem Grimmen
ein Grimm der Hölle nicht von hier.
Ganz rein, ganz planlos frei von Zukunft stieg
ich auf des Leidens wirren Scheiterhaufen,
so sicher nirgend Künftiges zu kaufen
um dieses Herz, darin der Vorrat schwieg.
Bin ich es noch, der da unkenntlich brennt?
Erinnerungen reiß ich nicht herein.
O Leben, Leben: Draußensein.
Und ich in Lohe. Niemand der mich kennt.

[Verzicht. Das ist nicht so wie Krankheit war
einst in der Kindheit. Aufschub. Vorwand um
größer zu werden. Alles rief und raunte.
Misch nicht in dieses was dich früh erstaunte]

Come, you last thing, which I acknowledge,
unholy agony in the fleshly weave:
just as I burned in spirit, look, I burn
in you; the wood has long held back,
long recoiled from those flames you blaze,
but now I feed you and burn in you.
Inside your rage my native mildness becomes
a raging hell, unlike anything here.
Without plan, completely pure, free of future
I mounted suffering's tangled pyre,
so sure of nowhere buying times to come
for this heart, its store so mute.
Is it still I, burning here beyond recognition?
I will not drag memories inside.
O life, life: externality.
And I in flame. No one knowing me.

[Renunciation. That's not how illness was
in childhood. Putting off. Subterfuge
for growing. Everything called and whispered.
Don't mix those early marvels into this]

Val-Mont, mid-December 1926
Last entry in last pocketbook

The last four lines (in brackets here) are canceled in the pocketbook.

THE BOOK OF HOURS

The Book of Hours (*Das Stunden-Buch*) is one of the strongest inaugural works in all of modern poetry. It arrives as if out of nowhere and seems to want to wipe the slate clean. When it appeared in December 1905, Rilke was already the author of some seven volumes of poetry, but none of them—not even the premature 1902 version of *The Book of Images*—suggests that anything serious is on its way. There are scattered moments of brilliance, to be sure, but the overall impression is of free-floating (and slightly inept) poetic ambition, a sort of would-be precociousness trying out subject matter and playing less impressively than it supposes with *Jugendstil* effects. Nothing prepares for the force and quiet authority with which the opening "Now" of *The Book of Hours* stakes its claim as *book*:

Now the hour bends down and touches me
with its clear, metallic ring;
my senses tremble. The feeling forms: *I can*—
and I grasp the malleable day.

The voice here is entirely new, and we recognize it in retrospect almost immediately as "Rilke." First-person utterance imbued with otherness and winding through sonic space rather than precipitating out a speaking self; clarity and simplicity of diction causing unexpected language choices—"metallic" (*metallenem*), "malleable" (*plastischen*)—to feel inherent, not ornamental: these will become signature traits of Rilke at his lyric best, and they trace their origin to the first poems of *The Book of Hours*.

 The Book of Hours presents itself as a single poem sequence divided into three sections. Rilke composed the first part, *The Book of a Monastic Life* (*Das Buch vom mönchischen Leben*), in Schmargendorf during September and October 1899 (sixty-seven poems in three weeks—his first experience of that creative fury he would undergo again at Muzot),[1] just after returning from his first trip to Russia and with his relationship with Lou Andreas-Salomé still alive but becoming difficult. The second part, *The Book of Pilgrimage* (*Das Buch von der Pilgerschaft*), he wrote in Worpswede in a single week of 1901,

during his first year of marriage with Clara Westhoff (and in exile from Lou). The third part, *The Book of Poverty and Death* (*Das Buch von der Armut und vom Tode*), Rilke again wrote in a single week—this time in 1903 during a brief respite in Viareggio, where he had fled the anxieties that were threatening to unhinge him during his first extended stay in Paris. Over the entire span of the poems' composition he kept them a secret from everyone—except Lou, to whom he went to great lengths to entrust them (there are times when she may have had the *only* copies), and to whom he always referred to them as "Prayers" (*Gebete*).[2] It was only in 1905, when Rilke decided on publication, that he retrieved the sequences from Lou and shaped them into their present form.

The poems' speaker is an unnamed monk and icon painter in the Russian Orthodox Church. In a sense, then, everything new in Rilke's voice could be explained as an accident of the book's fictive premise. If his poetry takes on the sound of "someone other" ("I circle around God, around the age-old tower; / I've been circling for millennia"), that's because the speaker is literally *not* Rilke. Likewise, the closeness to metaphor, the almost naive transparency, the spirituality that seems to resonate in the matrix of language, prior to any statement that forms from it: these would seem "in character" for a self-abnegating religious artist whose sensibility has been formed by Rilke's imaginary Russia.[3]

But a more complex alchemy seems at work in *The Book of Hours*, at least in its most memorable poems. One feels Rilke sloughing off ego and tapping into deeper places, not so much ventriloquizing a fictional persona as conjuring an "authentic" voice that will be his own (*whoever you are*) for the rest of his poetic life.[4] Indeed, one could claim that all Rilke's subsequent development takes place within the sonic register set down in *The Book of Hours*. Consider these two openings of poems from *The Book of Hours* and *The Book of Images*:

I live my life in widening circles
that drift out over the things.

And again my deep life rushes louder,
as if it moved now between steeper banks.

Though ostensibly a religious persona speaks in the first and Rilke-the-poet in the second, this distinction and the terms that maintain it are essentially mean-

ingless to the reading experience. We hear *the same voice* (how irresistibly it enters us!) "progressing" in the later poem (its title is "Fortschritt"), and we name this crafted voice "Rilke" in both instances without hesitation but only by default. Even in the objective, self-effacing *New Poems*, the *felt*-ness of the things described (which is their magic) resides in their *voicing*—

> With a canopy and its shade it turns
> for a short while, this little herd
> of many-colored horses, all from the land
> that lingers long, then disappears.
>
> <div align="right">("The Carousel")</div>

—and this voicing (here a speakerless, pitch-perfect surround) still bears the feel of that Rilke whose cadences *The Book of Hours* brought into being:

> You mustn't worry, God. They say *mine*
> to all patient, unprotesting things.
> They're like the wind that gusts through branches
> and says *my* tree.

Even "Rilke himself" regarded *The Book of Hours* as his origin, and remained true to it (alone among his early work) to the very end. Writing to his Polish translator in 1925, a year before his death, Rilke went so far as to characterize even the *Duino Elegies* as "a further shaping of those fundamental inspirations that had already been bestowed in *The Book of Hours*."[5]

It would be difficult to overstate the importance of *The Book of Hours*, both for Rilke's work and for modern poetry in general. It opened up whole new lyric possibilities for saying "I" and "You." And though those possibilities have since been endlessly exploited, its successes can still startle with their audacity. Poems like "You mustn't worry, God" and "What will you do, God, when I die?" pull off something that had never been thought of in poetry before, and though they perform with guileless simplicity, we are not sure yet how the trick is done. (And so we mumble "naive," "sentimental," "subjective," "solipsistic.") It's true that not many of the poems in *The Book of Hours* achieve its highest level of success, but those that do are so strong and break such crucial ground that it seems justified to call the book "one of the masterworks of modern German poetry."[6]

1. Even as late as 1913, when Rilke attempted to convey to Lou Andreas-Salomé how the "dictation" at Duino broke off and left him barren, it is the poems of 1899 that come to mind by way of contrast: "Yes, the two elegies are there—, but I can tell you in confidence how small and sharply riven a fragment they form of what was then delivered into my power. Had circumstances and forces been as they were when *The Book of Hours* began—: who knows what could have been achieved!" (letter of January 13, 1913).

2. See the end of Rilke's great Paris letter to Lou of July 22, 1903:

> Once I did succeed, if only for a short time. When I was in Viareggio—yes, the fears broke out there too . . . and yet it came. Prayers came into being there, Lou, a book of Prayers. I have to tell you this, because my first Prayers rest in your hands—those Prayers I have so often thought of and clung to from afar. Because they chime out so strongly and because they are so at peace with you (and because only you and I know about them)—that is why I could cling to them. And perhaps one day I might be allowed to come and place new ones, Prayers that have since come into being, with the others, with you, in your hands, in your quiet house.

It should be added that Rilke's calling these poems "Prayers" does not in itself impute to them a religiosity. Compare, from the same letter, his use of the term in his account of the closeness he felt in Paris to Baudelaire ("of all my forebears perhaps the most alien"):

> And at night I got up and looked for my favorite volume of Baudelaire, the *petites poèmes en prose*, and read aloud the most beautiful poem, the one titled *A une heure du matin*. Do you know it? It begins: *Enfin! seul!* . . . And it ends magnificently: rises, stands, and strides off like a Prayer. A Prayer of Baudelaire's; a real, unpolished Prayer, shaped by the hands, artless and beautiful like the Prayer of a Russian. —He had to go a long way to reach that poem, did Baudelaire, and he went there on his knees and crawling.

3. Russia was many things to Rilke; his second trip there triggered in him the conviction that all his former experiences had been small and false, and that creation had to be relearned in "Russian" terms:

> On the Volga, on this restfully rolling ocean, to be days and nights, many days and many nights; a broad, broad stream, high, high woods along the one shore, along the other a deep moorland in which even great cities stand like mere shacks and tents. — One learns all dimensions anew. One discovers: land is huge, water is something huge, and above all the sky is huge. What I have seen until now was no more than an image of land and river and world. Here, however, everything is itself. —I feel as if I had been witness to the creation; a few words for all existences, the things in the measure of God the Father . . .
>
> (*The Schmargendorf Diary*, September 1, 1900)

4. The revisionary process by which Rilke secured the voice of *The Book of Hours* uncannily *defines* it as voice untethered from both the person writing it and the persona speaking it. The initial draft of the 1899 poems included prose glosses that approximated, in Ralph Freedman's words, "a narrative accompaniment to the text in the manner of Dante's *Vita nuova*" (Freedman, "*Das Stunden-Buch* and *Das Buch der Bilder*: Harbingers of Rilke's Maturity," in *A Companion to the Works of Rainer Maria Rilke*, ed. Erika A. Metzger and Michael M. Metzger, [Rochester, N.Y.: Camden House, 2001], p. 94). Thus the opening poem ("Now the hour bends down and touches me") is followed by "On the evening of September 20, when, following a long rain, the sun passed through the forest and through me" (trans. Freedman)—and so on, throughout "The Prayers." On the opposite front, similar prose glosses characterize the monk (who in this earliest version is named "Apostol") and contextualize his exchanges with others and his solitary utterances. Jettisoning this entire apparatus and letting the poems float free was one of the most momentous writerly gestures Rilke ever made.

5. Letter to Witold Hulewicz, November 13, 1925.

6. Wolfgang Leppmann, *Rilke: A Life*, trans. Wolfgang Leppmann and Russell M. Stockton (New York: Fromm International, 1984 [1981]), p. 115.

THE BOOK OF IMAGES

The Book of Images (*Das Buch der Bilder*) is Rilke's most varied work. Callow *Jugendstil* pieces about young maidens and abandoned brides coexist with deftly poised lyrics that seek a complex relation with otherness and the outside world. And all *kinds* of poems are present. Short lyrics, dialogues, interior monologues, poems in fictionalized voices, quasi-ballads, narrative excursions into myth and history, religious poems (serious and wry), psychological portraits, a long requiem, three different poem cycles, and odd stream-of-consciousness pieces ("About Fountains," "Fragments from Lost Days") fill out the four sections of *The Book of Images*.

Such heterogeneity mirrors the circumstances in which the volume was composed. Unlike most of Rilke's great works, which came into being rapidly, in short, creative bursts, *The Book of Images* evolved gradually, over a seven-year period (June 1899 to August 1906) that spans experiences which mark the great transition in Rilke's early life: his complicated relationship with Lou Andreas-Salomé, their two trips to Russia together, and their gradual estrangement; his stay at Worpswede, an artists' colony near Bremen where he met Clara Westhoff and Paula Becker; his marriage to Clara and his rejection of or by Paula, the two events obscurely related; his residence in

Paris, where he fell under Rodin's spell, became obsessed with a poetry of sculptural "thingness," and had his first Baudelairean experiences of inner-city estrangement; the birth of his daughter, Ruth, followed by his gradual distancing of himself from his wife and child—a sacrifice to vocation hopelessly entangled with elements of cowardice and bad faith.

Amid all this eventfulness, *The Book of Images* appeared twice, in very different versions. A first edition was published in July 1902 (Rilke was twenty-six at the time) and contained forty-five poems written between 1898 and 1901, the majority of them taken from the diaries Rilke kept at Berlin-Schmargendorf and Worpswede. A second edition appeared four years later, in December 1906, greatly altering and expanding the first. (Thirty-seven new poems were added.)

In the period of revision between the two editions, Rilke was at work on a myriad of other projects, putting old concerns behind him and feeling his way into new ones. The third and final section of *The Book of Hours* was written in 1903, and the completed volume was published in 1905. A second edition of the popular *Stories of God* (first published in 1900) appeared in 1904. *The Lay of the Love and Death of Cornet Christopher Rilke*, written in 1899 and a favorite whenever Rilke gave readings, was published in its final form in 1906. A monograph on Worpswede, in which concerns with landscape and painting produce intense visual description, appeared in 1903, along with the first edition of Rilke's book on Rodin, so crucial to the aesthetic of the *New Poems*. The *New Poems* themselves were begun during this period (some thirty existed by the time Rilke wrote "The Voices," the last piece composed for *The Book of Images*), and *The Notebooks of Malte Laurids Brigge*, which would not be published until 1910, had by 1906 become a major preoccupation.

It is no wonder, then, that *The Book of Images* should make such a varied impression. In a very real sense the volume spans whole phases of Rilke's career and can be felt to trace their arc: reaching back to the art nouveau mannerisms of the earliest poems, containing in its interstices the spirituality of *The Book of Hours*, overlapping the first of the ego-effacing *New Poems*, and pointing beyond them (in such poems as "Human Beings at Night," "The Ashanti," "Pont du Carrousel," "The Neighbor," and especially "The Voices") to *The Notebooks of Malte Laurids Brigge*, with its feelings about the city's estranging power and the unsettling presence there of God's "cut ones."

And yet the best poems in *The Book of Images*—some thirty mesmerizing lyrics, the majority first appearing in the 1906 edition—give the book a core

identity that still resonates. Indeed, these lyrics could be said to epitomize what we mean when we characterize something—a mood, a stance, a cadence, a quality of voice, a way of looking—as "Rilkean." The poet of memory, of childhood, of leave-taking and looking back; the poet of night and its vastnesses, of human separations, of landscapes charged with remoteness and expectancy; the poet—especially—of solitude, in its endless inflections: all are found here, in poems as carefully proposed as anything Rilke ever wrote. The impulse that shapes their cadences seems to come from a place so unwavering that there is almost a complete break with the fragile lyrics of the early work. Even when one turns from *The Book of Hours* to the best of these poems, the evolution in voice is dramatic. It is as if there has been a "ripening in silence," to adapt a phrase from "Entrance." Last vestiges of piety and persona fall away, and a poem like "Evening" suddenly stands free, addressing both poet and reader with an immediacy and closeness not so much spoken as shaped by and invested with the qualities of voice:

Slowly the evening puts on the clothes
held for it by a ridge of ancient trees;
you watch: and the lands divide from you,
one going heavenward, one sinking down;

and leave you, not quite belonging to either,
not quite so dark as the house cloaked in silence,
not quite so surely pledging the eternal
as that which becomes star each night and climbs—

and leave you (inexpressibly to untangle)
your life, immense and ripening and fearful,
so that now closed in, now reaching everywhere,
it grows alternately stone in you and star.

Little in the early work prepares us for this stately, unforced solemnity, so mature in relation to the tangle of emotions it expresses. And it is as beautifully crafted as anything in the soon-to-come *New Poems*. The main difference is that while the most radical of the *New Poems* will exploit syntax and semantic density to achieve their version of sculptural "thingness," "Evening" works in the vocal register. Its focus may be visual, specific, oriented outward, but timing and cadence are its métier. It *shapes* voice, and this as much as anything

else is what gives the poem its anti-impressionistic feeling, its eerie sense of being "modern"—even now.

Note: *Das Buch der Bilder* can mean either "the book of pictures" or "the book of images." It is translated here as *The Book of Images* so as not to trivialize the key term *Bild*, whose complications the poems knowingly exploit. The word can designate a picture, a portrait, or any other form of pictorial representation (sculptural, architectural), and thus suggests a strong "belonging" to the visual world. But it can also designate an image that works as a metaphor—a figurative entity pointing to realities beyond or behind it. *Bilder* in this sense can populate the visual realm with traces, invisible connections, imaginings, remembrances, and intimations of things lost or unrealized, waiting to be recalled or brought (back) to life. These latter connotations are in play throughout the poems—so much so that a reader looking through the book for "word pictures" might indeed feel baffled by its title.

NEW POEMS

Rilke arrived in Paris for the first time in September 1902, commissioned by a German publisher to write a monograph on Rodin. The two met and grew close, and Rilke's interest soon deepened into discipleship. As his enthusiasm for the sculptor's work increased, so did his dissatisfaction with his own. Rodin was a laborer, a craftsman, and the energy and dedication with which he immersed himself in the actual process of making seemed to Rilke a rebuke to his own lyric dexterity and abject dependence on inspiration. With Rodin's *"travailler, rien que travailler"* ringing in his ears, he set about acquiring an entirely new set of working habits—forcing himself to write every day during regularly scheduled hours, wandering about Paris practicing the art of observation, taking notes, making lists of subjects for poems. Meanwhile he began to entertain the idea of a poetry that would answer to what he described as Rodin's "art of living surfaces"—a poetry that would somehow manage to belong to the world of things rather than feelings. The results—appearing slowly at first, then coming to fruition in a burst of creative brilliance that spanned the summers of 1906 and 1908—were the two volumes of the *New Poems*, which together constitute one of the great instances in modern literature of the lyric quest for objective experience.

What specifically is "new" about the *New Poems?* The most striking transformation occurs in Rilke's language, which grows simultaneously more lucid

and complex. Compression of statement and elimination of authorial self are taken to their extremes in the pursuit of an objective ideal. Only a few of these *Dinggedichte*, or "thing-poems," as they soon came to be called, are actually about objects, but all of them have a material quality and confront the reader with a sculptural, freestanding presence. Even their semantic densities communicate a sense of volume and contour. One is always aware of them as things made. Syntax, especially, becomes a tensile material capable of being worked into structures that remind one more often of the space-mobilizing forms of Arp than of Rodin's massive presences. Even in a poem like "The Capital," devoted entirely to the description of a static object, visual image interacts with a kinesis of line and syntax to transform the thing into a force field of opposing impulses:

> . . . the vaulting's ribs
> spring from the tangled capital
>
> and leave that chaos of densely intertwined,
> mysteriously winged creations:
> their hesitance and the suddenness of the heads
> and those strong leaves, whose sap
>
> mounts like rising anger, finally spilling over
> in a quick gesture that clenches
> and thrusts out— . . .

Several of the *New Poems* participate even more directly than this in the movements and energies they describe; the flamenco gestures of "Spanish Dancer" are an especially brilliant instance. Seldom is visual perception an end in itself, and often it is the focus of a poem's deconstructive energies: a gazelle dissolves into the stream of discontinuous metaphors that evoke it; a marble fountain becomes a complex microcosm of fluid interchanges and secret relations. "As ifs" proliferate through the poetry, keeping the reader's attention fixed not so much on the object world as on the zone where it and the imagination interact.

This interanimation of object and consciousness is, finally, the great theme of the *New Poems*, in spite of their apparent worship of states of withdrawal, apartness, and fulfilled isolation. At their most radical they seek to open the dimensions of what a phenomenologist would call the "lived world," where subject and object are inseparable aspects of an imaginatively engen-

dered unity. In "The Bowl of Roses," the "new poem" that perhaps goes fur-
thest in this direction, what begins as an object of perception is gradually
transformed by the descriptive impulse it releases into a multifarious world
teeming with metamorphic energies:

> What can't they be: was that yellow one,
> which lies there hollow and open, not the rind
> of a fruit in which that very yellow,
> more intense, more orange-red, was juice?
> And was mere opening too much for this one,
> since touched by air its inexpressible pink
> has taken on the bitter aftertaste of lilac?
> And that cambric one, is it not a dress
> in which the shift still clings, soft and breath-warm,
> both of them cast off together
> in the morning shadows by the old woodland pond?
> And this one, opalescent porcelain,
> fragile, a shallow china cup
> and full of tiny brilliant butterflies,—
> and that one, containing nothing but itself.

The transformative capacities of the roses are, of course, those of the imagi-
nation that beholds them, but the effect is the opposite of mere projection: the
act of viewing seems lured into a prior dimension where reality and imagina-
tion have yet to face each other off as opposites. Self-containment, arrived at
from this direction, feels like the opposite of itself, and triggers one of the
great moments of ontological redefinition in Rilke:

> And aren't they all that way: simply self-containing,
> if self-containing means: to transform the world outside
> and the wind and rain and patience of Spring
> and guilt and restlessness and muffled fate
> and the darkness of the evening earth
> out to the roaming and flying and fleeing of the clouds
> and the vague influence of distant stars
> into a handful of inwardness.

> Now it lies carefree in these opened roses.

Rilke sent the finished manuscript of *New Poems: The Other Part* to his publisher on August 17, 1908, less than a year after completing the original *New Poems*, and scarcely eight months after the first volume's December 1907 publication. All 99 of the poems in the second volume (106, if one counts the poems that form sequences) were composed between one August and the next, and in periods of sustained creative output even more intense than those that produced the first volume: 40 poems in August 1907 alone, followed by another 46 in the summer of 1908. The two volumes thus issue virtually uninterrupted from the same initial impulse. And they pursue the same "new" project—to subordinate lyric "expression" to workmanlike "making" ("not feelings," Rilke wrote in retrospect, "but things I had felt")—and achieve in poetry the same objective, freestanding integrity Rilke admired in Rodin's sculpture and Cézanne's paintings, his constant touchstones during this period:

> Somehow I too must find some way to make things; written, not sculpted things—*realities* that emerge from handcraft. Somehow I too must discover that smallest basic element, the cell of *my* art, the tangible immaterial means of representation for everything . . .
>
> (Letter to Lou Andreas-Salomé, August 10, 1903)

Given, then, all that the two volumes have in common, it seems inevitable that the boundary between them should have blurred: we now routinely refer to the poems of both as the *New Poems*, and at most distinguish them as parts 1 and 2 of a single work. Yet when Rilke sent the manuscript of the companion volume to his publisher, what he stressed was its separateness and distance from the original work:

> As I arranged the poems, I had the impression that the new volume could quite suitably join up with the earlier one: the course is almost parallel—only somewhat higher, it seems to me, and at a greater depth and with more distance. If the third volume is to join these two, a similar intensification will still have to be achieved in the ever more objective mastering of reality, out of which, entirely of its own accord, the wider significance and clearer validity of all things arises.
>
> (Letter to Anton Kippenberg, August 18, 1908)

It is hard to know what to make of language so abstract, but close attention to *New Poems: The Other Part* does confirm its difference. Its mood and personality are so different, in fact, from the 1907 *New Poems* that it can feel "other" in the same nontrivial sense that both volumes feel "new." This is nowhere truer than in the poems with explicit parallels in the first volume. "Archaic Torso of Apollo," for instance, introduces *New Poems: The Other Part* in the same way that "Early Apollo" begins the original *New Poems*. But in making this connection, it creates a virtual paradigm for how the second volume will "intensify" and differ from the first:

Early Apollo

As sometimes between still leafless branches
a morning looks through that's already
consummate Spring: so nothing of his head
could prevent the splendor of all poems

from striking us with almost lethal force;
for there is yet no shadow in his gaze,
his temples are too cool still for the laurel,
and only later from his eyebrows' arches

will the rose garden rise up on long stems,
from which petals, released, one by one
will drift down on the trembling of his mouth,

which now is still quiet, never-used, and gleaming
and only drinking something with its smile
as though the song were being infused in him.

Archaic Torso of Apollo

We never knew his head and all the light
that ripened in his fabled eyes. But
his torso still burns like a streetlamp dimmed
in which his gaze, lit long ago,

holds fast and shines. Otherwise the surge
of the breast could not blind you, nor a smile

run through the slight twist of the loins
toward that center where procreation flared.

Otherwise this stone would stand cut off
and cold under the shoulders' transparent drop
and not glisten like a wild beast's fur;

and not break forth from all its contours
like a star: for there is no place
that does not see you. You must change your life.

Both poems present the sculptural object as a first gesture, but "Archaic Torso" has a drive and a weight that can make "Early Apollo" seem almost coy and languorous by comparison. Its language is richer and more impacted and pursues its course with reckless daring. Assonance and alliteration are pushed to near limits in the search for a dense internal music. In line 1, "*unerhörtes Haupt*" is typical, especially in its rhyme with "*zurückgeschraubt*." A similar impacting occurs at the level of image. *Kandelaber* can mean either "candelabra" or "streetlamp," and this visual choice is woven into the subsequent texture of the poem, becoming explicit in the contrast between the solitary standing presence of line 9 and the glittering beast's pelt of line 11, and condensing again in the ambiguous "*durchsichtigem Sturz*" of line 10, which can conjure up either the glittering cascade of a waterfall or the airless drop of a bell jar. *Zurückgeschraubt* itself epitomizes the poem's daring. It refers to the candelabra/streetlamp's "lowered" light, but by way of a metonymic, elliptical allusion to the "screwing back" of a control knob. The disconcerting, almost ruthless kinesis of the idea (reinforced by the very sound of the word) informs one's sense of how tenaciously the gaze inwardly endures. It also forges a link with the poem's own turnings, and with the "slight twist of the loins" that in line 8 leads to the fertile center (itself an absence).

Zurückgeschraubt, in fact, could describe in general the difference between the poems in the two volumes. Those in the second tend, like "Archaic Torso," to feel indrawn and "screwed tighter" in relation to those in the first. Grammar and syntax become more convoluted and prolonged and at the same time move faster. An inner momentum bordering on the compulsive often hurtles the reader through a poem—sometimes toward a breaking point, as in "Night Drive," sometimes toward a final, unexpected reversal, as in "Archaic Torso" or "Black Cat." This intensification is a matter of content as well as of texture. The object of description in "Early Apollo" more or less passively

accepts the metaphors it elicits; they embellish it (however brilliantly) as their occasion and ground. But the metaphors of "Archaic Torso" inhere fiercely in their object, as if they were the very principle of its being. One can feel something of the same difference in many of the volumes' finest companion poems—"The Courtesan" (1907) and "The Lute" (1908), for instance, where the "objects" describe themselves:

The Courtesan

In my hair the sun of Venice will
prepare a gold: all alchemy's
illustrious outcome. My eyebrows
are like her bridges. See

how they span the silent danger
of my eyes, which have a secret
commerce with her canals, so the sea
rises and falls and changes in them. Whoever

sees me once is envious of my dog,
since often on him in distracted pauses
my hand, never singed by any heat,

invulnerable and bejeweled, rests—.
And boys, the hopes of ancient houses,
perish at my mouth as if from poison.

The Lute

I am the lute. Should you wish to describe
my body, with its lovely arching stripes:
speak of me as you would of a ripe
full-bodied fig. Underscore

the darkness you see in me. This was
Tullia's darkness. There was so little
in her secret places, and her lustrous hair
was like a light-filled hall. Sometimes

she'd absorb some sound from my surfaces
into her features and sing while I played.
Then I'd tense myself against her easefulness,
and finally my soul found itself in her.

"The Courtesan" is a wonderful mood piece and something of a tour de force in its evocation of Carpaccio's Venice. But one is never really tempted to hear the voice as more than a conceit. No "real" courtesan speaks in the poem, and not much otherness of any kind interferes with the pleasure of image and rhythm. Even the sexuality and the seductiveness are very much surface gestures. But in "The Lute" the object *exists*, and the voice of the poem belongs to it. The narcissism, the self-possession, the combination of frankness and disregard, the absorption in distant memories—all are elements of a powerful inwardness and help define the lute in its tantalizing inaccessibility. The sexuality in the poem, though less stressed, seems more immediate and real, largely because it is conceived in terms of tensions that inhere in the poem's own address. Yielding and resistance, invitation and evasion, easy surfaces and unexpected depths—these compose the lute's relation to both "Tullia" and the would-be describer and give the poem a charged separateness that "The Courtesan" lacks. The brilliant reversal in the final lines (again there is a *turning* on the reader), where the gender of the lute seems to change (or does it?) and the narcissistic object of admiration turns into an avatar of sexual straining and release, dictates an entirely new set of terms to the reader, who is left suspended among feelings of consummation and escape.

Such troping becomes more common in the second volume, as what draws the self takes on the power to question, displace, evade, estrange, undo, or otherwise disrupt it. The interpenetration of object and consciousness in *New Poems* is mainly a visionary theme: there is a euphoric sense of "reseeing" the world in ways that transcend the opposition between inner and outer, empty and fulfilled. But *New Poems: The Other Part* seeks out darker, more problematical versions of that relation. Many of the most striking poems—"Foreign Family," "The Site of the Fire," "Corpse-Washing," and "Snake-Charming," for instance—construct relation out of estrangement; *fremd* (foreign, alien, strange) is the word that appears over and over again. "Foreign" figures compel recognition and draw the viewer into mixtures of fascination and dread. The seductiveness of "One of the Old Ones" is an especially vivid Baudelairean instance:

Sometimes at evening (do you know how it feels?)
when they suddenly stop and nod backward
and show you under their half-hats
a smile that seems all patches . . .

Next to them there's always a building,
endless, and they lure you along
with the riddle of their scabs—
with the hat, the shawl, and the gait.

With the hand, which curled under the collar
waits in secret and longs for you:
as if it wished to wrap your hands
in a scrap of picked-up paper.

Against these uncanny figures with their pull on the viewer are the figures
of enduring isolation that either assume aloneness or "pull in" around grief,
pain, deprivation, and disfigurement. Holding on, to memory and to the aches
of an interred life, becomes a means of cohering, of keeping both relation and
the place of feeling alive. This theme, though less apparent than some of the
others in *New Poems: The Other Part*, may ultimately go deepest. In place of
übersteigen, "to transcend," we tend to get *überstehen*, with its untranslatable
combination of "to endure," "to live through," and "to survive." What
makes the theme so rich is the way this pulling in and hardening around sev-
erance and loss can unexpectedly bring forth the vital core (most sublimely in
"Archaic Torso"). Likewise, avatars of impenetrable singleness can become
centers of emanation and move toward exaltation. The last two poems in the
volume consummate this theme beautifully—first with the cradled sleep of an
ancient beetle stone, then with the unattached Buddha installed in glory, wel-
comed as "center of all centers, core of cores." And perhaps the theme's most
powerful instance comes just before them, in "The Solitary," where an open-
ing gesture of refusal imagines the destructive element—here conceived of as
distances—driving aloneness further and further on:

No: my heart shall be a tower,
and I myself set at its highest rim:
where nothing else exists, once again pain
and the unsayable, once again world.

Still one thing alone in immensity,
growing dark then light again,
still one last face full of longing
thrust out into the unappeasable,

still one uttermost face made of stone
heeding only its own inner gravity,
while the distances that silently destroy it
drive it on to an ever deeper bliss.

DUINO ELEGIES

The Duino elegies take their name from Castle Duino, an ancient fortresslike structure set high atop hills overlooking the Adriatic near Trieste. It was once a Roman watchtower, and Dante supposedly wrote parts of *The Divine Comedy* there. During the winter of 1911–12, Rilke, feeling empty and despondent since completing *The Notebooks of Malte Laurids Brigge* in 1910, was residing there when the inspiration for the *Elegies* came to him. Princess Marie von Thurn und Taxis-Hohenlohe (1855–1934), the friend and patron who made the castle available to him, related in her memoir the story of their genesis:

Rilke later told me how these elegies arose. He suspected nothing of what was taking hold inside him; though he may have hinted at it in a letter he wrote: "The nightingale is approaching—." Had he perhaps felt what was on its way? But things seemed again to fall silent. A great sadness came over him; he began to think that this winter too would be fruitless.

Then one morning he received a troublesome business letter. He wanted to be done with it quickly, and had to concern himself with sums and other such tedious matters. Outside, a violent north wind was blowing, but the sun shone and the blue water had a silvery gleam. Rilke climbed down to the bastions which, jutting to the east and west, were connected to the foot of the castle by a narrow path along the cliffs. The cliffs fall steeply, for about two hundred feet, into the sea. Rilke paced back and forth, deep in thought, since the reply to the letter so concerned him. Then, all at once, in the midst of his brooding, he halted suddenly, for it seemed to him that in the raging of

the storm a voice had called to him: "Who, if I cried out, would hear me among the Angels' orders?" He stood still, listening. "What is that?" he half whispered. "What is it, what is coming?"

He took out his notebook, which he always carried with him, and wrote down these words, together with a few lines that formed without his intervention. Who had come? And then he knew the answer: the god . . .

Very calmly he climbed back up to his room, set his notebook aside, and replied to the difficult letter.

By that evening the entire elegy had been written down.[1]

Rilke was elated; he copied the poem into a green leather-bound notebook that he and the princess had bought together in Weimar and sent it to her in Vienna on January 21 as "the first Duino work (and the first for a long time!)." Within days he had composed the effortless-seeming "Second Elegy" as well, along with fragments of the third, sixth, and ninth and the opening lines of the tenth. His task as a poet had been announced to him.

But nothing further would materialize at Duino. Rilke left the castle in May with no more written and recommenced the wanderings that had preceded his stay there. Though he continued to write poems in his notebooks, the elegies and his failure to sustain them were what obsessed him now. ("Yes, the two elegies are there—," he wrote Lou Andreas-Salomé from Spain in January 1913, "but I can tell you in confidence how small and sharply riven a fragment they form of what was then delivered into my power.") During the next few years he would make sporadic progress: he forced the uneven "Third Elegy" to completion in October 1913 in Paris and composed more lines of the sixth; in November 1915 he wrote the terse, elliptical "Fourth Elegy" in just two days in Munich. But that would be all for more than six years, until in February 1922, in another castle solitude in Switzerland, the floodgates broke.

Rilke had been living alone since July 1921 in the Château de Muzot, a small medieval tower in the Rhône Valley near the village of Sierre, Switzerland, where he had deliberately isolated himself in hope of recapturing the inspiration of the elegies. ("I am now taking root and spinning a web around myself inside a primeval tower . . . in the midst of this incomparably grand, magnificent landscape," he wrote to Francisca Stoecklin on November 16.) There, during three weeks in February, he experienced a creative storm so extraordinary that his later mythologizing of the resulting work as "given" to him, a "dictation" for which he served as medium or scribe, is understandable.

It began on February 2, when he unexpectedly began writing sonnets. After three days he had produced twenty-five of the twenty-six poems that would form the first part of the *Sonnets to Orpheus*. On the morning of February 7, "The Seventh Elegy" came (all but the final lines, which he would add on February 26). The same day he began "The Eighth Elegy," the masterwork of the sequence, and finished it the following afternoon. On February 9, after completing "The Sixth Elegy," he composed the difficult ninth and all but four lines of "Antistrophes," a poem that would temporarily serve as the fifth. That evening he wrote excitedly to his publisher, Anton Kippenberg, that the *Elegies* were done ("My dear friend, I am over the mountain! The *Elegies* are here! . . . I went outside into the cold moonlight and stroked little Muzot like a big animal, its old walls which granted this to me . . . And my dear friend: *this*: that you have made this possible for me, have been so patient with me: ten years! Thanks! . . . And that you always believed in me—*thanks!*").

The next day was uneventful. Then, on February 11, Rilke returned to his draft of "The Tenth Elegy." He kept the first fifteen lines, which had existed since Duino, and composed a completely new version of the rest that same day (later, when asked, he would name the tenth as his favorite). He wrote at once to Princess Marie, who had remained for him, in an almost courtly sense, the patron of the *Elegies*:

At last,

 Princess,

At last, the blessed, so blessed day, when in this letter the conclusion—so far as I can see—of the

 Elegies

 I can announce to you:

 TEN!

From the last, great one (with the opening begun back in Duino: "Someday, at the end of the nightmare of knowing, may I emerge singing praise and jubilation to assenting angels . . ."), from this last one, which even then was meant to come last,—from this—my hand is still trembling! Just now, Saturday the eleventh, at six in the evening, it is finished!—

Everything in only a few days, it was an indescribable storm, a hurricane in my spirit (like that time in Duino) all the sinews and tissues in me groaned,—there was no thinking about food, God knows who fed me.

But now it *is*. Is. Is.

Amen.

So this is what I've survived for, through everything, on and on. Through Everything. All for this. *Only* this.

One of them I have dedicated to Kassner. But the whole is *yours*, Princess, how could it not be! Will be called:

The Duino Elegies.

In this book there will be no dedication (for I can't give you what has been yours from the beginning) but instead:

From the property of . . .

That same evening Rilke wrote similar letters to Lou Andreas-Salomé and two other close friends—as if the accomplishing of the *Elegies*, which required total solitude, was nonetheless a drama in which a whole circle of acquaintances had to be absorbed. Then on February 14 a final elegy came, the fifth, or "Saltimbanques," which he placed at the center of the cycle, discarding "Antistrophes," a poem that now felt to him inappropriate there. With the *Elegies* complete (save for a handful of lines), there was a last surprise: the sonnets returned, and Rilke found himself writing nonstop again. Between February 15 and 23 he composed another cycle of twenty-nine poems that would form the second part of the *Sonnets to Orpheus.*

After the second group of sonnets, the tempest at Muzot subsided, and Rilke's elation reached again toward friends. He copied out the last six elegies and sent them to Kippenberg on February 23, "for publication when he saw fit"; on the same day he sent the sonnets to Kippenberg's wife, Katharina (with whom he enjoyed a years-long friendship and correspondence), along with a separate letter asking her to judge if they were suitable for publication. (Both volumes were published sumptuously in 1923.) There was, of course, to be a copy for the princess, but Rilke waited until she could visit him at Muzot, so that he could present the poems to her in person and read them to her aloud. That "great day" occurred on June 7. Princess Marie would remember it vividly:

Secretive, tiny, low rooms with old furniture—flowers, many flowers everywhere, among them the five-petaled, flame-colored rose . . . We went up to the study—a room filled with books, filled with devotion. Adjacent to it the narrow bedroom and the little chapel . . . Everything seems as if created for the poet. And finally, standing at his desk as he always does, he began to read . . . As he read—wonderfully, as only he

can read—I felt my heart beating more and more strongly, felt the tears running down my cheeks. There are no words for this experience. The next day—in the charming hotel at Sierre—it was the sonnets' turn. Fifty-seven, and not a single one too many. Every word a jewel. Some of them make one's heart stand still.[2]

In July the Kippenbergs visited, and again Rilke read—the *Elegies* one evening for the two of them, the *Sonnets* the next morning for Katharina alone. Plans were discussed for the publication not only of the elegies and the sonnets but of a five-volume edition of his complete works—so convinced was Rilke that all he had been given to say had been said.

In truth Rilke would continue to write poems prolifically at Muzot. But he never allowed any of this unpublished work to infiltrate his life's story as a poet, which *had* to climax with the *Elegies*. (Even the sonnets he would think of as a "bonus" or "reward" that came with the *Elegies'* completion.) So many ethical evasions, disappointments, and things undone he had rationalized in terms of the "waiting" required of him by the task of the *Elegies*, that it was only by rehearsing the drama of their composition that he could feel himself justified and redeemed—even, albeit in a wishful sense, exemplary:

> That a man who has felt himself . . . cloven to his foundations [Rilke is looking back from December 1925, scarcely a year away from death, on how he was "saved" that February in Muzot] into a Formerly and an incompatible, dying NOW: that such a man should experience the grace of being able to perceive how, in still more secret depths, beneath the torn-open cleft, the continuity of his work and of his mind was being restored . . . , seems to me more than a merely private occurrence; for by that token a measure is provided for the inexhaustible layering of our nature; and how many who, for one reason or another believe they have been torn asunder, might not draw from this example of "continuability" their own particular consolation.
>
> (I would like to think that this consolation has also somehow become an aspect of the accomplishment of the great Elegies, so that they express themselves more completely than, without endangerment and rescue, could have been possible.)[3]

Despite Rilke's personal, sometimes almost hermetic investment in the *Elegies*, he believed that his poetry spoke for itself. He distrusted commentaries

as dilutions and foreclosures of the individual's reading experience. When a friend wrote to him that she felt the key to one of the *Sonnets to Orpheus* lay in the idea of the transmigration of souls, he responded: "You are thinking too far out beyond the poem itself . . . I believe that no poem in the *Sonnets to Orpheus* means anything that is not fully written out there, often, it is true, with its most secret name. All 'allusion' I am convinced would be contradictory to the indescribable 'being-there' of the poem."[4] In another context he wrote that his most recalcitrant obscurities might require not elucidation (*Aufklärung*) so much as "submitting-to" (*Unterwerfung*).[5] In this spirit I have held explanatory notes to the *Duino Elegies* to a minimum: a few passages to give the flavor of Rilke's thinking, a gloss on the difficult ending of "The First Elegy," and an attempt to address what may be a major misconception about a trope in "The Fifth Elegy."

NOTES

1. Fürstin Marie von Thurn und Taxis-Hohenlohe, *Erinnerungen an Rainer Maria Rilke* (Munich and Berlin, 1932), pp. 40–41. Rilke and this remarkable woman, twenty years his senior, became intimate friends; she was arguably the most important abiding presence in the last fifteen years of his life. They corresponded about practically everything. (There are 120 letters from 1912 and 1913 alone: see *Briefwechsel mit Marie von Thurn und Taxis*, 2 vols. [Frankfurt, 1986 (1951)].) Here is Princess Marie answering, in a letter of March 9, 1913, one of Rilke's frequent "complaints":

> Oh Dottore Serafico [her nickname for him], I envy you! I think you are the most fortunate man on God's earth (now you are getting mad as a bug—*con rispetto parlando*—but nevertheless it is true,—if only your remarkable eyes, which see everything with such extraordinary clarity, could see yourself as well). Very well, I will enumerate. You are a great poet, you know it perfectly well. You are in love (*don't* protest, you *are* in love and always will be, where or with whom or for how long is beside the point). You have a small atelier in Paris—and it is March—the whole glorious Spring is knocking at your door—Come in! I'm Dottore Serafico! Consider *me*—I'm a woman—and a woman my age should tear out every hair on her head every time she looks at herself in the mirror and then hang herself with the nearest rope. I have had so much trouble and worry in my life . . . And yet a blossoming fruit-tree and a golden sunbeam *make me wild with delight!* [in English in the original]. But, on the other hand, if you weren't so desperate you probably wouldn't write so wonderfully. So *be* desperate! Be *really* desperate, be even *more* desperate!

2. Thurn und Taxis-Hohenlohe, *Erinnerungen*, pp. 93–94.

3. Letter to Arthur Fischer-Colbrie, December 18, 1925.

4. Letter to the Countess Sizzo, June 1, 1923, quoted and translated in Rilke, *Sonnets to Orpheus*, trans. M. D. Herder Norton (New York, 1943), pp. 10–11.

5. Letter to Clara Rilke, April 23, 1923.

SONNETS TO ORPHEUS

I would like to step out of my heart
and be under the great sky.
　　　　—Rilke, "Lament"

I

How to account for the *Sonnets to Orpheus*? Rilke himself regarded them with amazement. They seem genuinely to have taken him by surprise. Since July 1921 he had been living in Muzot, creating conditions hospitable to the resumption of what would eventually be the *Duino Elegies*, the "task" he had been given almost a decade earlier at Duino Castle. This meant gradually divesting himself of human contact and conversation, "gathering himself" into an absolute solitude (one wondrously efficient housekeeper excepted). If he could not will the *Elegies* to completion, he could at least try to turn himself into a core of undistracted readiness.

Meanwhile serendipity was at work, scattering the most diverse influences (at least in retrospect they seem so) into this scene of attempted concentration. For Christmas 1920, Rilke's lover, the painter Baladine Klossowska ("Merline"), had given him a French prose version of Ovid's *Metamorphoses*, which prominently features the story of Orpheus. When she departed from Muzot at Rilke's urging in November 1921, she left pinned to the wall opposite his writing table a postcard reproduction of a Renaissance drawing of a youthful, almost carefree Orpheus (though his expression *could* be anguished) sitting at the base of a tree, singing and playing a stringed instrument, while a gathering of animals (one bird, two deer, and a pair of rabbits) listens attentively. The image would remain in place throughout the winter months of 1922, a token of Merline's absence. Increasingly, Rilke translated. By the end of 1921 he had finished a version of Michelangelo's *Sonnets*, which left him thinking about the strictness of the sonnet form and the extent to which it might be freed. He immersed himself in the work of Paul Valéry (by 1921 his most important artistic "other"), a poet who had remained silent for almost twenty-five years, while he studied mathematics, and who had only recently

resumed writing. Rilke found in the French poet's new work a "masculine" exactitude and measure that was precisely what he felt missing in things German ("and now the pace of every one of his lines is enriched by that deep balanced repose which none of us can muster").[1] At the same time, when he translated Valéry he felt an almost bodily sense of "fit." In the early winter he agreed, at Valéry's request, to translate the latter's *Eupalinos* dialogue into German, and in January he copied out *L'âme et la danse* (*The Soul and the Dance*), which he would translate in 1926, the last year of his life.

The decisive influence came in the form of the record of a young girl's approaching death. Rilke knew Vera Ouckama Knoop, the daughter of friends from his prewar Munich days and the playmate of his own daughter Ruth, when she was still a child and already a dancer of great promise. He had learned in 1919 from Vera's mother, Gertrud, of her daughter's recent death at age nineteen from leukemia, but it was not until November 1921, on the occasion of Ruth's engagement, that he chose to write in consolation. A heartfelt correspondence ensued between these two people who only casually knew each other, and one of Rilke's letters culminated in a wish for some keepsake by which he might remember Vera ("some little thing that was dear to Vera, if possible something that she often had with her").[2] Gertrud complied with a gesture whose very extravagance could almost be construed as a protest against the sentimentality in Rilke's request. On January 1, 1922, he received from her a package, without any cover letter, containing sixteen closely written pages on which Gertrud had chronicled, day by day, the last stage of Vera's leukemia, with "its torturous alternations of pain and despair, remission and hope."[3]

The effect on Rilke was overwhelming, and Vera took on an almost hallucinatory reality: "Now it is about Vera," he wrote her mother, "whose dark, strange, vivid loveliness is so hauntingly unforgettable and so prodigiously evocable that in the very moment of writing this I am afraid to close my eyes, lest I should suddenly, in my own here and now, feel myself completely overwhelmed by it."[4] Orpheus and Eurydice, Rilke and his own dead love, Paula Modersohn Becker—all mingle strangely in this awakened vividness. And as Rilke goes on to draw out for Gertrud the significance of her daughter's dying testament, phrases appear that he would later employ to articulate the "meaning" of the *Elegies* and the *Sonnets* themselves:

How much, how much, how much she *was* all that, *that* to which these memorials of her agony bear such deep and irrevocable witness,—and (isn't it so?) how wonderful, how unique, how incomparable a human

being is! For when everything in her should have been consumed, suddenly there arose in her heart a great flood of light, so much that otherwise it would have sufficed to brighten a long existence here (where?); and in it appeared, so infinitely illumined, the two outermost boundaries of her pure intuition: *this*, that suffering is an error, a dull misapprehension arising from the physical that drives its wedge, its stony wedge, into the unity between heaven and the earth; *and*, at the other extreme, the oneness of her wide-open heart with the existing and enduring world, this assent to life, this joyous, impassioned communing to the very last moment with her native earth—ah, with only the earth? Nay (and this she could not know in these first attacks of breakup and parting)—with the *Whole*, with much more than the earth. Oh, how, how she loved, how she reached out with the antennae of her heart beyond all that which can be grasped or encompassed here . . .[5]

He closed by accepting Gertrud's pages with "an immense obligation to my inmost and gravest self as well as (even if I can only attain it from afar) to my serenity."[6] It would be one obligation, at least, that no one could accuse Rilke of shirking.

11

On February 2 the door finally opened. Only a day earlier Rilke had been complaining (again) about the difficulty of concentration, and when he sat down at his appointed time to write, his hope as usual was to coax the *Elegies* out of hiding. Instead, he began writing sonnets. One followed another, and suddenly Rilke was in the midst of a creative release so extraordinary that he felt himself transcribing, not composing. He wrote continuously, "letting the stream of the sonnets gush over me like a deluge,"[7] and by February 5 he had completed, in order, without altering a line, all but one of the twenty-six poems that would form the first part of the *Sonnets to Orpheus*.[8] "It was the most enigmatic dictation I have ever undergone," he would say later.[9] And though the source of the poems was a mystery to him, he understood them as inspired by Vera. He quickly made a hand copy of the entire sequence and sent it to Gertrud on February 7, as an acknowledgment of her daughter's role in its creation:

Dear, honored friend,—In a few thrillingly impassioned days, when I actually intended to take up some other work, these sonnets were given to me. You will understand with only a glance why you must be

the first to possess them. For, elusive as the relationship is (only one sonnet . . . summons Vera's own figure into this excitation dedicated to her), it nevertheless governs and moves the course of the whole and suffused more and more—although so secretly that I recognized it only gradually—this irresistible creation that so staggered me.[10]

If these sonnets were to be published one day, he concluded, there was no question that they would be in memory of Vera—it was only left for Gertrud to agree on the form the dedication should take.[11]

The same day that Rilke sent the sonnets to Gertrud, elegies—*mirabile dictu!*—began arriving. Between February 7 and 11 he composed, again in a tempest of creation, the seventh, eighth, ninth, a first version of the fifth, the remainder of the long-unfinished sixth, and all but the fifteen opening lines of the concluding tenth. On February 11, with all the Duino elegies at last in place, Rilke felt himself *finished*, and that evening could write letters to close friends and supporters, all striking the same note of a life of waiting at last justified. On the fourteenth a last elegy arrived "in a radiant afterstorm,"[12] and Rilke, thrilled with this free-form meditation on Picasso's *Saltimbanques*, substituted it for the poem that had been serving as the fifth.

But then, with the work that had become Rilke's life project achieved, something truly unpredictable occurred. "Scarcely was the Fifth on paper," he wrote Lou Andreas-Salomé, when the stream of the sonnets *returned*, at full strength, apparently unfazed by the interruption of the elegies.[13] Again Rilke was writing nonstop. By February 23 he had produced twenty-nine *more* sonnets, which he arranged (moving the last poem written to the beginning of the sequence) to form a matching group. As the creative storm at Muzot now finally subsided, Rilke found himself with a second major work, the two-part *Sonnets to Orpheus*.

III

Given the circumstances of their creation, it seems inevitable that the *Sonnets to Orpheus* and the *Duino Elegies* should be considered companion works. Rilke himself regarded them as "of the same birth," and was anxious to stress their connectedness:

> *We are*, let it be emphasized again, *in the sense of the Elegies, we are the transformers of the earth; our entire existence, the flights and plunges of our love, everything qualifies us for this task* (besides which there is, es-

sentially, no other). (The Sonnets show particular instances of this activity, which here appears placed under the name and protection of a dead girl, whose incompletion and innocence holds open the grave door so that, having passed on, she belongs to those powers which keep the one half of life fresh, and open toward the other, wound-open half.) Elegies and Sonnets support each other constantly—, and I consider it an infinite grace that with the same breath I was permitted to fill both these sails: the little rust-colored sail of the Sonnets and the Elegies' gigantic white canvas.[14]

Certainly there is much in common. Both works inhabit the same "transvaluing" landscape, where praise and lament (and by extension love and parting, desire and loss, life and death) are not in opposition but internal to one another, the latter not the negation of the former but its matrix, the space in which it intensifies. (One wonders what Rilke would have made of Vermeer's *Girl with a Pearl Earring*, with its eidetic infoldings of grief and desire, departure and resuscitation, loss and new life.) The sonnets seem especially attuned to "The Ninth Elegy," with its realm of transformation and fleetingness ("*Once* for each thing, only once. Once and no more. And we too, / only once. Never again"), where feelings resolve blissfully into things and things seek both rescue and rapture in language ("What if we're only *here* to say: *house,* / *bridge, fountain, gate, jug, fruit tree, window,*— / at most: *column, tower* . . . but for *saying,* understand, / oh for such saying as the things themselves / never dreamt so intensely to be").

Yet once all the similarities are enumerated, what remains most remarkable about the *Sonnets* is how completely *other* they are from the *Elegies* (even from those only days away from them). Their very exhilaration lies in being so. It is a difference less of vision than of stance or demeanor. "The First Elegy" opens as if under way, with a strong, first-person voice speaking in extremis (*Wer, wenn ich schriee, hörte mich denn aus der Engel / Ordnungen?*),[15] and its surges toward clarification and breakthrough remain so intensely vocal that one tends to hear oneself actually *saying* it as one reads.[16] But the first of the *Sonnets to Orpheus* seems to open at some farther place, unrushed and self-pronouncing: *Da stieg ein Baum.* (Could one imagine a more different beginning?) This too is utterance, but the ego and exposed subjectivity of the *Elegies* are absent. The poem proceeds more like choreography: an abrupt statement that *posits* with the force of a speech act ("A tree arose"), then transforms at once into invocation and apostrophe

("O pure transcendence!"), modulates back seamlessly into hushed, perfectly paced narration ("And all was silent") before becoming in its very last line direct address ("you built temples for them in their hearing"). If one needs a speaking voice to ground such utterance, best seek it among those ancient sarcophagi welcomed in Sonnet 1.10: "all that's been wrested from doubt / I greet, the mouths opened again / after knowing well what silence means."

All the best sonnets possess this magisterial aplomb, which gives even the gravest or most elegiac of them a lightness and translucence. Their pace seems heightened *both* by the "deep, balanced repose" that Rilke admired in Valéry *and* by the "art of movement and metamorphosis" that Vera's mother described to him as "innate in her body and mind."[17] Even when, as in Sonnet 1.14, the content is a train of thought that ends in questions, there is something thrilling about following it—like the trees following Vera in Sonnet 2.28—as the poem winds its way without misstep through enjambment, stanza break, and medial pause to the last strophe's "final whirl":

> We puzzle over flower, vine-leaf, fruit.
> They speak not just the language of the year.
> A thing of succor rises from the dark
> and its hues may gleam with the jealousy
>
> of the dead, those who strengthen the earth.
> What do we know of their share in it?
> It has long been their practice to enrich
> the loam with their own free marrow.
>
> The question is: do they do it willingly? . . .
> Does this fruit, a work of sullen slaves,
> push through clenched to us, to their masters?
>
> Or are *they* the masters, sleeping among
> the roots and granting us from their profusion
> this hybrid of mute strength and kisses?

Has a conundrum ever been articulated with greater equanimity? Or the rhetorical "we" ever felt closer, less coercive?[18]

Because the *Sonnets to Orpheus* are so predominantly poems of invocation,

apostrophe, and direct address, much of their freedom lies in the way they play with the terms of subjectivity and relation—especially at the level of pronoun. "I," "we," "you," "she," and "friend" (which in the *Sonnets* acts like a pronoun) often feel like *positional* terms in a situation that is always changing. Whatever identifications they facilitate are more fluid and provisional than those induced in the *Elegies*. Consider the opening of Sonnet 1.16, which is both exemplary and problematic:

> You, my friend, are alone, because . . .

Who speaks here, and to whom? Do we align with the speaker or feel ourselves addressed? For the moment we are in two places at once, as yet "unidentified." The remainder of the stanza—almost as if starting over—locates us "over here" with the speaker in an emphasized plural (though the tendency to feel ourselves addressed by "you" will subliminally persist), but in the process it defers the identity of the "friend":

> *We*, with words and pointing fingers,
> gradually make the world our own—
> perhaps its weakest, most hazardous part.

These lines, which could be spoken to anyone or no one (or by "us" to "us"), are then readdressed by the next stanza to the "friend"—who is still "you" but now in opposition to "us," though not entirely other:

> Who points fingers at a smell?
> Yet you feel so many of those forces
> that threaten us . . . You recognize the dead,
> and you cower before the magic spell.

Herein lies the crux. Do we "guess" at some point during these lines that a *dog* is being addressed? We know this to be true from Rilke's letters,[19] but how clearly does the animal take on outline in the poem? Rilke would seem to need it both ways. *Without* the dog, much of the feeling in the poem remains unattached and the sense, if not the poignancy, of the final lines is lost. But *with* the dog, positions harden and the play of pronouns and identities is foreclosed. (As readers we may even go back and start over.) Yet the poem seems to want to keep this play open to the very end:

Look, now we together must manage
with piecework and parts, as if they were the whole.
Helping you will be hard. Above all:

don't plant me in your heart. I'd grow too fast.
But I will guide *my* master's hand and say:
Here. Here is Esau in his pelt.

The sestet begins by reconfiguring the speaker with the "you" in an intimate twosome diametrically opposite to the "we" of the opening stanza.[20] With that, the cadence changes slightly, the tone deepens, and just for a moment the "you" threatens to float free or "refer" someplace else entirely: "Helping you will be hard. Above all: / don't plant me in your heart. I'd grow too fast" could almost have migrated from Rilke's 1909 *Requiem for a Friend*, his poem to Paula ("Don't come back. If you can bear it, stay / dead among the dead. They have their own concerns. / But help me . . ."). And when, at the very end, the sonnet retrieves the situation and formally introduces its addressee, it does so falsely, in a scenario of deliberate subterfuge: "But I will guide *my* master's hand and say: / Here. Here is Esau in his pelt." In the Old Testament story, Rebecca disguises her younger son Jacob in goatskins so that he can gain the inheritance due his older brother Esau, the "rough" or "hairy" one. In Rilke's appropriation, substitution multiplies. The Greek Orpheus replaces the blind patriarch Isaac, the first-person speaker performs Rebecca's function, and "you" takes the place of the already disguised Jacob. Is it "really" Esau this time or is he being cheated once again?[21] Does the poem's final gesture repeat or rectify the original subterfuge?

None of the other sonnets plays quite so openly with its terms of address, but time and again the poems create the same freedom at the level of the utterance, an ebb and flow across the boundary between "you" and "I" that makes identification seem unnecessary and reductive. This may be what more than anything else makes the *Sonnets* feel so "reader-intimate" even when they are perceived as difficult. When we reach the opening address of the magnificent final sonnet, its indeterminacies draw us into what has now become familiar territory: "Silent friend of the many distances, / feel how your every breath enlarges space." Who speaks here? and to whom? are questions that seem part of a way of thinking long outgrown.[22] To persist with them, and especially to resolve them with proper names, feels reductive and hopelessly archaic—as in this all-too-common gloss: "By the end of the book Rilke is no longer addressing Orpheus. He has become Orpheus, and can

652

speak to his personal self from the center of the universe."[23] Such a formulation exiles the reader and weighs the poem down (one can feel it sinking) with ego, reigning authorial presence, and fixed identity—exactly reversing the process of disencumberment through which the poem and the entire sequence reach their conclusion:

> And if the earthly should forget you,
> say to the silent loam: I flow.
> To the rushing water speak: I am.

With these lines a final paradox: *someone* tells *someone else* to *say* something *under certain conditions*, and what emerges is one of the most beautiful instances of absolute utterance in all of poetry.

While I was working on these sonnets, I found a constant source of inspiration in Denise Levertov's great poem "A Tree Telling of Orpheus," with its exquisite feel for language moved by the enlivened body. To her memory I dedicate this translation.

NOTES

1. Letter to Lou Andreas-Salomé, January 13, 1923.

2. Letter to Gertrud Ouckama Knoop, November 26, 1921.

3. Ralph Freedman, *Life of a Poet: Rainer Maria Rilke* (New York: Farrar, Straus and Giroux, 1996), p. 481. Gertrud's pages were a doubly fateful gift. Something similar had arrived in the mail for Rilke once before. In 1916 he received unforewarned from the mother of Paula Becker (with whom as a young man he had had a brief, hopelessly complicated romantic relationship, and whose death in 1907 had haunted him with grief and guilt ever since) a large packet of Paula's letters and journals, asking him if he would edit them for publication. (It was not that strange a request. In 1913 Rilke had urged her brother, who had published a sampling of Paula's writings, to release a more comprehensive selection. For the details, see Eric Torgersen, *Dear Friend: Rainer Maria Rilke and Paula Modersohn Becker* [Evanston, Ill.: Northwestern University Press, 1998], pp. 238–45.) In the end Rilke cravenly evaded this more fearful obligation, declining the task after a six-month delay and urging *against* their publication, on the grounds that they would only damage Paula's artistic reputation. It is hard to imagine Rilke in 1922 *not* registering this coincidence. And just four years later, in December 1926, Rilke himself would die from a type of leukemia (undiagnosed as such until the last month of his illness) similar to Vera's, experiencing agonies as extreme as hers. Obviously Rilke could not have known that in Vera's dying he was reading his own death, but with hindsight his passionate articulation of her courage and openness feels uncannily like a challenge he is issuing to himself.

4. Letter to Gertrud Ouckama Knoop, undated.

5. Ibid.

6. Ibid.

7. Quoted in Freedman, *Life of a Poet*, p. 483.

8. On February 9 Rilke sent Gertrud a copy of what is now Sonnet 1.21, asking her to "paste it over" the initial version, which he had already characterized in his letter of the seventh as something that "only served to conduct the current and [that] essentially remained empty after its passing." Later in the month he added Sonnet 1.23 and substituted a new version of Sonnet 1.7.

9. Letter to Xaver von Moos, April 20, 1923.

10. Letter to Gertrud Ouckama Knoop, February 7, 1922.

11. Rilke obviously took this dedication very seriously: it appears on the title page as if it were a subtitle, just below the title and in the same typeface.

12. Letter to Lou Andreas-Salomé, February 19, 1922.

13. Ibid.

14. Letter to Witold Hulewicz (Rilke's Polish translator), November 13, 1925. Here Rilke characterizes the *Sonnets* as "instances" of what the *Elegies* propose. Elsewhere he tends to refer to them as a "bonus" or an unexpected "reward." Given this need on his part to subordinate the *Sonnets* to the autobiographical drama of the *Elegies*, it is worth reminding oneself that the *Sonnets* both initiated the great creative outpouring of February 1922 and brought it to a close, and that their creation occupied approximately twice as many days of the period between the second and the twenty-third as did the *Elegies*.

15. "Who, if I cried out, would hear me among the Angels' / Orders?"

16. I am drawing on William Gass's keen account of what it is like to read the *Elegies*: see his *Reading Rilke: Reflections on the Problems of Translation* (New York: Knopf, 1999), especially pp. 94–102.

17. Rilke, letter to Countess Margot Sizzo-Norris-Crouy, April 12, 1923, recounting the stages of Vera's illness: "This beautiful child, who had just begun to attract the attention of everyone who saw her, by the art of movement and transformation that was innate in her body and mind [*Geist*]—unexpectedly declared that she no longer could or would dance (this happened just at the end of childhood). Her body changed, grew strangely heavy and massive, without losing its beautiful Slavic features; during the time that remained to her, Vera devoted herself to music; finally she only drew—as if the denied dance came forth from her ever more quietly, ever more discreetly." Rilke's locutions here seem to be describing not so much the degeneration caused by a specific disease as some strangely fantasized maturational process. At any rate, would not the poet be almost bound to imagine one *further* stage—lines of *writing* in which the denied dance would come forth even *more* quietly, even *more* discreetly?

18. The same could be said of "The Eighth Elegy," which stands out from the other elegies in the evenness and regal poise it shares with the best sonnets.

19. "One has to know—or surmise—that Sonnet XVI is addressed to a dog. I didn't want to add a note to this effect, precisely because I wanted to take him completely into the whole. Any hint would just have isolated him again, singled him out. (This way he takes part down below, belonging and warned, like the dog and the child in Rembrandt's Night Watch.)" (Letter to Clara Rilke, April 23, 1923.)

20. Rilke's German manages this plural in a locution that avoids pronouns altogether.

21. Confusion multiplies in one of Rilke's later explanations of the poem, where he seems to mistake the two brothers in the original Old Testament story: "In the poem *to the dog*, . . . the poet wants to guide this hand so that it may, for the sake of his infinite sympathy and devotion, bless the dog, who, almost like Esau, has put on his pelt only so that he could share, in his heart, an inheritance that would never have come to him: could participate, with sorrow and pity, in all of human existence." (Letter to Countess Margot Sizzo-Norris-Crouy, June 1, 1923.) However, this is Rilke thinking about the poem more than a year after the original inspiration and both rationalizing and sentimentalizing in the process of commenting; the poem itself seems clear about the unnamed Jacob.

22. In a brief handwritten note about the poem, Rilke seems to go out of his way to be unhelpful: "To a friend of Vera."

23. Stephen Mitchell, in the introduction to his translation of *Sonnets to Orpheus* (New York: Simon and Schuster, 1985), p. 10.

UNCOLLECTED POEMS

After Rilke completed the second part of the *New Poems* in 1908, he virtually ceased publishing volumes of poetry. *Requiem for a Friend* (occasioned by the death of Paula Becker) appeared in 1909, the poem cycle *The Life of the Virgin Mary* in 1913, but nothing major until the sudden appearance in 1923 of the *Duino Elegies* and the *Sonnets to Orpheus*—and then nothing further from the time of their publication until Rilke's death from acute leukemia in December 1926.

The story we tell of these circumstances (largely at the prompting of Rilke's own letters) goes something like this: After more than a decade of free, uninterrupted productivity, Rilke was gradually drawn by his work on *The Notebooks of Malte Laurids Brigge* into a realm of conflict and self-doubt—to such a degree that after that prose work's publication in 1910 he found himself directionless and existentially exhausted, a beginner unable to begin, feeling more and more estranged from the task of poetry and yet looking to it increasingly for some definitive, life-answering statement. The years from 1910 through 1922 thus become Rilke's "crisis" years, the crisis deep-

ened by his failure to sustain work on the elegies begun at Duino in 1912, and not resolved until the whirlwind completion of those poems at Muzot in February 1922, accompanied by the virtually unwilled dictation of the *Sonnets to Orpheus*, the latter a kind of gift or bonus confirming the high oracular achievement of the *Elegies* and taking its own place as Rilke's one great "post-crisis" work.

So powerfully does this narrative influence our conception of the later Rilke that it can come as something of a shock to learn that the poet, both during his crisis years and after them, was writing poems continuously, often prolifically—in letters, in guest books, in presentation copies, but above all in the pocketbooks he always carried with him. Both the quantity and the variety of this uncollected poetry are astonishing.[1] There are over five hundred pieces, ranging from completed poems of great fluency and poise, to headlong statements that hurtle through their subjects, to brief, unassuming epiphanies that traverse consciousness like fireflies, to hard aphoristic kernels ("The transformed speaks only to relinquishers. All / holders-on are stranglers"). It is a formidable body of work. For all its miscellany, there is the sense of an alternate aesthetic informing it, easing distinctions between the finished and the incomplete and allowing poetry to evolve with minimal stress on opening and coming to a close.

Surprise deepens as one encounters one superb poem after another in this assemblage—not just large-scale masterpieces such as "The Spirit Ariel" and "Christ's Descent into Hell," but also a host of small, unprepossessing stunners like "Early Spring":

Harshness vanished. Suddenly caring
spreads itself over the field's uncovered gray.
Little rivulets change their intonations.
Tendernesses, inexpertly,

reach toward the earth from space.
Roads run far into the land, foretelling it.
Unexpectedly you see its rising's
visage in the empty tree.

After enough such beautifully pitched poems, one has to wonder what accounts for this body of work's neglect—by Rilke himself and in Rilke criticism and biography up to the present day.

Explanations range from the mundane to the obscure. The poems themselves were assembled only gradually after Rilke's death, in awkward stages (the pocketbooks were not made available until 1945, and those from entire years may be lost), and J. B. Leishman's rushed translation of the entire corpus, for all the bravery of the undertaking, has served in its near unreadability as a kind of death's-head that keeps English-speaking readers away.[2] More subtly estranging is the German edition's division of the work into separate sections it designates "completed works" (*Vollendetes*), "dedications" (*Widmungen*), and "drafts" (*Entwürfe*)—an arrangement that makes it impossible to experience the poems in their temporal succession and imposes on them the very distinctions they so curiously blur.[3]

Beyond such problems of access and presentation, however, there is the ever-present myth of Rilke's Duino crisis and that myth's way of obscuring whatever might contradict it or undermine its drama. Rilke's own neglect of the uncollected poems seems to stem from this phenomenon. Consider his complaint in a letter of 1915 to Princess Marie, his host and benefactor at Duino: "For five years now, ever since *Malte Laurids* closed behind me, I've been standing around like a beginner, though as a beginner who can't begin."[4] Rilke must have truly felt this blockage, since he expressed it so often in his letters. But viewed in the light of the uncollected poems composed during the years he mentions, it is sheer mythologizing. Immediately after *Malte Laurids* there is not stagnation but modest output. And then in 1913 and 1914—hard on the heels of the first suspension of the Duino project—there is an explosion of creative brilliance. Rilke composed more than 150 poems during these two years, many of them among the greatest he ever wrote: "The Spanish Trilogy," "The Raising of Lazarus," "The Spirit Ariel," "Christ's Descent into Hell," "The Great Night," "Turning," "Exposed on the mountains of the heart"—to cite only a few of the best-known. Evidently Rilke, once he had become obsessed with the project of the *Duino Elegies*, could not accept these poems as validations. There is no indication that he ever considered publishing them together in a volume, and the self-fashioning aspect of his consciousness seems to have all but erased them.[5] But they are a major accomplishment, and one would expect even the briefest treatment of Rilke's poetic career to spotlight the period between late 1912 and early 1915 as one of its great florescences. Instead, the work from these years is typically placed within the sad aftermath of the *Elegies'* initial waning ("The avalanche of poetry subsided and, instead of the 'dictated' flow and compulsive utterance, scraps of material had to be laboriously quarried"),[6] or treated as "crisis po-

ems" (especially crisis poems *about* being blocked), or assimilated in some other way to the Duino mythos: "It might therefore be said that much of the poetry [Rilke] wrote between 1912 and 1914 is about the price he would have to pay in order to be able to complete the *Duino Elegies*, in order to achieve what might be called the 'angelic vision,' in order to be and remain the only kind of poet he now cared to be."[7]

But there was obviously another kind of poet Rilke cared very much to be: the fact that he kept writing in the manner of the uncollected poems testifies to that. For one of the striking things about those poems is their *difference* from the high vatic mode of the *Duino Elegies* and the *Sonnets to Orpheus*. The two bodies of work seem to stand over against each other, in necessary counterpoise. Against the oracular utterance of the *Elegies*—still sometimes thought of as Rilke's only voice—the uncollected poems articulate a realm of pure occasion: the flooding or flaring of an emotion or a memory, the flash of an idea, the urgency of something willed or wanted or held in wait, acts of attention triggered by or issuing in surprise, upsurges of bitterness or revulsion—even, as in the following quatrain, moments of tough-minded scorn for the gentler self:

> God won't be lived like some light morning.
> Whoever climbs down the shaft must give up
> earth's repleteness for the craft of mining:
> stand hunched and pry him loose in tunnels.

Such poems tend to be fast, headlong, in transit. They touch down at full throttle. Often they appear to compose themselves before one's eyes. An initial impulse, rather than undergoing "development," seems to play itself through, without premeditation, often elliptically and toward no predestined end. Consider the following untitled poem (or "draft"), written the same year as the first of the Duino elegies:

> O the curves of my longing through the cosmos,
> and in every streak: my being's
> flung-outness. Many of them returning
> only after a thousand years on the sad ellipse
> of their momentum and passing on.
> Hastening through the once-existent future,
> knowing themselves in the seasons

or airily, as a precisely timed influence
almost starlike in the overwakeful
apparatus for a brief moment trembling

Here especially there is an eerie sense of closeness to the poem in process. The first line flings itself out lavishly (one is reminded of some of the great opening lines of Donne's *Holy Sonnets*), and what follows seems to ride that first surge, as it devolves in self-propagating metaphors toward the single, short-lived, unpunctuated light point, "trembling." It is an eloquent, beautifully paced poem, but it follows its own obscure trajectory, and what it "says" remains suspended in images that images beget, only half translated into some understanding *behind* the poem.

The uncollected poems could thus be said to give us the opposite of "angelic vision." For the most part they aren't interested in consolidating a transcendental consciousness, especially one with visionary wisdom or ex cathedra powers of speech.[8] Everything in them tends to be registered at ground level (which makes all the more remarkable their vivid feelings for the self's sidereal existence and the proliferation in them of arcs, trajectories, bridge systems through space), and some of their most memorable imagery is of dispersal and lavish, even wasteful expenditure.

There *are* intrusions of second-level consciousness in the poems, but the experience—far from orphic—is usually of a descriptive voice interrupting itself, surprised, as the evoked moment speeds on:

Do you still remember: falling stars,
how they leapt slantwise through the sky
like horses over suddenly held-out hurdles
of our wishes—did we have *so* many?—
for stars, innumerable, leapt everywhere;
almost every gaze upward became
wedded to the swift hazard of their play,
and our heart felt like a single thing
beneath that vast disintegration of their brilliance—
and was whole, as if it would survive them!

So much contributes to this poem's complex epiphany: again the ex nihilo opening, the single trajectory, the poem playing itself through; the long-ago other still present in conversation; the heart-catching, throwaway trope,

sweeping through three enjambed lines and then caught up in thought before even one's astonishment can register; a universe where swiftness, chance, and play reign, with the "suddenness" thrust into it by the human game of wishes a strangely integral component; memory not thinking back but confirming the moment's life in consciousness; the elation over something "then" felt "now," and the poem in fact producing that elation; cosmic disintegration as something lavished on the transient human self, *bestowing* the feeling of survival; the subjunctive that frames that feeling somehow not qualifying or undermining it but allowing exclamation.

Rilke wrote "Do you still remember" in 1924 ("Early Spring" belongs to the same year), in the midst of another great creative surge that is all but passed over in the canonical story of his later years. So much narrative force tends to get invested in the climactic, crisis-resolving "dictation" of the remaining elegies and both parts of the *Sonnets to Orpheus* in that three-week period during February 1922 that Rilke's fate seems to close: there seems no *reason* why any poetry should intervene between this consummation and his death in 1926. But in this gap the uncollected work proliferates: some thirty poems in the latter months of 1923, and then, amazingly, more than a hundred in 1924, scarcely any of them negligible and many among Rilke's best: altogether a body of more than two hundred last poems, stretching from the final completion of the Orpheus sonnets to the last pocketbook's final entry, a fiercely apocalyptic poem Rilke wrote only weeks before his death.[9]

It seems important to call attention to these last poems, if for no other reason than to stress the fact of their existence. But it would be misleading to regard them as a separate group, given the degree to which they *continue* the mode of the uncollected poems, virtually unaffected by the spectacular orphic interruptions of early 1922. If anything, they seem to intensify, distill, and define more sharply the character of the uncollected work. But the poems of 1923 and 1924 do seem to enter a new zone, or at least take on a new coloration. Language lightens yet grows dense with neologism, ellipsis, and wordplay. The change in feeling is elusive; Leishman, attempting to describe it, has recourse to the late Beethoven: "There is an *Umschlag*, a turn, a peripeteia: the prevailing mood is no longer one of strain and tension and effort, but of acceptance, or—to use Rilke's favorite word—of *consentment*: now almost ecstatically joyful, now gravely tranquil, now sadly resigned; often, as in the last music of Beethoven, so much all of these together than [*sic*] one cannot say which prevails."[10] An even apter analogue might be Klee's last

paintings, which, like Rilke's poems, are content to stay small, and which also proliferate, the apparent ease and *slightness* of the thing producing, again as with Rilke, disproportionately intense effects. (Klee's angels, so alien to those of the elegies, would be uncannily at home in the world of the uncollected poems.) Consider "Wild Rosebush," the kind of poem that Rilke seemed able to write at will in 1924:

> How it stands out against the darkenings
> of the rainy evening, young and pure,
> its tendrils arched everywhere in givingness
> yet absorbed in its rose-being;
>
> the shallow flowers, already open here and there,
> each unasked for and untended;
> thus immeasurably exceeded by itself
> and indescribably self-aroused,
>
> it calls to the wanderer, who in his evening
> meditating comes past along the road:
> Oh look at me, see, over here, how safe I am
> and unprotected and having all I need.

This deceptively simple poem is all contradiction, opposition, counterpoise. The isolated rosebush is heightened by its background and yet stands there *against* it, perhaps, vulnerably *near* it both in space and in time (the *Verdunkelungen* at work behind the rosebush can suggest not just "darkenings" but deepenings, blackings-out, suppressions, obscure inflictions of harm). The rosebush itself is pure contradiction, a confluence of opposed motives pushed to their extremes: both "absorbed" (*versunken* can range from "sunk" to "immersed" to "engrossed") in its rose-being—and thus both like and unlike the human being who walks past deep in thought—and extravagantly arched out in gestures of self-offering (*ausgeschwungen*, a Rilkean coinage suggesting not only the outward curve of the tendril but the motive force that extends it and perhaps even the desire that signals through it): gestures, it would seem, that go unheeded. The "shallowness" of the open flowers counteracts the bush's "sunkenness" in its rose-being, and contradictory senses of abandonment (achingly forsaken or blissfully outside need) grow almost explicit in the paired participial adjectives (*ungewollt und ungepflegt*): either "un-

premeditated and uncultivated"—hence spontaneously wild—or "unwanted and uncared for," as with an orphan.

As all this descriptiveness builds up in arcane formulations of self-exceeding and self-excitement, the poem crosses over unexpectedly into the realm of voicing. As it does so—producing another quietly intense epiphany—new oppositions configure. Within the rosebush's articulation of itself, are not "safe" and "unprotected" in blatant opposition? Or does it only seem so from one's human standpoint? And if the rosebush is set apart from us in the unconflictedness of its contradictions, why the calling out so fervently to the human passerby, the intense desire to make itself seen and heard? Does it wish to offer itself up as an exemplum (as in "See how it might be for you"), or does it long for some connection? Either way, there is a pull. The rosebush and the solitary wanderer are themselves in counterpoise: the one possessing speech but sunk in silent thought, the other mute but calling fervently; the one passing by oblivious, the other straining from its rooted place; both of them solitary against the background "darkenings." And if it is in the nature of things that the wanderer *not* hear the wild rosebush's call, how then account for the poem's own urgently imagined voicing of it? What *human* split does this configure? And last: as the poem rounds to its climax, how is it that the rapture in the voice prevails over its lostness on the human passerby?

The counterpositioning that makes "Wild Rosebush" so rich weaves through the whole of the uncollected poems; it is an obsessive leitmotif. *Gegenüber* is the key German term, whose slight distinctions Rilke seems always to mobilize: opposite, vis-à-vis, over against, facing, compared with, in relation to. Divides become the space of both severance and relation, longing and equipoise; opposites seek (sometimes mutually, sometimes one-sidedly) to bridge, cross over, bind, balance, renew, even stretch taut their "betweenness." Male is posed against female, the face against the universe or the vast night sky. Women renew their tension with their mirror images, Narcissus views his lying lifeless on the water's floor. Cups penetrate each other without clinking, the interval between them remains unchanged. Signals from the other side fail to reach us, change us anyway. The gods learned quickly to simulate halves, while wholeness may have been our worst mistake. "Brother body" must be humored in his sickness by his friend and fellow recluse "consciousness," who is already a peculiar "we." From over there in the creature world, "Everything tempts," while from over here on our side, "even in the lightest things we waken counterweight."

From this first leitmotif it would be only a step to the uncollected poems'

total weave: rising and falling, remembering and forgetting, gazing and heart-work, consent and refusal, renunciation and intractability, shelter and exposure, departure and arrival, holding on and letting go—on and on, in seemingly endless refiguration. Perhaps it is unremarkable that the poems should possess so elaborate an inner architecture. After all, a single poet wrote them. But the meshwork feels more ardent than matter-of-fact. The sensation of a body of work is stronger than that of scattered moments of a life in crisis. And what this body of work gives us seems to come from a side of Rilke—one could even claim his strongest side—that is not otherwise apparent. Among the uncollected poems there seems to me to be at least a hundred that, if Rilke *had* published them together, would stand as one of the great volumes of poetry in twentieth-century literature.

NOTES

1. By the uncollected poetry I mean, following J. B. Leishman (note 2 below), all the German poems not collected and published in book form by Rilke himself. Rilke did from time to time allow individual "uncollected" poems to be published in the *Insel-Almanach* and other periodicals.

2. Rainer Maria Rilke, *Poems, 1906 to 1926*, trans. and ed. J. B. Leishman (Norfolk, Va.: New Directions, 1957). Leishman gives a concise summary of the poems' bibliographic history in the opening pages of his long introduction to this volume.

3. Rainer Maria Rilke, *Sämtliche Werke*, ed. Ruth Sieber Rilke and Ernst Zinn, 6 vols. (Frankfurt: Insel, 1955–66), vols. 2 and 6.

4. Quoted and translated by Michael Hamburger, *An Unofficial Rilke* (London: Anvil Press Poetry, 1981), p. 17.

5. On three different occasions Rilke did make unpublished selections from the uncollected work. During the war he put together a small collection for Rudolf Kassner entitled *Poems to Night*. In 1922 he and his publisher Anton Kippenberg assembled a group of poems for a proposed appendix to the *Duino Elegies*—an idea that was subsequently discarded. Shortly before his death he transcribed in a leather-bound volume a set of poems and prose pieces, *From Pocketbooks and Writing Pads (Aus Taschenbüchern und Merkblättern)*, which he sent to Katharina Kippenberg for occasional publication in the *Insel-Almanach*.

6. Siegfried Mandel, *Rainer Maria Rilke: The Poetic Instinct* (Carbondale: Southern Illinois University Press, 1965), p. 102.

7. Leishman, in Rilke, *Poems, 1906 to 1926*, p. 23.

8. There are, of course, exceptions, such as the programmatic "What birds plunge through" and "As once the winged energy of delight"—though even in these poems the oracular imperative voices sphinxlike conundrums.

9. The profusion of German poems scarcely indicates just how prolific Rilke was during

1924—the very year when the severity of his illness became unmistakable and his transit between the castle haven in Muzot and the nearby sanatorium at Val-Mont began. That year, in addition to the German poems, he composed *Vergers* and *Quatrains valaisans*, French poem sequences of fifty-nine and thirty-six poems, respectively. He also entered into the two-year verse correspondence with Erica Mitterer that elicited some forty poems from him between June and August of 1924.

10. Leishman, in Rilke, *Poems, 1906 to 1926*, p. 37.

Zornige sahst du flackern, sahst zwei Knaben, 214